About This Book

Why is this topic important?

To comply with federal and state laws, every organization must be able to conduct a competent and thorough workplace investigation into harassment and discrimination complaints. To prevent harm to workers and productivity, organizations must know how to use an investigation to hold people accountable and provide healing in their workplace. This book is a comprehensive guide to achieving these goals. It not only provides tools and guidelines for investigations, but it also provides a summary of the psychological and intercultural research to help investigators and managers understand and interpret the behaviors of their employees. With this book, leaders and human resource professionals will be able to respond to complaints fairly and with confidence.

What can you achieve with this book?

This book enables both the novice and experienced investigator to understand and investigate the dynamics of harassment in the workplace. It provides organizations with a roadmap that can help prevent as well as address and resolve harassment. The book also helps workplace leaders and human resource professionals with tools to understand and apply complex laws and psychological research. Throughout the book, checklists, in-depth examples, and focused case studies provide the reader with practical tools and insights with which to approach any investigation. The accompanying CD provides organizations with tools with which to share knowledge and ensure competent, consistent investigations.

How is this book organized?

This book first sets the stage for an investigation by helping experienced and novice investigators understand the legal and psychological knowledge and skills a good investigation requires. The chapters then lay out the stages of investigation until the final chapter on the investigator as witness. Unlike any other investigation guide, this book includes a tested training module for teaching in-house investigators the art and science of investigating. Finally, up-to-date case law reviews and sample policies and forms complete the book.

About Pfeiffer

Pfeiffer serves the professional development and hands-on resource needs of training and human resource practitioners and gives them products to do their jobs better. We deliver proven ideas and solutions from experts in HR development and HR management, and we offer effective and customizable tools to improve workplace performance. From novice to seasoned professional, Pfeiffer is the source you can trust to make yourself and your organization more successful.

Essential Knowledge Pfeiffer produces insightful, practical, and comprehensive materials on topics that matter the most to training and HR professionals. Our Essential Knowledge resources translate the expertise of seasoned professionals into practical, how-to guidance on critical workplace issues and problems. These resources are supported by case studies, worksheets, and job aids and are frequently supplemented with CD-ROMs, websites, and other means of making the content easier to read, understand, and use.

Essential Tools Pfeiffer's Essential Tools resources save time and expense by offering proven, ready-to-use materials—including exercises, activities, games, instruments, and assessments—for use during a training or team-learning event. These resources are frequently offered in looseleaf or CD-ROM format to facilitate copying and customization of the material.

Pfeiffer also recognizes the remarkable power of new technologies in expanding the reach and effectiveness of training. While e-hype has often created whizbang solutions in search of a problem, we are dedicated to bringing convenience and enhancements to proven training solutions. All our e-tools comply with rigorous functionality standards. The most appropriate technology wrapped around essential content yields the perfect solution for today's on-the-go trainers and human resource professionals.

Essential resources for training and HR professionals

Investigating Harassment and Discrimination Complaints

A Practical Guide

Jan C. Salisbury
Bobbi Killian Dominick

Pfeiffer
A Wiley Imprint
www.pfeiffer.com

Library of Congress Cataloging-in-Publication Data
Salisbury, Jan.
   Investigating harassment and discrimination complaints: a practical guide / by Jan Salisbury and Bobbi Killian Dominick.
      p.; cm.
   "A Wiley Imprint."
   Includes bibliographical references and index.
   ISBN 0-7879-6874-9 (alk. paper)
1. Discrimination in employment—Investigation—United States. 2. Sexual harassment—Investigation—United States.
   I. Dominick, Bobbi Killian. II. Title.

HD4903.5.U58S24 2003
658.3'008—dc22   2003015264

Acquiring Editor: Martin Delahoussaye
Director of Development: Kathleen Dolan Davies
Developmental Editor: Susan Rachmeler
Production Editor: Nina Kreiden
Editor: Rebecca Taff
Manufacturing Supervisor: Bill Matherly
Editorial Assistant: Laura Reizman
Illustrations: Lotus Art

Printing 10 9 8 7 6 5 4 3 2 1

Contents

CD Contents   xi

Dedication   xiii

Preface   xv

Acknowledgments   xvii

Introduction   xix

PART ONE   ESSENTIAL INFORMATION

1   Investigator Fears, Motivations, and Jargon   3
    An Investigator's Greatest Fears 3
    An Investigator's Greatest Motivations 5
    Interpreting Legal Jargon 5

2   The Law of Harassment and What Investigators Need to Know   9
    Why Investigators Need to Know the Law 9
    Relevant EEO Laws 9
    Definition of Harassment Under Title VII 11
    Employer Liability for Supervisory Harassment 12
      and the Affirmative Defense
    EEOC's Guidance on Supervisory Harassment 17
    Other Types of Harassment 19
    Retaliation After the Original Complaint 22
    Special Problems in Harassment Law 25

3   The Psychology of Harassment   30
    The Nature of Harassment 30
    Harassers 33
    Coping with Harassment 37

The Impact of Harassment on Individuals and Workgroups 39

Environmental Factors Affecting Harassment 40

Implications for Investigators 41

4   Diversity and Harassment   42

The Diversity of Race, Ethnicity, and Other Cultural Differences 44

Differences Between Men and Women 46

Tips for Investigators 47

PART TWO   PRIOR TO THE INVESTIGATION

5   Characteristics of Effective Investigators   51

Unbiased Pursuit of the Facts 51

Superior Communication Skills 52

Ease with Difficult Behaviors and Emotions 52

Legal Knowledge 53

Excellent Relationship with Management 54

Knowledge of Hierarchy and Culture 55

Presentation Skills 55

Emotional Maturity and Detachment 55

Valuing and Understanding Diversity 56

Choosing the Right Investigator 56

6   Organizational Settings Conducive to Effective Investigations   59

A Dynamic Organizational Model 59

Policies to Prevent Discrimination, Harassment, and Retaliation 61

Procedures for Investigating Allegations 63

Role of Leadership 65

Role of Training 66

Role of HR and the Investigators 67

PART THREE   THE INVESTIGATION

7   The Investigative Plan   71

When to Do an Investigation 71

Intake of Complaints 72

Developing an Investigative Plan 72

Setting Up Interviews 77

Size of the Investigation 78

Other Legal Issues to Consider 79

8   Documentation   81

    Record Keeping 81

    Attorney-Client Privilege 83

    Writing an Investigative Report 85

    Disseminating the Written Report 88

9   Tips and Techniques for Conducting the Investigation   89

    Confidentiality 89

    Civil vs. Criminal Investigations 91

    Conducting the Investigation 99

    The Interviewing Process 107

    Interviewing the Complainant 110

    Interviewing the Alleged Harasser 112

    Interviewing Witnesses 113

    Completing the Process 114

    Gathering Factual Documentation 114

10   Making the Determination   116

    Deciding When You Are Finished 116

    Policy Violations vs. Violations of the Law 116

    Determining Credibility 117

    Deciding What Is Relevant 120

    Corroborating Evidence 120

    Boorish Behavior and Bad Management 121

    Risk Factors 121

    Making a Determination 122

PART FOUR   BEYOND THE INVESTIGATION

11   Prompt, Corrective Action   125

    A Working Definition of Zero Tolerance 125

    Presenting the Issues to Top Management 126

    Judging the Severity of the Behavior 126

    Disciplinary Considerations 127

    Types of Discipline 129

    Training for Workgroups 130

    Training for Individual Harassers 131

12   Remedies, Healing, and Follow-Up   132

Remedies for Aggrieved Employees 132

The Need for Debriefing 133

Leading the Debriefing 134

Debriefing the Complainant 134

Debriefing the Accused 137

Debriefing Workgroups 138

Debriefing Employees and Witnesses 142

13   The Investigator as Witness   143

Testifying During Trial 146

Surviving Cross-Examination 146

Conclusion 147

Training Program: Training Internal Investigators   149

Training Internal Investigators Handouts   170

Appendix   197

Sample Policy   199

Sample Investigative Forms   203

Sample Report   208

Federal Cases of Importance for Sexual Harassment Issues   211

Federal Cases Addressing the Affirmative Defense, 1998–2002   214

Enforcement Guidelines Issued by EEOC   234

Policy Guidance on Current Issues of Sexual Harassment (1990)   267

The U.S. Equal Employment Opportunity   283
     Commission Enforcement Guidelines

Bibliography   291

Index   299

About the Authors   305

How to Use the CD ROM   307

NOTE TO READER: The information on CD can now be found on http://booksupport.wiley.com (http://wiley.mpstechnologies.com/wiley/BOBContent/searchLPBobContent.do)

CD Contents

Training Program: Training Internal Investigators Handouts

    Handout A: Self-Evaluation Form

    Handout B: Microcosm Respectful Workplace Anti-Harassment Policy

    Handout C: Case Studies

    Handout D: Four Layers of Diversity

    Handout E: Stereotypes and Generalizations

    Handout F: You as a Diverse Entity

    Handout G: Triad Role Play

    Handout H: Forming an Investigative Plan

    Handout I-1: Witness Summary: Willima Michaels

    Handout I-2: Witness Statement: Tom Torrance

    Handout I-3: Witness Summary: David Lee

    Handout I-4: Witness Summary: B.J. Raymond

    Handout I-5: Witness Summary: Michelle Cline

    Handout J-1: Role Play Preparation and Feedback Forms

    Handout J-2: Role Play Feedback Guidelines

    Handout K: Remedies, Healing, and Aftermath

    Handout L: Debriefing the Workgroup Exercise

    Handout M: Your Organization's Follow-Up Issues

Sample Policy

Sample Investigative Forms

        Investigation Activity Log

        Investigator's Checklist

        Checklist for Interview with Complainant

        Checklist for Interview with Accused

        Checklist for Interviews with Witnesses

Sample Report

In Memory of My Parents, Bob and Wilma Salisbury

To Tom, Sam , Matt and Asuka, David and Lori, Bob and Mary,
My Inspirations

Preface

THIS MANUAL WAS CONCEIVED shortly after the 1991 Hill-Thomas hearings on the sexual harassment of Anita Hill by now Supreme Court Justice Clarence Thomas. The hearings were a national teach-in for sexual harassment, and organizations and the Equal Employment Opportunity Commission (EEOC) found itself deluged with complaints from women of every age. Lawsuits increased and organizations became concerned about investigating the complaints correctly. They clamored for training on how to handle the complex, messy, and emotionally laden discriminatory harassment complaints. Mary Sebek, a former EEOC judge, and Jan Salisbury worked with organizations on harassment for over a decade. During the 1992 conference, Sex and Power Issues in the Workplace, held in Seattle and chaired by Jan, it became clear that the combined disciplines of human resources, psychology, and the law were the keys to preventing and resolving sexual harassment in the workplace. Because there were no publications available that included the insights and skills from these disciplines, Mary and Jan began to write a manual to use for training investigators.

This manual developed slowly because it took hundreds of investigations and experience with harassment complaints *of all types* to understand how to effectively prevent, investigate, and resolve harassment in the workplace. These situations were often painful, and the lawsuits that followed provided expensive lessons on what not to do. The investigator workshops developed into intense hands-on experiences for trainees, because investigating skills could not be effectively developed through lectures and discussion. As Jan Salisbury became involved as an expert in lawsuits, she realized that the role of the investigation was becoming more prominent: investigations served as the foundation for decisions made by organizations and for liability standards on prompt corrective action.

When Jan moved to Boise, Idaho, she sought a local attorney who also believed in the multidisciplinary approach to investigating. She met Bobbi Dominick, an employment defense attorney for twenty years, and Bobbi co-facilitated the investigator training and helped to co-write the manual. Finally, after five years of working together, Jan and Bobbi decided that the manual was ready to publish.

Acknowledgments

WE (JAN AND BOBBI) RESPECT OUR DIVERSITY and the power it brings to our teaching, thinking, and writing.

We are grateful to the thousands of employees, human resource professionals, and organizations who let us work alongside them so that we could learn from their experiences and skills. We also appreciate the lawyers and judges who included our opinions in their deliberations. This manual is for all of them.

Much of the psychological research and wisdom contained in this manual developed from research conducted by Jan and by her research colleagues. The first research group in Seattle included Helen Remick, Angela Ginorio, and Donna Stringer. This group banded together to publish their experiences in the harassment workplace wars and were pioneers on the front lines coping with harassment in the 1980s. In the 1990s, Jan's colleagues in the Psychology Department at the University of Illinois, including Louise Fitzgerald, Fritz Drasgow, and Chuck Hulin and their talented graduate students, invited Jan's practical experience into their studies and lab and created brilliant psychological models from extensive research with employees from diverse workplaces. Their commitment to outstanding science continues to illuminate our understanding of the psychology of harassment. Without the dedication and partnership of these psychologists, this manual would not have been written.

There are, of course, many people in our personal lives who deserve credit and multiple thanks. I (Jan) thank my daughter Cameron Cook and her father Jeff Cook for understanding and supporting the time and effort it took to gain the expertise and to write the book. My friends were always there for me and never stopped believing that this book was worth writing and would be written. Finally, I want to thank my mentor in graduate school in psychology, John Silva, who taught me to love the science and to give psychology away wherever it is needed.

I (Bobbi) thank my spouse, Thomas Dominick, who has been my rock throughout my legal career, supporting my efforts to learn and grow in the law, and my children Sam and Matt, who put up with a mother who, at times, seems obsessed with harassment and discrimination. I also thank all of my colleagues in the law on both sides of this issue, who continually challenge me to grow in my thinking about how the law impacts the lives of both supervisors and employees.

Introduction

of the law, observation, and retaliation...

RIGHT AT THIS MOMENT, at hundreds of thousands of companies, on the desks of thousands of human resource professionals or company leaders, sits a piece of paper that strikes fear into the hearts of many. The paper represents an internal complaint about harassment, discrimination, or retaliation. Over the last twenty years, the authors have seen corporate executives, managers, and HR professionals struggle with what to do with that little piece of paper. Until now, there has been no roadmap, no authoritative guideline, telling that lonely manager or HR professional what to do. Attorneys have told them for years, "When you get a complaint, you must investigate." But how? Whether the complaint is received at a Fortune 500 company, a small high-tech startup, or a government agency, *something* needs to be done with that piece of paper. This manual provides the roadmap that has been so necessary. We want to provide those who investigate complaints with a lifeline, a resource that is both informative and useful, both authoritative and practical. We want to provide those who investigate such complaints with an in-depth understanding of the law and psychology surrounding these complex issues, but at the same time make the concepts clear and understandable to the novice investigator. No resource has existed up to now; we believe our experience and knowledge make this manual possible.

How This Book Is Organized

We follow the logical process of investigating complaints in organizing this book. The first section provides preliminary information that is essential to understanding complaints of harassment, discrimination, and retaliation. Chapter 1 addresses the fears and motivations of investigators. Chapter 2 summarizes the critical aspects of the law, discrimination, and retaliation that any investigator must understand. Chapters 3 and 4 address the psychology of harassment and the way diversity affects harassment. Both chapters are essential in understanding human behavior at the crux of every complaint.

The next section discusses the pre-investigation stage and describes steps that an organization can take prior to an investigation to strengthen the company's ability to prevent harassment and to effectively investigate and correct it after it occurs. This section includes chapters on assessing the strengths and characteristics of investigators (Chapter 5) and assessing the organization's systems (Chapter 6).

The next section covers the investigation itself. It begins by allowing the investigator to focus on creating a plan for the investigation (Chapter 7). Then the crucial issue of documentation is thoroughly explained in Chapter 8. Chapter 9 lays out the infrastructure of an investigation and contains detailed explanations for how the investigation can be completed. Finally, Chapter 10 addresses a rarely discussed subject that has become prominent—how to draw conclusions from the information gathered.

The final section recognizes that the investigation is just a stage of resolving harassment and discrimination complaints. Chapters 11 and 12 address discipline for any policy violations uncovered in the investigation and the remedies for any aggrieved employees. Finally, Chapter 13 addresses another subject that has recently become more significant—the investigator's role if litigation arises out of the complaint.

This manual is accompanied by a wealth of valuable resources. The Appendix includes a sample policy, sample forms to use in an investigation, and a sample report. The Appendix also includes a summary of cases that have discussed investigations and the outcome of internal complaints of harassment, discrimination, and retaliation, as well as some helpful resources in the form of government publications from the Equal Employment Opportunity Commission.

Finally, this manual provides something no other manual does: *a training program.* We have used a variation of this program for many years to train investigators, and it has been very well-received by both experienced and inexperienced investigators. It provides an outline for your organization to train investigators by having them actually complete a realistic role-play investigation as part of the training, a type of hands-on learning that has been largely ignored in this field up to now.

How to Use This Book

Following are our suggestions for users of this book:

First-Time or Novice Investigators Who Have a Complaint on Your Desk Right Now You don't have time for training, you don't have time to read the whole manual, you need to start this investigation right now. What should you read? We suggest that you turn immediately to the Appendix and make copies of the checklists and log that are provided. The log is explained in Chapter 8. Those forms will serve as your lifelines while you conduct the investigation. Then read Chapter 9 in its entirety. That chapter will take you through the entire process of the investigation. Chapter 9 includes some references to information in other chapters; read that information as well. Once you have completed the investigation using the checklists and log, read how to write a written report in Chapter 8. If you are involved in deciding what should be done about the complaint, read Chapters 11 and 12 on corrective action and remedial measures.

Once you have taken care of the crisis, immediately examine the remaining chapters. Remember, the process of investigating is improved by practice. If you find things in reviewing the remaining chapters that you did wrong, don't despair. You will do it better next time. Suggest to your organization that it conduct the training explained in the materials so that all investigators will be better prepared. If your organization cannot conduct such training, find an outside training program.

First-Time or Novice Investigators Who Do Not Have a Current Crisis Find a training program and attend it, or encourage your company to organize one. Read the entire manual and think about how you would apply it in practice.

Experienced Investigators Who Have Never Received Training Encourage your organization to use this manual to begin a training program for all investigators. We have found that even seasoned investigators will benefit from increased training. Many times these investigators are the ones who benefit most from our training sessions, because they know first-hand the problems they have encountered, and after training have better tools to deal with those problems. Also, the interaction between investigators provides ideas for best practices. Finally, we have found that even experienced investigators are sometimes surprised by the information we reveal in Chapters 2, 3, 4, and 12. Read those chapters and think about how the intersection of both law and psychology shaped your past investigations. We have found that experienced investigators will benefit from the organizational tools provided and the tips on documentation and investigations provided in Chapters 8 and 9. Finally, many investigations have uncovered problems, but the issue festers in the workplace. Even experienced investigators are frustrated by what to do after the investigation is over. Pay close attention to Chapter 12, and try to learn what your organization can do to heal workplaces affected by complaints.

The principles of this manual have successfully been used a hundred times. We hope you will adopt its practices so that your workplace will be more respectful and productive.

Part One
Essential Information

Chapter 1

Investigator Fears, Motivations, and Jargon

INVESTIGATING HARASSMENT AND DISCRIMINATION CLAIMS can be intimidating and stressful. Very personal and intimate details of co-workers' lives can be revealed. Employees are often angry, embarrassed, and emotional. Investigations may affect people's lives and the workgroup's ability to interact and accomplish objectives. The liability of the organization is also at stake. The conclusions of an investigation can determine the future of all of those involved, including the organization itself. Over the years of teaching the art of investigating to many different people, the authors have learned that investigators are plagued by many similar fears and motivated by differing values and needs.

An Investigator's Greatest Fears

The task of investigating can be daunting. Here are some common fears that both experienced and inexperienced investigators have.

Am I Doing It Right? With so much at stake, it is not surprising that investigators are most concerned about whether their investigations are competent. Training and knowledge are critical to building confidence, and this manual provides the tools to conduct proficient investigations. In addition, the courts have recently concluded that organizations must conduct only a "reasonable investigation," *not* a perfect one. Finally, the organization, not the individual investigator, is ultimately responsible for the adequacy of the investigation and its outcomes.

Do I Have What It Takes? Investigators often ask themselves: "Am I emotionally biased?" "Am I too impatient?" "Am I a good listener?" "Can I deal with the embarrassment or anger that employees may feel?" "Can I ask the tough questions?" There is no way to judge a particular investigator's emotional responses to investigations without actual experience. This manual can help the investigator control his or her emotions and judge the appropriate response to these questions. For instance, understanding the psychological impact of harassment, described in Chapter 3, can help an investigator anticipate emotional responses without taking the anger or emotion personally. This manual will show the investigator how to build a support team (attorneys, management, other investigators) so that one person's limits or shortcomings do not undermine the investigation.

Will I Harm People? Because investigations can have a significant impact on employees and on the organization, it is natural to fear harming others. Investigators play only one role in what should be a team of managers deciding what the evidence means and how to remedy the complaint. The team approach provides some protection against a mistaken decision that may cause unintended harm to those involved. A thorough and proficient investigation is also the best tool to ensure that employment actions are fair. This manual will help prevent undeserved harm and promote fairness.

Will Management Do the Right Thing? This manual can be used to train management as well as investigators. When the investigator, human resources, and management work as a team to resolve complaints, it is more likely that management will make good decisions. Most poor decisions are made because management is not trained and thus does not understand harassment and discrimination, the issues underlying the behavior, and appropriate corrective responses. This manual enables the "investigative team" to be on the "same page," operating from the same set of principles and goals.

Will My Investigation Make the Problem Worse? Sometimes investigations discover a "tomb of skeletons." For instance, ethical or financial misconduct might be uncovered. More victims and perpetrators may be identified. The investigator must understand that such revelations do not result from a poor investigation. Instead, uncovering additional misconduct may result from a good investigation. Uncovering such misdeeds provides an opportunity for management to correct and remedy many things that are damaging the employees or the organization.

Will This Investigation Harm Me? Many investigators fear that playing the role of an "internal cop" may damage their own careers, reputations, relationships with others, or emotional well-being. These fears are realistic only when the organization allows an investigator to become a scapegoat for inappropriate behavior or to become the focus of controversy. This manual describes what organizations should do to create a culture of respect and adequate systems to prevent and resolve harassment and discrimination.

An Investigator's Greatest Motivations

Given the fears investigators commonly hold, why do people choose to be investigators? We have also learned over the years that investigators have many different reasons for wanting to practice this art. These include the following:

The Challenge and Excitement Investigations are intellectually and emotionally challenging and are rarely boring. The art of investigating appeals to highly analytical and curious people who enjoy new and stimulating tasks.

Making a Difference Investigators tell us they believe their work helps to eradicate discrimination and harassment and solve workplace problems. These investigators make a positive contribution to their organizations when they eliminate barriers and promote a respectful culture.

Studying People Many investigators are drawn to the work because they have a fascination for people. They like engaging with diverse people and enjoy the challenge of understanding people's behavior.

By reading this manual, the investigator may come to understand many other motivations for continuing to perform the investigative role.

Investigating harassment claims in organizations can be a complex and difficult task. The fears described in this chapter are common and real. But these fears need not be realized when investigators have learned what is presented here.

Interpreting Legal Jargon

Sometimes investigators fear making a mistake because they misunderstand legal issues or terms. Understanding legal jargon helps eliminate the mystery of the legal system. Listed below are terms used in this manual.

Names Used for the People or Entities Involved

Complainant The person who brings forward a complaint of discrimination, harassment, or retaliation. Many administrative agencies use this term to avoid any connotation that might imply, prior to investigation, that the complaint is valid. Thus, in conducting an investigation, avoid using the term "victim," because to do so implies you have drawn a conclusion about the claim's validity.

Respondent This is the name given the responding party when a complaint is filed in an administrative agency like the EEOC. Generally, the respondent is the employer.

Plaintiff The person or entity who initiates legal action in court by the filing of a complaint. In the discrimination and harassment area, this is generally the employee.

Defendant The person or entity sued by the plaintiff in court. In discrimination and harassment cases, this is generally the employer and any supervisors who are sued for their participation in the harassment and discrimination.

Names Assigned to the Entity That Will Adjudicate Disputes

EEOC (Equal Employment Opportunity Commission) This is the U.S. governmental entity that investigates claims of discrimination in employment. The agency also issues regulations interpreting the discrimination laws and provides the public with interpretive guidance on compliance with these laws. Complaints generally may be filed with the EEOC within 180 days of the time of the discriminatory act, or within 300 days if the EEOC has an agreement with a state agency to process claims. Proceedings in the EEOC do not involve a jury trial or result in a judgment, but instead generally involve an investigator interviewing witnesses and producing a summary report. The EEOC can, however, decide to sue an employer as the plaintiff if the agency believes that the issue at stake is an important one.

Trial Court When a complaint is filed in court, the first court to hear the case is called the trial court. This is the court that will rule on any motions and make any other necessary rulings. This is also the court where a jury trial will take place, if necessary.

Appellate Court After the trial court has completed processing of the case, the party who loses often has a right to appeal the case to a higher court. The appellate court will not take additional testimony, but instead will rule solely on the legal theories applicable to the case.

Administrative Agency Often a complaint about discrimination or harassment will first be presented to an administrative agency prior to being filed in court. The EEOC is such an administrative agency. Many states also have administrative agencies assigned to process complaints of discrimination and harassment. These agencies do not hold jury trials, and often they do not even have the power to make a binding determination of the issues.

Human Rights Commission Many states have state agencies such as a Human Rights Commission, a Fair Practices Commission, or a similar agency. This agency generally functions the same as the EEOC, except on a state level. Many times, a complainant will file a complaint with both the EEOC and the relevant state agency.

Common Terms Used in Litigating Claims

Affidavit When a party wants to submit information to a judge in a court case, to ask a judge to make a particular ruling prior to trial, the request may be accompanied by a statement by witnesses who can verify the facts important to the request. Attorneys will draft a document with the relevant facts, and the witness will swear to the veracity of the facts.

Affirmative Defense A term used to describe the burden of the employer to disprove that discrimination or harassment occurred. In the legal world, a claim must be proven by providing evidence that meets the criteria outlined by statute or the courts. In defining the elements of proof necessary, the courts define the elements by identifying which party has the burden of proving each fact. When the elements of proof are called an "affirmative defense," this means that the defendant, generally the employer, has the burden of proving those facts. This term is important in understanding liability for harassment, as described in Chapter 2.

Deposition This is a technique used in litigation, after a court complaint is filed, to discover information known by the other parties. In a deposition, the person giving testimony is placed under oath and asked questions and must respond by providing the information. This process is described more fully in Chapter 13.

Discovery The formal process by which the parties gather information from opponents in a court case. The taking of a deposition is one method of discovery. This is described more fully in Chapter 13.

Additional Terms Defined in the Manual

In addition, the following terms are defined throughout the text.

ADA (Americans with Disabilities Act) Defined in Chapter 2.

ADEA (Age Discrimination in Employment Act) Defined in Chapter 2.

Attorney-Client Privilege Defined in Chapter 8.

Attorney Work Product Defined in Chapter 8.

Burden of Proof Defined in Chapter 2.

Corroboration Defined in Chapter 10.

Credibility Defined in Chapter 10.

Cross-Examination Defined in Chapter 13.

Discrimination Defined in Chapter 2.

Harassment Defined in Chapter 2.

Hostile Work Environment Defined in Chapter 2.

Liability Defined in Chapter 2.

Prompt Corrective Action Defined in Chapter 11.

Protected Class Defined in Chapter 2.

Quid Pro Quo Defined in Chapter 2.

Retaliation Defined in Chapter 2.

Titles VI, VII, IX Various Congressional Acts that define discrimination in employment and education, defined in Chapter 2.

Experience with investigations will help to dispel many of the fears a novice investigator may have. With experience, the investigator will come to understand the "jargon" and become adept at handling difficult investigations. The remainder of this book provides the necessary guidance to reduce the fear of the unknown, and allow the investigator to enjoy the investigative process.

Chapter 2

The Law of Harassment and What Investigators Need to Know

HARASSMENT AND DISCRIMINATION are legally defined by several federal, state, and local laws. This manual addresses only U.S. federal law. An investigator should also become familiar with state and local laws in the jurisdictions where the company operates. Some states, cities, or counties have additional protected classes other than those described below. Other states may have more stringent antidiscrimination provisions. Thus, consult with your HR department or legal counsel to determine appropriate state laws.

Why Investigators Need to Know the Law

Investigators need not be attorneys, but they must understand the law of harassment and discrimination. Many questions that arise during the investigation should be answered with a basic understanding of the legal concepts surrounding harassment. For example, during the course of an investigation, a complainant may ask the investigator to stop the investigation. The proper response to that request hinges critically on an understanding of what the law requires. Thus, investigators must understand the law, not so that they can defend the employer in court, but so that they can conduct a legally sufficient investigation.

Relevant EEO Laws

Various federal and state Equal Employment Opportunity (EEO) laws govern discrimination and harassment. The various laws create what are known as "protected classes." If a person is in a "protected class" and is treated differently because of his or her membership in that class, then that treatment violates these laws. Generally "protected classes" created by these laws include gender (including pregnancy), race/color, national origin, religion, age, and disability.

Title VII of the Civil Rights Act of 1964 prohibits discrimination in employment on the basis of race/color, gender, national origin, and religion. Sexual harassment is a form of gender discrimination. Harassment on the basis of race/color, national origin, or religion is also a prohibited form of discrimination under Title VII.

The Americans with Disabilities Act (ADA) prohibits employment discrimination and harassment on the basis of a disability. It also provides that businesses offering accommodations to the public make physical changes to allow access for the disabled. Complaints of discrimination in providing public access should also be investigated, and any discrimination or barriers eliminated, because the next person affected could be an employee.

The Age Discrimination in Employment Act (ADEA) prohibits age discrimination in employment. It also prohibits harassment on the basis of age.

Title VII, the ADA, and the ADEA also prohibit retaliation for prior protected EEO activity. Protected EEO activity includes complaining about harassment, opposing a practice an individual reasonably believes violates the EEO laws, or cooperating in an EEO investigation.

Title VII's prohibitions cover employers with fifteen or more employees, plus labor unions and employment agencies. State and local EEO laws generally cover the same entities and often reach down to cover employers with fewer than fifteen employees. State and local EEO laws often include similar prohibitions against discrimination and harassment.

If the employer is covered, every employee and applicant for employment is protected from discrimination, harassment, and retaliation on the bases listed above. Former employees also are protected when they experience retaliation from a former employer because of prior protected EEO activity.

Student interns and cooperative students often are protected from EEO discrimination and retaliation under Title IX of the Civil Rights Act of 1964. Titles IV and VI of the Civil Rights Act also protect students from discrimination and harassment. Volunteers and independent contractors generally are not protected against discrimination or harassment.

The U.S. Equal Employment Opportunity Commission (EEOC), the U.S. Department of Justice, and/or the U.S. Department of Labor, Office of Federal Contract Compliance Programs, enforce most of the federal EEO laws, including Title VII. The U.S. Department of Education enforces Title IX and other EEO-related laws with respect to students.

State and local human rights agencies enforce their respective state and/or local EEO laws and often have agreements with the EEOC that allow them to enforce federal EEO laws. Because of these work-sharing agreements between the EEOC and state agencies, complainants are more likely to contact the state agencies with their complaints.

In addition, in some states, complainants can go directly to state court to privately enforce their EEO rights and/or they may access federal and/or state courts after exhausting their administrative remedies with federal, state, and/or local EEO enforcement agencies.

Definition of Harassment Under Title VII

A significant focus of the development of harassment law has been on sexual harassment. Because sexual harassment is the most litigated form of harassment, it is discussed in more detail here. However, the analysis that the courts have used to determine liability for sexual harassment also applies to other forms of prohibited harassment.

Title VII of the Civil Rights Act of 1964 is a federal equal employment opportunity (EEO) law. Among other things, it prohibits sexual harassment in the workplace of employers covered by the law.

Sexual harassment is defined under federal law as any unwelcome sexual advances, requests for sexual favors, or any other verbal or physical conduct of a sexual nature when:

- Submission to such conduct is explicitly or implicitly made a term or condition of employment;

- Submission to or rejection of the conduct is used as a basis for any employment decision; or

- The conduct has as its purpose or effect the unreasonable interference with the work environment, or the creation of a hostile, intimidating, or offensive work environment.

Under federal law, the gender and sexual orientation of the parties is irrelevant for purposes of sexual harassment liability.

Most state laws on sexual harassment are consistent with this federal law definition. Gender demeaning behavior is another form of sexual harassment prohibited by federal law and by most state laws.

There are two basic kinds of sexual harassment: (1) quid pro quo (literally, "this for that" in Latin); and (2) hostile work environment.

Quid Pro Quo Sexual Harassment

Quid pro quo sexual harassment occurs when a manager, supervisor, or other agent of the employer uses his or her power to request or demand sexual favors from a subordinate in exchange for providing employment benefits or withholding employment detriments.

Hostile Work Environment Sexual Harassment

Hostile work environment sexual harassment occurs when unwelcome sexual or gender-demeaning conduct so pervades the workplace that a hostile, intimidating, or offensive work environment results. In judging whether a plaintiff has shown a hostile working environment, the courts will rely heavily on factors such as the pervasive nature of the conduct and the severity of the behavior. (See discussion in Chapter 11 concerning levels of severity.) The courts will use the same criteria in judging hostile work environment based on other protected cases.

> The fact that the complainant once welcomed or tolerated the conduct is irrelevant. Once the complainant notifies the offender or a manager, supervisor, or other agent of the employer that the conduct is unwelcome, the conduct must stop, or harassment may be proven.

Employer Liability for Supervisory Harassment and the Affirmative Defense

Since 1986, courts have held employers liable for hostile work environment harassment under a negligence theory. That is, the employer would be liable when it knew or reasonably should have known about the harassment and failed to take prompt corrective action. The employer was deemed to know about the harassment if any of its managers, supervisors, or other agents actually knew, or if they would have known with due diligence.

On June 26, 1998, the U.S. Supreme Court changed the standard for employer liability when a hostile work environment results from supervisory misconduct within the complainant's chain of command. In *Burlington Industries v. Ellerth* and in *Faragher v. City of Boca Raton, Florida,* the Supreme Court held that, where a hostile work environment results from misconduct by a supervisor in the complainant's chain of command, the employer will be vicariously liable, unless it can make the affirmative showing described later in this section.

The U.S. Supreme Court also resolved the quid pro quo liability issue. In Ellerth, the Supreme Court held that quid pro quo sexual harassment occurs only when a supervisor actually uses his or her authority against a subordinate to affect a "tangible employment action." This is sometimes also known as a "tangible job injury." The Court defined "tangible employment action" to include an economic detriment resulting from a significant change in employment, such as hiring, firing, failing to promote, or reassignment with significantly different responsibilities. The Court held that when there is a tangible job injury, the employer is automatically liable, and there is no defense to the claim, if the harassment occurred.

After *Faragher* and *Ellerth*, to prove quid pro quo sexual harassment, the complainant must show that:

- She or he was subjected to unwelcome sexual advances because of her or his sex by a manager, supervisor, or other agent of the employer, and

- She or he suffered a tangible employment action—an economic detriment resulting from a significant change in employment, such as hiring, firing, failing to promote, or reassignment with significantly different responsibilities—because of how she or he responded to the advances.

If the complainant can show only unwelcome sexual advances coupled with unfulfilled threats of a tangible employment action, the complaint becomes one of hostile work environment sexual harassment.

Under *Faragher* and *Ellerth*'s new standard, the complainant must prove a hostile work environment by showing that:

- She or he was subjected to unwelcome sexual or gender-demeaning conduct because of her/his sex, and

- The conduct was sufficiently severe or pervasive to unreasonably interfere with the terms, conditions, or privileges of her or his work environment or create an abusive work environment, and

- For harassment by non-supervisory personnel, the employer should be liable for the conduct under a negligence theory because it knew or should have known about the conduct and failed to take prompt corrective action, or

- If the offender was a supervisor in the victim's chain of command, the employer should be vicariously liable for the conduct, subject to the affirmative defense noted below.

An example demonstrates these two different standards of liability. At a bar after work, several employees were drinking beer. John, the supervisor, began making lewd comments about Ann, his subordinate. Another co-worker of Ann's, Steve, joined in the comments and made several of his own. If a lawsuit arose out of this situation, the court would judge liability for John and Steve's conduct separately. Assuming that the court found a hostile work environment existed, the court would find that the company was vicariously liable for John's conduct, unless the company could prove the affirmative defense noted below. This would be the standard of liability applied, even if this is the first time that John had engaged in such behavior. For Steve's conduct, the company would only be found liable if Ann could prove that Steve had previously engaged in similar conduct and that the company knew of the behavior, but did nothing to stop it.

If the complainant meets the burden of proof under a negligence theory, the employer has no defense to liability. If the complainant meets the burden of proof under a vicarious liability theory, the employer can avoid liability if it can make an affirmative showing the following affirmative defense:

- The employer exercised reasonable care to prevent and promptly correct any sexually harassing behavior in its work environment, and

- The complainant unreasonably failed to take advantage of any preventative or corrective opportunities provided by the employer or to avoid harm otherwise.

The *Faragher* and *Ellerth* Affirmative Defense

The employer must prove that it:

1. Exercised reasonable care to prevent and promptly correct any sexually harassing behavior

AND

2. The employee unreasonably failed to take advantage of any preventive or corrective opportunities provided by the employer or to prevent harm otherwise.

In a recent case, the court found no liability when the employer could show that it did everything correctly. In Van Alstyne v. Ackerly Group (2001), the employer had an effective policy, and it had been communicated to the employee. Once the employee complained, the employer conducted an immediate investigation, immediately met with both the complainant and her attorney, and both the investigator and other supervisors continued to check in with the complainant while the investigation was ongoing. She was assured that no retaliation would occur. She was also told that she did not have to attend meetings alone with her supervisor. She was offered counseling, and the harasser was eventually terminated. The court held that the employer had established the affirmative defense and dismissed the case.

Vicarious liability is a legal device for holding an employer responsible for the acts of its employees. In holding employers vicariously liable for supervisory misconduct within the chain of command, the Supreme Court relied on the fact that it is the supervisor's agency relationship with the employer that affords him or her access to and power over subordinates. This employer-sanctioned access and power facilitates the supervisor's harassment and makes it more difficult for the subordinate to check or avoid the abuse, as she or he might with a co-worker, for example, by walking away, telling him or her where to go, or reporting the abuse to a supervisor. These court decisions further emphasize the importance of training supervisors and holding them accountable for their behavior. (See Chapter 6 discussion of the organizational response to harassment.)

The Court noted that, as in quid pro quo sexual harassment, the supervisor's power to supervise, hire, fire, and set work and pay schedules does not disappear when she or he is engaged in abusive sexual behavior rather than in the legitimate work of the employer. The Court found that it makes sense to hold the employer vicariously liable for supervisory misconduct because the employer has a much greater opportunity to guard against the misconduct by screening supervisors, training them, and closely monitoring their performance, which it cannot do to the same degree with general workers. As a result, most cases that reach the courts involve a supervisor harassing a subordinate.

In *Faragher v. City of Boca Raton,* the U.S. Supreme Court noted that one incident of unwelcome offensive conduct generally will not be sufficient to create a hostile work environment unless the conduct is very severe, threatening, or egregious. It found the same to be true for conduct that occurs only sporadically. In determining what conduct is sufficient to create a hostile work environment, many courts have adopted the perspective of a "reasonable person" of the complainant's gender.

Figures 2.1 and 2.2 represent the liability standards imposed by the Supreme Court after *Faragher* and *Ellerth.*

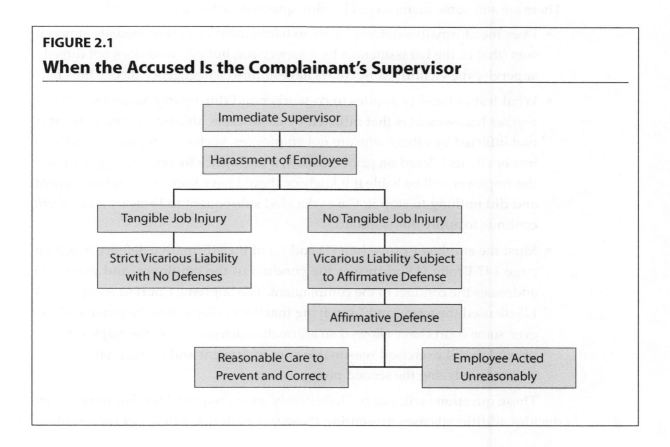

FIGURE 2.1

When the Accused Is the Complainant's Supervisor

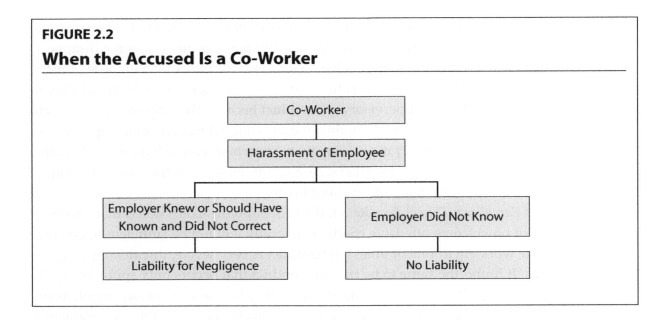

FIGURE 2.2

When the Accused Is a Co-Worker

Unanswered Questions About Liability

There are still some unanswered liability questions after *Faragher* and *Ellerth.*

- Does the affirmative defense apply to harassment by non-immediate supervisors (that is, the harassment is by a supervisor, but one who does not directly supervise the victim)? Most courts have applied a negligence theory thus far.

- What test of liability applies to co-worker and third-party harassment? (Co-worker harassment is that inflicted by co-workers; third-party harassment is that inflicted by others who are not employees, such as independent contractors or clients.) Based on prior case law, a negligence theory will apply, in that the employer will be liable if it knew or should have known of the harassment and did nothing to stop it. Cases decided subsequent to *Faragher* and *Ellerth* continue to apply this standard.

- Must the employer prove *both* (1) and (2) of the affirmative defense noted on page 14? Prong (1) addresses the conduct of the employer, and prong (2) addresses the conduct of the complainant. The Supreme Court in *Faragher* and *Ellerth* used the term "and," implying that both criteria must be proven. However, some courts have allowed an affirmative defense where the employer only proved that it exercised reasonable care to prevent and correct harassment, without analyzing the second prong.

These questions will not be definitively answered until the Supreme Court decides additional cases presenting these fact patterns. Attorneys representing employers should ensure that their knowledge on these issues is current, and that they inform management of any relevant new developments.

EEOC's Guidance on Supervisory Harassment

In June of 1999, the EEOC issued an Enforcement Guidance interpreting the elements of the *Faragher* and *Ellerth* affirmative defense. This is what the EEOC said about important issues relating to the affirmative defense.

Supervisory Capacity

The EEOC's Guidance indicates that a person will be considered a "supervisor" when:

1. The person has the authority to undertake or recommend tangible employment actions affecting the employee, or

2. The individual has authority to direct the employee's daily work activities.

Thus, while an employer may not consider a "crew chief," "shift leader," or "line supervisor" a true supervisor, the EEOC will treat that person as a supervisor for purposes of liability if the above criteria are met.

Tangible Employment Action

According to the Guidance, a tangible employment action:

- Requires an official act of the enterprise;
- Is usually documented in official company records;
- May be subject to review by higher level supervisors; and
- Often requires the formal approval of the enterprise and use of its internal processes.

A tangible employment action also:

- Usually inflicts direct economic harm; and
- Can only be caused by a supervisor or other person acting with the authority of the company.

Examples of "tangible employment actions" given in the Guidance include:

- Hiring and firing;
- Promotion and failure to promote;
- Demotion;
- Undesirable reassignment;

- A decision causing a significant change in benefits;
- Compensation decisions; and
- Work assignments.

The Courts have struggled with whether a "constructive discharge" constitutes a tangible employment action. A constructive discharge occurs when the complainant quits to avoid the harassment, retaliation, or other unlawful activity. Most courts have held that this does not constitute a tangible employment action, probably because it is not an official act of the enterprise. Regardless of whether constructive discharge is a tangible employment action, it remains a serious liability issue, because even if the standard of liability is judged under the affirmative defense, employers found liable will be responsible for damages arising from the complainant's loss of income.

Policy and Complaint Procedure

The Guidance provides suggested content for an employer's policy and complaint procedure. This is the *minimum* standard set by the EEOC, but additional steps should also be taken, as discussed in Chapter 6. Such policies and procedures are a method of preventing harassment, in accordance with the obligation imposed by *Faragher* and *Ellerth*.

The Guidance indicates that the following policy elements must be present:

- A clear explanation of prohibited conduct;
- Assurance that employees who complain will be protected against retaliation;
- A clearly described complaint process that provides an accessible way to complain;
- Assurance that the employer will protect the confidentiality of harassment complaints to the extent possible;
- A complaint process that provides a prompt, thorough, and impartial investigation; and
- Assurance that the employer will take immediate and appropriate corrective action when it determines that harassment has occurred.

See Chapter 6 for a further discussion of appropriate policies and procedures.

Effective Investigative Process

The Guidance states that an effective investigative process is essential for the affirmative defense to succeed. The investigation must be prompt, thorough, and impartial. The employer is encouraged to consider intermediate measures to prevent further harassment. Employers are directed to perform credibility determinations and reach a determination based on all the relevant facts. See the discussion in Chapter 10 of credibility and relevance issues.

Effect of Employee's Failure to Complain

The Guidance also addresses the effect of the second prong of the affirmative defense: the employee's failure to complain. The Guidance makes it clear that the EEOC feels the failure to complain should be excused when:

- Using the complaint mechanism entails a risk of retaliation;
- There are obstacles to complaints; or
- The complaint mechanism is not effective.

Thus, the courts are interested in whether the complaint procedures really work, not just in the language employers have included in their policies.

Other Types of Harassment

Harassment based on other protected classes also violates discrimination laws. Following *Faragher* and *Ellerth*, courts across the country have indicated that they will use the same standard of liability for supervisory sexual harassment in cases addressing other forms of harassment. They will also use the same burden of proof. In its Enforcement Guidance on Supervisory Liability, the EEOC has also signaled that it will apply the same standards to all types of harassment. This means that employers must take reasonable care to prevent or correct promptly any harassment in these areas as well.

Race/Color Harassment

Jokes, innuendoes, or demeaning comments based on race/color are prohibited by Title VII and constitute unlawful harassment if they meet the criteria for harassment.

In 2000–2002 the EEOC publicly settled several prominent racial harassment cases, noting a disturbing increase in racial harassment allegations. The EEOC settled a racial harassment and retaliation suit against Metairie, Louisiana–based Lakeside Toyota, one of the state's largest car dealerships. The suit alleged that a white former used car manager subjected six black employees to a racially hostile work environment that included repeated verbal harassment, racial slurs, physical threats, intimidation, and assaults with a bat. The EEOC also settled a suit against Georgia Pacific, where a white manager in the company's fabrication shop subjected African-American employees to severe and repeated acts of racial harassment, consisting of racial slurs, jokes, comments, and graffiti. The EEOC obtained a $1,825,000 settlement in a racial harassment lawsuit on behalf of thirty-two current and former African-American employees of Scientific Colors, Inc., doing business as Apollo Colors. According to the suit, the egregious harassment included racist graffiti, display of hangman's nooses, and racial epithets at the employer's facility in Rockdale, Illinois. The EEOC also settled a case against a nursing home where the administrator had frequently used racial slurs to refer to black employees and ordered white supervisors and charge nurses to discipline black employees without cause. The administrator also required applications to be coded with smiling faces for white applicants and frowning faces for black applicants.

Religious Harassment

Jokes, demeaning comments, or taunting on the basis of religion can also constitute harassment if it creates a hostile working environment. However, an employer also has an obligation to provide reasonable accommodation to its employees' religious beliefs. Thus, the employer must tolerate some religious expression when it does not create undue disruption or hardship. Employers seeking to prevent religious harassment must thus tread very carefully in walking the line between accommodation of religious beliefs and the protection against harassment on the basis of religion. Generally, if religious expressions by one employee create a hostile environment for another, the employer can curb the expression to eliminate the hostile work environment. Most, if not all, courts have considered the creation of a hostile work environment to be undue disruption or hardship. There was a significant rise in religious discrimination issues following September 11, 2001; thus employers should be especially vigilant to ensure that employees who practice Islam and other religions closely identified with terrorism by some Americans do not become the targets of harassment. In addition, derogatory jokes about religion, hostility toward religions, stereotyping, and discrimination because of religion are not uncommon in workplaces; employers must take steps to address *all* religious harassment.

Joy was a Unitarian who believed in religious diversity and inclusiveness. These beliefs led her to react strongly to a Christmas Nativity scene in the workplace, as well as other Christmas decorations and events. She complained to her supervisor, who said that her complaints were trivial. All she wanted, Joy stated, was to have religious displays out of the workplace. While it often is very easy to accommodate religious beliefs in the workplace, ignoring simple requests can get the employer in trouble. This supervisor should not have demeaned the employee's complaints, and instead should have looked for an accommodation that would satisfy the employee's religious objections, if possible.

National Origin Harassment

Jokes about an employee's country of origin and demeaning comments about those from other countries could lead to claims of national origin harassment, which will be judged on the same grounds as noted previously. Current international events often enhance the potential for national origin harassment. For example, since the terrorist attacks on the World Trade Center on September 11, 2001, and the war in Iraq, derogatory comments about other countries have become particularly problematic, and claims have risen dramatically. Many Americans feel strongly that certain world nations may be more responsible for terrorist events, or that some countries should have taken a different position on the war effort, and those employees may be tempted to vent frustrations against co-workers from those nations. Employers must take special care to prevent and correct such harassing behavior.

A French high-tech company with a production facility in the United States had an employee who created and distributed flyers that accused the French of exploiting Americans by fighting to keep unions out of their manufacturing plants, while at the same time accusing the French of being cowards and harming American interests by not supporting the war in Iraq. The resulting polarization of the French and American employees and their French management created a hostile environment for many employees because of these national origin issues.

On December 2, 2002, the EEOC issued a new section for its Compliance Manual on national origin discrimination. This manual is intended to provide guidance to employers on dealing with national origin issues in the workplace. In the manual, the EEOC noted that harassment was one of the most common claims raised in national origin discrimination charges filed with that agency. The EEOC noted that 2,719 charges of national origin harassment had been filed in fiscal year 2002.

The EEOC indicated that a number of factors would be examined in determining whether national origin harassment occurred. Among the factors listed were:

1. Whether the conduct was physically threatening or intimidating;

2. How frequently the conduct was repeated;

3. Whether the conduct was hostile or patently offensive;

4. The context in which the harassment occurred; and

5. Whether management responded appropriately when it learned of the harassment.

The fifth factor noted by the EEOC is an incorporation of the principles of *Faragher* and *Ellerth* into the national origin area. The EEOC suggested that one of the best ways to prevent harassment was to have a clearly communicated policy prohibiting it and to train managers on how to identify and respond effectively to harassment.

Age Harassment

Jokes, innuendoes, or demeaning comments based on a person's advanced age are prohibited by the Age Discrimination in Employment Act and, if they meet the criteria for harassment, constitute unlawful harassment. The ADEA protects those over 40 years of age against discrimination on the basis of their age.

Disability Harassment

While the Americans with Disabilities Act is relatively new to the discrimination scene, recent cases confirm that harassment on the basis of disability is actionable if it meets the hostile work environment test. This is an especially critical issue for employers, who must provide reasonable accommodations for employees with disabilities; these accommodations may in turn lead to resentment and comments from other employees. This text cannot deal in depth with the complicated issue of reasonable accommodations; thus, employers addressing this issue should consult other texts or seek legal assistance from counsel.

> The EEOC found an employer liable for disability harassment based on demeaning and mean-spirited comments from a number of male co-workers who expressed resentment toward the complainant, for whom accommodations had been made. The Commission found that a supervisor participated in and encouraged the harassment (*Horkan v. United States Postal Service*).

Retaliation After the Original Complaint

Often, once a complaint of harassment or discrimination is made, the original problem is resolved, but the most dangerous behavior remains unresolved. For this reason legal claims alleging retaliation often succeed, even when the original discrimination was corrected by the employer. Employers must not ignore the potential for retaliation complaints whenever harassment or discrimination is alleged.

When an employee files a harassment complaint, participates in a harassment investigation, or opposes a practice he or she reasonably believes violates EEO laws, he or she is protected from retaliation because of that activity. Examples of retaliation include:

- Discharge;
- Failure to promote;
- Change of job duties; and
- Isolating, ridiculing, or demeaning an individual because of prior EEO activity.

To prove retaliation, the complainant must show that:

- She or he engaged in prior protected EEO activity;
- The employer was aware of such activity;
- She or he suffered an adverse employment action; and
- There is a causal connection between the prior protected EEO activity and the adverse action.

The adverse actions listed above do not necessarily have to be actions of a supervisor. Recent cases have made it clear that employers also have an obligation to stop retaliation where the perpetrators are co-workers.

On May 20, 1998, the EEOC issued a new section for its Compliance Manual that addressed retaliation under all the EEO laws enforced by that agency. The Manual now indicates that protected activity includes both filing a charge under Title VII and opposition to activities that are reasonably believed to constitute discrimination. The EEOC recognized that any opposition must be "reasonable" and based on a good-faith belief that discrimination is occurring. The Compliance Manual also indicates that the person entitled to protection need not be the person who engaged in the opposition, so long as there is a nexus between the opposition and the retaliation. For example, an employee tells a supervisor that she does not like it when the supervisor refers to a co-worker with a limp as "gimpy." If the supervisor retaliates by naming the complaining employee "wimpy" and then refers to the two employees as "wimpy" and "gimpy," that would be a violation of these laws against retaliation.

In addition, the practices opposed need not be practices of the offending employer. This means that an employer will be guilty of retaliation against an applicant when it uses that person's opposition to a former employer's discriminatory practices as a reason to refuse to make a job offer.

Finally, the Compliance Manual now confirms that participation is protected regardless of whether the original allegation of discrimination is valid or reasonable. Thus, employers who attempt to discipline employees who file "false" charges take a real risk of retaliation liability, because of the difficulty of proving falsity. Some employers will take action against complaints deemed malicious and false, but it is very difficult to discern the difference between those complaints that are simply unverified and those that are maliciously false. Employers who wish to discipline employees for allegedly malicious complaints should seek legal counsel regarding that issue.

Important Things to Remember About Retaliation Complaints

1. Victims do not have to be members of a protected class;

2. Victims do not have to raise viable complaints of discrimination;

3. Victims can sue current or former employers;

4. Victims can base claims on an associate's protected activity; and

5. There is a wide range of protected activity included such as:

- The person protected does not have to use the word "discrimination," just include complaints about differing treatment for a protected class

- Complaints about discrimination against self

- Complaints about discrimination against others

- Threatening to file a charge of discrimination

- Complaining about discrimination of a former employer

For investigators, the critical issues are

1. If a complaint of harassment is under investigation, the investigator must be careful to collect information about possible retaliation as well, including facts such as adverse actions taken against the complainant after the complaint was lodged and/or any anger or animus directed at the complainant by the alleged harasser(s) or co-workers, including any information indicating that they might act on that anger or animus. All of this information is important in making sure that a complete investigation is conducted. Separate findings should be made on both the harassment and the retaliation.

2. If information concerning potential retaliation is gathered in the investigation, the investigator must be sure to communicate that information to the decision maker so that an interim decision can be made concerning the protection of the complainant against further retaliation.

Sometimes, retaliation is not unlawful. The manner of opposition must be reasonable and motivated by opposition, not some other agenda. However, this exception is narrowly drawn and should not generally be relied on in conducting investigations.

One of the most important criteria in determining whether retaliation has occurred is the timing of the protected activity and the adverse action. For example, if an employee complains of harassment and is disciplined the next day, the timing raises a strong presumption of a retaliatory motive. Thus, in a retaliation investigation, pay attention to the timing of events. In addition, the involvement of the target of the harassment complaint in the adverse action is critical. Generally, retaliation includes some motive, revenge, or "payback" and generally is more likely to occur when the target of the harassment or discrimination complaint is involved in the decision-making process for the adverse action. These are important facts to gather in investigating alleged retaliation.

Special Problems in Harassment Law
Third-Party Harassment

Third-party harassment, where the alleged harasser is not an employee, creates special problems for employers. Many employees may have contact with customers, clients, consultants, suppliers, members of the general public, or independent contractors who work for other employers.

Third-party conduct that meets the definition of harassment and that creates a hostile work environment is conduct that must be investigated and remedied, just as with any other harassment. However, when the harassing behavior is that of a third party, the courts will likely not apply the *Faragher* and *Ellerth* affirmative defense test. Instead, they will likely apply a test of whether the employer "knew or should have known" of the harassment and failed to take reasonable steps to stop known harassing behavior. This is the same test that will likely be applied to co-worker harassment.

Cases where employers have been found liable for third-party harassment have been those for which the employer failed to stop the harassment when a complaint was received and instead encouraged the employee to continue dealing with the offending party and make him or her "happy." The employer has been absolved of liability when the employer took strong steps to stop the harassment immediately.

> In an Oklahoma case, a waitress at Pizza Hut was subjected to lewd comments and sexual touching by two regular customers. The employee told her manager, but the manager insisted that she continue to wait on the customers. The manager's response ignored a company manual describing the appropriate response, which included sending a male waiter to wait on the customers, having the manager wait on them, or asking them to leave. The employer was ordered to pay $200,000 in damages to the waitress (*Lockard v. Pizza Hut*).

Thus, when an allegation involves third-party harassment, the investigator must treat the complaint the same as any other complaint and conduct a thorough investigation. Special care must be used to ensure confidentiality, to the extent possible, when dealing with those who are not employed by the organization.

Sexual Favoritism

Allegations of sexual favoritism may also lead to a harassment complaint. The EEOC has issued a guidance on this subject titled "Policy Guidance on Employer Liability Under Title VII for Sexual Favoritism," which states:

> *Where employment opportunities or benefits are granted because of an individual's submission to the employer's sexual advances or requests for sexual favors, the employer may be held liable for unlawful sexual discrimination against other persons who were qualified for but were denied that employment opportunity or benefit.*

Thus, the EEOC has attempted to prohibit, as sex discrimination, the adverse effect on the workgroup when one employee gains promotions or other job benefits because of submission to sexual advances. The EEOC has said that isolated instances of favoritism are not prohibited. Liability can arise when the favoritism is widespread and an offended party can show that the discriminatory or demeaning attitude was pervasive enough to create a hostile work environment.

The important thing to remember when there is a problem with sexual favoritism is that, like a harassment complaint, this allegation must be investigated. Simply because the primary relationship appears to be consensual does not mean that no potential coercion exists. Thus, employers should take steps to talk with the involved employees to ensure that the relationship itself is consensual. Finally, the victim of this type of behavior may be the person who did not receive job benefits because of favoritism.

Workplace Dating

Romance in the workplace has become a major issue for employers, with increasing awareness of the potential for sexual harassment claims. The danger of liability for sexual favoritism, even with a consensual relationship, looms.

In 2001, the Society for Human Resource Management (SHRM) teamed up with CareerJournal.com to conduct a survey of Human Resource (HR) professionals and executives on workplace romance concerns. When asked about their reasons for concern regarding workplace romance, 95 percent of the HR professionals indicated a concern about potential claims for sexual harassment. Of the executives polled, 76 percent cited the same concern about sexual harassment. Yet many companies had not yet instituted a written policy concerning workplace romance. Only 20 percent of the HR professionals indicated that their company had either a written or verbal policy on the issue (15 percent had a written policy, and 5 percent had a verbal policy).

While workplace romance has always existed, employers have become increasingly uncomfortable with its existence. At times, it can result in unequal treatment, or the appearance of unequal treatment, for those not involved in the relationship. Workplace romance can also result in the appearance of unfair reprisals against subordinate employees once the romance ends.

According to the developing law in this area, it is generally permissible for employers to prohibit dating between some classes of employees, based on the premise that dating and romantic relationships interfere with company morale, increase the risk of favoritism, and reduce the productivity of the couple involved. However, some employee challenges to anti-fraternization rules have been successful, especially where public employment is involved, with an accompanying constitutional right to privacy or freedom of association.

Thus, if a complaint arises concerning a romantic relationship, even if it appears consensual, the employer must take it seriously. An investigation must be done. Some employers, even upon a finding that the relationship is consensual, have taken steps to ensure that no supervisor-subordinate relationship exists and have had the involved employees sign an agreement indicating that the relationship is consensual.

If you have a policy on workplace dating, *you must be prepared to enforce it*, and enforce it fairly against all employees. Each organization must examine its own culture to determine if such a policy is enforceable. There may be many circumstances where a policy is unenforceable or impractical. For example, if the company is a family-owned business, then there are likely to be many family members already working together, and it would be difficult to ban employees from the same kinds of relationships. Also, if the company is very small, imposing a workplace dating rule could have disastrous consequences if the enforcement of the policy requires the employer to terminate a key employee. If the employer may not want to enforce the policy in every circumstance, then it would likely be futile to have such a policy.

Temporary Workers

If a temporary worker is considered an "employee" for purposes of EEO laws, then the employer's duty with respect to sexual harassment is identical to its duty to regular employees. Thus the employer must take steps to stop harassment of a temporary worker. If harassment occurs, the employer must investigate it and act promptly to correct it.

The EEOC has issued a Guidance explaining how the law of harassment applies to temporary workers. The Guidance places temporary workers in the "employee" category unless they are considered "independent contractors." If the employer retains the right to control the means and methods by which the worker accomplishes the work, then the worker is an "employee." The label used to identify the worker is not determinative. In other words, the employer can call a worker an independent contractor, but if the worker works on the employer's premises, uses the employer's equipment, and performs the same tasks as a regular employee, then the worker will be deemed an employee for purposes of EEO laws. If both a temporary staffing firm and the employer have control, then both have the obligations of an employer under EEO laws.

Nontarget Harassment

Hostile work environment harassment can occur regardless of whether the victim was the target of the harassment.

When jokes, comments, and innuendoes are directed at Employee A, but Employee B finds the conduct offensive, the conduct may be pervasive enough that it creates a hostile working environment for Employee B. Liability can be assessed regardless of the fact that Employee A may find the conduct humorous and non-offensive. Thus, an employer must correct the harassing behavior, even when an employee is not the "target" of the behavior. This situation calls for an investigation.

Same Sex Harassment

In *Oncale v. Sundowner Offshore Services, Inc.* (1998), the U.S. Supreme Court determined that a male could maintain a claim for hostile work environment sexual harassment, even when the alleged harassers were also male.

The Court held that the prohibition against discrimination "because of sex" protects men as well as women. However, the Court made it clear that Title VII is directed at discrimination because of sex, and thus a plaintiff claiming same sex harassment must still prove that he or she was treated differently because of his or her gender. Thus, a complaint from a male employee about conduct of other males must still be investigated and remedied if necessary. The same is true for complaints from females about the behavior of other females.

> *Oncale* involved a situation where a male worker on an offshore oil rig was subjected to behavior and comments that were both demeaning and sexual in nature. The male employee was physically assaulted by other employees and threatened with rape by male co-workers. All of the employees on the oil rig were male. The court held that this behavior was sufficiently hostile or abusive to support a complaint of hostile work environment.

Off-Duty Conduct

Employers must regulate conduct of their employees that creates a hostile work environment for any employee.

Courts often judge liability for harassment based on both on-duty and off-duty conduct. For example, in *Reed v. MBNA Marketing Systems, Inc.*, the court viewed a demand for oral sex that occurred off-duty as part of a pattern of increasingly suggestive behavior at work. The court also cited another case, *Crowley v. L.L. Bean* where the court had looked at non-workplace conduct to help determine the severity and pervasiveness of the hostility in the workplace.

The obligation to prevent harassment is not diminished or eliminated because some of the offensive conduct occurred off-duty or off the employer's premises between two employees. If the conduct affects the workplace and the working relationship between the two employees, then it must be addressed. Thus the investigation will focus not only on the nature of the off-duty conduct, but also on how it affected the workplace and the working relationship between employees.

Illegal Aliens

When illegal aliens are employed in a workforce, they do not lose their protection against sexual harassment. The same prevention and correction obligations of an employer apply when the victimized employee is an illegal alien. Thus, an investigation must be completed and corrective action taken.

In 1999, the EEOC issued an Enforcement Guidance that took the position that illegal aliens who are subjected to workplace discrimination or harassment are entitled to all of the monetary remedies, including back pay, as any other employee discriminated against in the workplace. However, on June 27, 2002, the EEOC rescinded that Guidance following a decision of the U.S. Supreme Court in a case involving the National Labor Relations Board. The EEOC took the position that illegal aliens are protected by discrimination laws, but the Supreme Court decision called into question whether they could be awarded monetary damages for discrimination. Investigators dealing with harassment or discrimination claims involving undocumented workers should therefore consult the latest Guidance in determining prompt corrective action. See Chapter 11.

This chapter provides a very brief summary of the law of harassment, discrimination, and retaliation. It will provide useful background knowledge for investigators who are completing their investigations. While the investigation should be designed to uncover potential policy violations, knowledge of legal standards guides the investigator in gathering appropriate information. This information should enable the organization to assess potential legal liability and decide what action should be taken.

Chapter 3

The Psychology of Harassment

GOOD INVESTIGATING IS AS MUCH AN ART as it is a technical skill. "People skills" and experience with many types of people and organizations enable an investigator to (1) develop rapport, (2) intuitively unveil truth, and (3) guide others through an emotionally strenuous process. Although nothing can substitute for experience, twenty-five years of social science research can help guide the task of investigating.

The Nature of Harassment

By far the most widely studied form of harassment is sexual harassment. Racial and national origin harassment are just beginning to be examined by social scientists. The study of harassment based on religion, age, and disability are still far behind.

Sexual Harassment

Extensive research categorizes sexual harassment into three main areas (Fitzgerald, Hulin, & Drasgow, 1995): (1) sexual coercion, including quid pro quo; (2) unwelcome sexual attention (sexual behavior intended to engage in a relationship); and (3) gender hostility (demeaning and derogatory behavior, such as stereotyping, hostile behavior based on gender). This last category is by far the most common form of sexual harassment, either by itself or combined with unwelcome sexual attention (Fitzgerald, Swan, & Magley, 1997).

Research has consistently found that more than 90 percent of sexual harassment involves men harassing women. Less than 2 percent of female targets are harassed by other women, but when men are the target, the harasser is also male as much as 50 percent of the time (Berdahl, Magley, & Waldon, 1996).

A newly appointed female warehouse manager named Sue Ferina frequently found her briefcase missing. In addition, sexual cartoons were attached to her office door with her name scrawled on various female characters. Some of the employees pretended not to hear her when she called out orders or messages. When she investigated the sexual cartoons, threatening messages were left for her to read. At first, Sue expected these behaviors and felt only mildly annoyed. She had worked in the environment for fifteen years and had developed a thick skin. Gradually, as others in the warehouse witnessed these events, she felt humiliated and angry. Not wanting management to see her as "weak," she tried to address the issue herself by reading and reinforcing the policy and being direct and clear about her instructions. It was not until the sexually threatening messages began that Sue felt compelled to report the behaviors to Human Resources. An investigation was begun but did not reveal the perpetrators. After reporting the incidents, Sue started experiencing headaches, found it difficult to get to sleep, and felt demoralized when she met with her male peers. She became both angry and depressed and wondered if moving into management was the right choice for her.

This example reflects the sexual harassment literature: where there is gender hostility, there are likely to be unwelcome sexual advances and behaviors as well. Research by Pryor (Pryor, LaVite, & Stoller, 1993) indicates that when sexual materials (for example, e-mails, calendars, and cartoons) pervade the workplace, interpersonal sexual behavior is more likely to occur. That is, sexual material in the workplace apparently sends a message to some that comments, physical behavior, or propositioning will be tolerated.

Racial, Ethnic, National Origin, Disability, or Age Harassment

Other forms of discriminatory harassment are usually defined in terms of epithets, jokes about the targeted groups, behavior that reflects stereotyping, or demeaning and derogatory looks, and behaviors and comments toward employees of a particular group. There is no scientific way to distinguish among people of the world based on their color or ethnic origin. The word "race" is now generally accepted as a social construct created centuries ago to distinguish between people of European ancestry and people of color; "race" often implied that people who were different were a lesser form of humanity (Mills, 1997). For example, the English declared themselves the English race and thought of those in Africa as the African race. Thus most of the claims that fall within the legal parameters of "race discrimination, or harassment" really address color, ethnicity, or national origin. (See Chapter 4 for a discussion about how to help identify these forms of harassing behaviors when they are more subtle.)

Incivility and Workplace Aggression

During the last few years, researchers have begun to examine common workplace behaviors that employees often regard as harassing but which are not included in legal definitions. Although physical violence and unlawful behavior in the workplace receive the most media attention, researchers have found that verbal, non-physical violence is much more prevalent and pervasive (Keashly, 2001). Aggressive behaviors of a psychological nature include supervisors or co-workers yelling, often in an angry tone of voice (Donovan, Drasgow, & Munson, 1998); giving dirty looks (Keashly, 2001); insulting or criticizing; making threats; using differential or unfair treatment; discounting other's contributions; demanding, unreasonable expectations; dishonesty; spreading rumors; and game playing (Glomb, 2002). Aggressive behaviors of a more physical nature include making angry gestures (pounding one's fist, pointing fingers, rolling eyes); using hostile body language (leaning across the desk); throwing something (a file or stack of papers); or physically assaulting another (Donovan, Drasgow, & Munson, 1998; Keashly, 2001).

More subtle disrespectful behaviors have been measured by a tool researchers call the Incivility Scale and include both respectful behaviors (employees praised for good work; questions and problems are responded to quickly) and disrespectful behaviors (supervisors play favorites; employees put each other down; supervisors swear at employees) (Cortina, Magley, Williams, & Langhout, 2001). Incivility and workplace aggression result in negative and harmful outcomes as much as discriminatory harassment. As a result, employers are increasingly including a general harassment clause in their policy to address general harassment. (See Chapter 6 for a discussion regarding general harassment clause.)

The manufacturing plant's corporate office received a complaint on their 800 number from a supervisor who was leaving his job because of the "abuse and stress" he had endured from his chain of command over the last two years. Because of the potential magnitude of the case, the company hired an outside investigator. Interviewing the supervisor led the investigator to ten more "victimized" employees that eventually led to over fifty interviews. Employees and lower managers alike described vulgar language, intimidating physical and psychological tactics, and a retaliatory environment that had kept employees from coming forward for years. While Title VII harassment was not a major part of the investigation, sexual and ethnic comments and jokes were not uncommon and, more important, no one in management intervened. The president of the company was shocked and dismayed.

He wondered how such an abusive, unproductive workplace was allowed to flourish when the corporate values did not support such a climate. After careful analysis, he realized that he had never personally talked to the employees and that the plant had received no management training for at least five years.

This example demonstrates an investigation in which general harassment was the primary culprit. Even if organizations do not have a policy that formally prohibits disrespectful behavior, many investigators find that these behaviors are part of the root problem that complainants want to be addressed. They also recognize that, if these behaviors are tolerated, protected class harassment is not far behind. Their importance and impact should not be underestimated.

Retaliation

Retaliation is a separate cause of action under the law (see Chapter 2 for a full discussion of relevant laws) and has been studied separately from harassment (Cortina & Magley, 2002). Retaliation may take many forms, including lowered performance reviews or even firing. It often takes the form of ostracization by management or employees or other hostile behavior. Regardless of the form, retaliation is likely to result in psychological and workplace effects as or more deleterious than the harassment itself.

The severe impact of retaliation is another reason why investigators and management must actively prevent and address retaliation during and after an investigation.

Harassers

Although many employers would like to be able to screen out harassers through personality or mental health devices, it is not possible to predict *any* kind of harassment through psychological assessments. Harassment behavior results from a complex array of personality, cultural, and other learned values and behaviors, and the extent to which it is likely to occur is heavily dependent on whether the environment tolerates such behaviors (Hulin, Fitzgerald, & Drasgow, 1996; Pryor & Whalen, 1997). However, psychological research helps us understand patterns and individual reasons for harassment.

Quid Pro Quo Harassers

John Pryor has studied men who are "likely to sexually harass" (Pryor, Gledd, & Williams, 1995). Pryor has identified these men by presenting them with "quid pro quo" scenarios and asking whether they would engage in the behaviors if they knew they would not be caught. These men completed psychological measures and also participated in experimental situations to further determine their propensity to harass.

According to this and other research, men who are likely to engage in coercive sexual harassment:

- View themselves as hyper-masculine (tough, self-reliant);
- See sex as a way to deal with boredom, as a way to impress others, or as a means of sheer physical gratification;
- Score low on empathy scales;
- Are conservative in their attitudes toward women's roles;
- Tend to perceive sex and dominance as indistinguishable; and
- When in power positions, are more likely to "objectify" women.

In experimental situations, Pryor also discovered that these men were more likely to touch others or make sexual comments when the environment was tolerant of such behavior (Pryor, LaVite, & Stoller, 1993). The challenge for the investigator is to realize that these characteristics are rarely visible to others and often contradict what others see. This is not unusual; most rapists are not distinguishable in sophisticated psychological testing and tend to appear "normal" to other people (Pryor, LaVite, & Stoller, 1993). Therefore, it should not be surprising to discover that CEOs or judges who are known for their competence and intelligence can use their power to coerce someone into sex. When such cases are investigated, the facts reveal the truth—character analyses are unhelpful. No matter what you think about the person or what your prior experience is, never *assume* that he or she is not capable of the behavior of which he or she is accused.

Individual Reasons for Harassment

Sometimes it is easier for the investigators to spot patterns of harassment if they can first discern why the person may have committed such behavior. Research and experience have helped us identify reoccurring reasons and causes of sexual harassment (Stringer, Remick, Salisbury, & Ginorio, 1990).

Power Issues

One of the most common reasons why effective managers and powerful leaders find themselves behaving in ways that are perceived as harassing is their blind spot to the impact of their power on others. We have discovered that these men and women see themselves as "one of the team" and do not see their jokes and comments as having any more influence on their employees than a co-worker's behavior. Although they are more likely to admit the behavior, they may rigorously minimize the fact that it frightened, offended, or even threatened someone.

Power almost always has an active role in harassment. Harassment of all types usually emerges in a situation in which one person has power over another. Supervisory power is only one kind. Age, knowledge, race, gender, membership in the majority group at work (occupation, sexual orientation, and so forth), perceived affiliation with others who have power, and the power of longevity in a workplace are only a few sources of power from which harassment emerges. Thus, co-workers can have significant power over one another and use that power to harass. Analyzing the power factors in a harassment complaint is important because it helps us understand the impact of the harassment and what may be necessary to correct the situation.

Personal Crisis

Sometimes someone sexually harasses for the first time in response to an emotional, legal, physical, or work crisis. Whether their motivation is to bolster their self-esteem or to desperately connect with someone else to satisfy their needs, persons in sudden crisis don't necessarily have a pattern of harassment. If you choose to retain such employees, referring them to an employee assistance program or counseling may help them.

Personality or Addictive Disorders

Most mean-spirited and outrageous harassing behavior emerges from a long-term personality disorder or from the impact of addiction. Drugs and alcohol remove inhibiting forces on the emotional part of the brain. Having destructive self-centered personalities often results in people disassociating from the impact of their behavior on others—simply put, people with character disorders or addictions focus totally on their own needs and often show little real interest in others. Personality disorders are often difficult to spot, because these individuals may appear very different at work. Serious individual problems are rarely changed through private counseling or other mental health resources. Addiction requires intensive inpatient or outpatient treatment and personality disorders take years to develop and years to change. Finally, individuals who do not see and take responsibility for their own behavior cannot benefit from counseling, therapy, or programs unless they really want to change.

Ignorance

Some people have no idea how sexual, racial, religious, or other jokes affect people from different backgrounds. Despite obvious verbal or nonverbal cues that others interpret their behavior as offensive or even threatening, they claim that their actions are reasonable because their "intent" is to joke, kid, or make others feel welcome. If they have a positive history of working with people and genuinely want to become more successful with people, training and individual coaching might help these harassers change their behavior. However, their behavior may also reflect underlying sexist or racist attitudes or a personality disorder, which are highly resistant to change.

A president of a small subsidiary of a high-tech company was accused of making demeaning comments about gender and race. He was astounded. He had a reputation for promoting women and people of many sexual orientations and believed he valued their contribution. The investigation showed that, by and large, gay and lesbian employees and women found him to be open and supportive. It was during off-site events, on the road, and at company parties that the executive made the remarks, which alienated many people. When questioned why he chose to make these comments, the president remarked that in these settings he felt less like a "president" and more like one of the team with whom he was interacting. He believed that his ability to "relate" made him likable. He believed his egalitarian attitude was part of what made him an effective president and did not realize that his power remained with him in every setting and that every comment potentially carried a powerful message. He also underestimated the effect his remarks had on others.

Sexism, Racism, or Stereotyping

Although power issues are also critical in analyzing nonsexual forms of harassment, the reasons for other types of harassment can be very different. Many of the "causes" of other forms of harassment lie in the web of our culture that institutionalizes stereotyping, racism, and oppression of those who are less privileged. *All* of us carry around stereotypes of groups that affect how we behave toward people. In debriefing some harassers who admit to their demeaning jokes and comments, they purport to have no idea why they said or did things. They are surprised that mimicking a Japanese accent in a joke, using the word faggot, or sharing stereotypes about a religion are against the company policy and are potentially illegal and harmful to others. Their willingness to look at the impact of their behavior and change their attitudes is key to whether or not these behaviors are likely to be repeated.

Coping with Harassment

Americans value individual responsibility and accountability. We tend to believe that most bad things happen as a result of our own behavior or failings and that we should be able to find some way to confront the situation. Also, American culture values directness and expects that, when people are unhappy, they should tell the person with whom they have had the problem. Such values lead investigators, managers, and co-workers to ask these questions:

- Why didn't the person come forward sooner?

- Why do some victims go along with the behavior or even participate in the behavior?

- Why do some confront the harasser and some do not?

- Why do people experience and describe sexual harassment but only label it as sexual harassment 20 percent of the time?

Most studies of what researchers label "coping" have examined sexual harassment, although some of the results can be applied to other harassment. This research validates that there is a notable discrepancy between (1) how people believe that they *would* respond to harassment if they were exposed to it and (2) how victims actually *do* respond (Fitzgerald, Swan, & Fischer, 1995). Studies across cultures have confirmed that avoidance (avoiding interacting with the person), denial (relabeling the situation as benign, putting up with the behavior, detaching from the harassment, self-blame, and minimizing), assertion (talking to the offender, complaining), advocacy seeking (getting help from a supervisor or co-worker; filing a complaint), and social coping (seeking social support at work or at home) are universal responses to sexual harassment (Wasti & Cortina, 2002). By far the most commonly used method of coping with sexual harassment is avoiding the harasser, denying that the harassment is happening, and minimizing the impact of the harasser.

When do victims seek out the organization to advocate for their needs? Most studies (Culbertson, Rosenfield, Booth-Kewley, & Magnuson, 1992; Gutek, 1985) document that few victims ever file formal complaints or even informally discuss harassment with organizational authorities. As a result of good training and organizational processes, and well-publicized events (such as the Hill-Thomas hearings and publicized lawsuits), these percentages have been increasing, but they are still quite low. Many victims prefer to handle the situation themselves or believe it was "not important enough" to report. They fear being labeled as "whiners" and believe that nothing can or will be done (Gutek & Koss, 1993; Martindale, 1990) or are reluctant to cause problems for the offender. The most common reason is fear—fear of retaliation, of not being believed, of damaging one's situation, or of being shamed and humiliated (Gutek & Koss, 1993). The dilemma for complainants is that assertive responses such as confronting the harasser or filing a complaint are not only frequently ineffective, but often actually make things worse and may prompt psychological and health-related effects (Hesson-McInnis & Fitzgerald, 1997). As Livingston (1982) remarked, "Given the immense psychological and economic costs to individuals who use formal action, in contrast to the potentially meager gains, it is not surprising that so few victims choose" these responses.

Racial harassment, on the other hand, is rarely viewed as irrelevant or benign by recipients (Branscombe, Harvey, & Schmitt, 1995). Resignation (accepting that harassment is happening), confrontation, and seeking social support were among the major coping mechanisms identified in racial harassment studies focusing on African Americans. While the dynamics of workplace abuse and other forms of harassment may create a slightly different pattern of coping, experienced investigators have found that harassment victims are prone to tolerate even horrendous behavior in their workplace.

Finally, recent research (Bergman, Langhout, Palmieri, Cortina, & Fitzgerald, 2002) documents that organizational procedures that result in clear outcomes influence whether or not employees report the harassment in the future. It also affects their satisfaction levels with work, supervisors, and co-workers. When organizations have lengthy, poorly defined, and ineffective processes, reporting can harm the victim in terms of job and psychological outcomes.

Although there are many factors that affect how people cope with the various forms of harassment, confronting the person early in the process is more the exception than the norm. Fear of retaliation is the number one reason why complainants do not come forward and why they choose more indirect, safer methods of coping. Another factor in whether women come forward with complaints is the tendency to not label behavior as sexual harassment, even when the behavior is unwelcome, derogatory, and sexual (Fitzgerald, Swan, & Magley, 1997). As cultures change, organizations improve complaint resolution processes, and new generations change their attitudes about harassment, methods of coping may also change.

For the present, investigators should thoroughly understand the implications of research on coping with harassment. They should be open and nonjudgmental when they inquire about how a complainant copes with harassment. Investigators should also use the research to help explain victim behaviors to management and advocate for speedy, full remedies when harassment has occurred (see Chapter 12 for a thorough discussion of remedies). Finally, they should consider not only the perspective of the individual involved, but also whether the work environment and complaint processes have created a safe climate in which complaints will be taken seriously.

The Impact of Harassment on Individuals and Workgroups

In the last two decades, the effects of sexual harassment, incivility, and racial harassment have become increasingly well-documented. Studies from many different workplaces have consistently shown that harassment can have traumatic effects on employees, both as individuals and as members of the workgroup in which the harassment is occurring. Identifying these effects is crucial for the investigator and for management. First, they help determine the severity of the harassment and the potential sanctions. Second, understanding the impact of harassment encourages the organization to take necessary steps (see Chapter 12) to heal employees and return them to their productive best!

Effects on Individuals

Compared with non-harassed employees, harassed employees experience:

- Less psychological well-being;

- More post-traumatic stress symptoms (anxiety, depression, sleep disturbances, and so on);

- Less commitment to the organization;

- Less satisfaction with work and supervisors;

- Greater likelihood of looking for or thinking about applying for a job elsewhere; and

- Greater likelihood of withdrawing from work (using more sick leave, being less responsive to work demands, and engaging in drug and alcohol behavior) (Fitzgerald, Hulin, & Drasgow, 1995).

These effects tend to occur even at the lowest levels of frequency and severity. Employees who suffer from workplace aggression, abuse, or incivility have very similar outcomes and emotionally can become shocked, embarrassed, disappointed, depressed, fearful, insulted, tearful, and so on (Glomb, 2002). The important point for employers is that any kind of harassment will affect an employee's ability to produce.

Effects on Workgroups

The effects of harassment extend far beyond the direct target. Other members of the workgroups are also affected, experiencing what is called "ambient" harassment (Glomb, Richman, Hulin, Drasgow, Schneider, & Fitzgerald, 1997). Ambient harassment refers to the impact of being in a workgroup in which a person is being harassed. When compared with workgroups where no harassment is occurring, workgroups in which harassment is occurring display similar symptoms and effects as targeted employees. Further, in organizations that tolerate harassment, do not train, and do not implement their policies and procedures, employees in general are less committed to the organization and are less satisfied with their supervisors and with their work, suggesting reduced cohesion and effectiveness (Magley, Salisbury, Zickar, & Fitzgerald, 1997; Schneider, Swan, & Fitzgerald, 1997). Experience shows that such workgroups also:

- Engage in rumors, gossip, and retaliation;
- Polarize, usually against the complainant;
- Lose their morale, concentration, trust, and productivity; and
- Escalate unresolved team/organizational issues.

To resolve harassment effectively, the investigator must determine the extent to which these effects of harassment exist in the work environment (see Chapter 9 for specific types of questioning). This information helps management fully appreciate the impact of the harassment and to commit to solutions that not only correct the situation, but also prevent it from reoccurring.

Environmental Factors Affecting Harassment

It is important for investigators to know that the combination of environmental *and* individual factors best predicts whether harassment is likely to occur. For example, when leaders fail to intervene and sanction behavior and when they fail to institute preventative measures, harassment is more likely to occur (Williams, Fitzgerald, & Drasgow, 1999). (See Chapter 6 for a full discussion of the importance of leadership.) Highly gender-segregated occupations are characterized by strong sex-role stereotyping that often leads to glass ceilings, discrimination, and gender hostility. In environments that have less than 20 percent of one gender, race, or other minority group represented throughout the management structure, sexual, racial, or other harassment is likely to occur (Gutek, 1985) because less diversity in the power structure creates a homogeneous environment where people in the majority group tend to establish a culture that can be insensitive to differences and where people think age, gender, and race-related comments and behaviors are more likely to be viewed positively (Gutek, 1985; McIntosh, 1986).

These factors help the investigator not only anticipate why harassment may be occurring, but also diagnose what is needed for change, thereby preventing further harassment. Recruiting and finding competent women or people of color for positions of power will change the culture and gradually change behavior.

In a sales environment, it was not unusual for the few women and people of color who worked there to hear sexual comments and other jokes about groups of people. In addition, female and non-white sales associates found themselves working with potentially less lucrative customers. The organization began to implement diversity initiatives and recruit diverse workers who more closely reflected their customer base. They also began to actively promote non-whites and women into leadership positions and, as a result, everyone found themselves reporting to a diverse group of managers. Over time, the employees intuitively knew that previous language and behaviors would not be tolerated and the integration of diversity brought a greater sense of equality, respect, and understanding for all the employees.

Implications for Investigators

Psychological research is a valuable tool for investigators as they search to create meaning from complex evidence presented by people they have interviewed. When investigators fail to understand the psychological dynamics of harassment, they risk misinterpreting evidence and allowing bias to affect it. To summarize, investigators can use this research:

- To help understand how common reactions and behavior are;
- To understand aberrant or deviant behavior;
- To develop indirect corroboration that harassing behavior occurred;
- To counter our own stereotypes about harassment;
- To guide questioning during an investigation;
- To diagnose what led up to the harassment;
- To develop effective strategies to prevent further harassment;
- To plan for healing the aftermath of harassment; and
- To identify how to help people recover or change.

Investigating techniques and strategies that use the knowledge described in this chapter will be described in more detail in Chapters 9 and 10.

Chapter 4

Diversity and Harassment

THE RESEARCH IN CHAPTER 3 summarizes the psychological ramifications of harassment for *most* people. Those ramifications should not be over-generalized—individuals or groups of people identified by their ethnicity, gender, religion, or other characteristics can differ in their response to harassment. Moreover, a more inclusive definition of diversity goes beyond the usual protected class categories (race, color, religion, disability, and so on). Thus, differences in styles, positions, occupations, and other cultural differences are very relevant to the investigator.

Harassment occurs in a context, and diversity is often a key to understanding the dynamics of that context. In Figure 4.1, Gardenswartz and Rowe (1994) create a layered approach to diversity that demonstrates that people are born with personality tendencies but form most of their values and behaviors through an array of diverse cultural influences. These layers of internal, external, organizational, and international influences form filters that greatly affect our interpretation of and reactions to our environment. Investigators should know that, although some behaviors are universally unacceptable and harmful, the power of other harassing behavior lies in our interpretation of the behavior, as seen through these filters. Investigators can apply these layers by remembering that, in order to understand how or why a person feels harassed, you have to understand everything you can about the situation, roles, and diverse filters within each person and how they interact. In addition, the investigator's ability to apply a "reasonable victim" (Chapter 2) standard may depend on his or her understanding of the cultural context of the harassment. Finally, the investigator should be very aware of his or her own filters and of when these may help him or her to understand the impact of a behavior and when these filters create a blind spot that prevents the investigator from seeing the situation objectively.

FIGURE 4.1

The Four Layers of Diversity

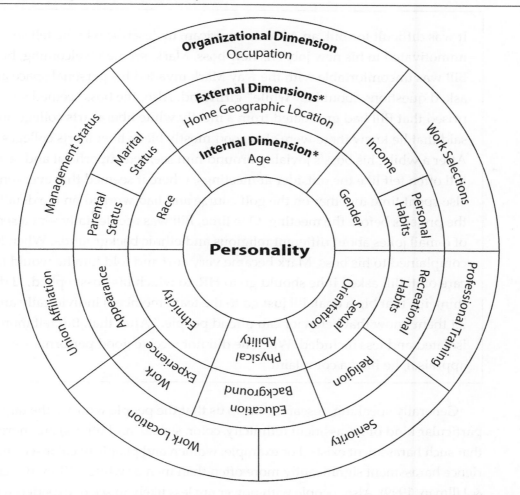

Reproduced with permission from Diverse Teams at Work: Capitalizing on the Power of Diversity *by Lee Gardenswartz and Anita Rowe, copyright 2003, Society for Human Resource Management.*

*Internal and external dimensions are adapted from Marilyn Loden and Judy Rosener, Workforce America! *(Irwin, 1991).*

The Diversity of Race, Ethnicity, and Other Cultural Differences

It was difficult for Bill, an African American, to describe why he felt so unmotivated in his new job. His new boss, Mark, seemed welcoming, but Bill was uncomfortable with the way Mark invaded his personal space and asked questions about his "white" girlfriend. Also, the boss seemed surprised that Bill had graduated from a mostly white liberal arts college and said that he knew there were also good mostly black liberal arts colleges. After a while, his boss's joviality around him seemed superficial and false. Bill often felt like the outsider at meetings, where it seemed that everyone else spent time together on the golf course and had worked on the details of the projects before the meeting. One time, Bill was accidentally sent a series of e-mail jokes about different religious and ethnic backgrounds. When he complained to his boss, Mark became very curt and told him he would take care of it. Bill asked if he should go to HR, to which his boss replied, "I don't think it's that big a deal. I'll just go to the team members individually and let them know that behavior can offend people." After that, Bill felt more isolated and less included. When he did not receive good performance appraisal, he filed a complaint.

Generally speaking, research shows us that the people who are the targets of a particular kind of harassment (ethnicity, color, sexual, and others) are more aware that such harassment exists. For example, women and people of color see and experience harassment significantly more often than men or whites (Klonoff, Landrine, & Ullman, 1999). Also, people with power are less likely to see or experience harassment because their power insulates them against such behavior. Unfortunately, many people assume that because they have never experienced or seen such behavior it does not happen. Investigators should anticipate that some managers may resist acknowledging the frequency and severity of harassing behaviors as a result of their own experiences. Armed with research and explanations, the investigator can help management correctly interpret the evidence gathered during an investigation (Murrell, 1996).

Sexual harassment in particular appears in different forms, depending on a person's gender or ethnicity. A study of Mexican-American women working in U.S. agricultural plants showed that women who were less acculturated (spoke and read less English, had fewer English-speaking friends) were less likely to be harassed, but more likely to be adversely affected when they were. Because of the strict sex-role norms of Mexican-American culture surrounding sex-related behavior and the harsh judgments of women who engage in any form of sexual behavior, women who endorse this traditional culture may understandably react severely to the harassment (Shupe, Cortina, Ramos, Salisbury, & Fitzgerald, 2002). In our growing multicultural workplaces where many languages are spoken, investigators should also consider the interpretation of words and their degree of offensiveness in a person's native tongue.

> A Costa Rican employee complained that his co-workers mimicked his effeminate gestures and called him "cuelero." Although he spoke Spanish, the employee didn't fully understand the term "cuelero," but knew it was derogatory. To understand the degree of offensiveness, the investigator asked several Mexican Americans, one of whom explained that cuelero (asshole) was a very derogatory word used in some parts of Mexico. Understanding the degree of cultural offensiveness of the term was very helpful when the investigator assessed the severity of the behaviors involved in the complaint.

Studies of African-American women have shown that when they are sexually harassed, there is often a "racial" component to the harassment. That is, sexual stereotypes (a legacy from the time of enslavement of African Americans) of black women are interlaced with the harassment. Moreover, the level of harm experienced in these kinds of harassment can be more severe because they include two types of discriminatory harassment, sex and race/color (Buchanan & Ormerod, 2001).

For example, a research participant reported changing into a red dress after work (for a dinner date with her husband) and a white colleague said, "You look like you're getting ready to go stand on the corner" (implying that she looked like a prostitute). Several women also reported comments on their shoes, such as their being "too exotic and offensive." One woman was told by a white male co-worker, "I bet you are a slave to sex" (Buchanan & Ormerod, 2001).

The level of offensiveness of the remarks quoted in Buchanan's study is severe because they not only sexualize these African-American women in a very demeaning way, but they attempt to reinstate them into the image of a black woman slave. It is thus very important for the investigator to understand both sexual and racial stereotypes, how they intermingle, and how they impact the investigation (Buchanan & Omerod, 2001). When behavior has implications of both gender and race/color harassment, both types must be investigated.

Generational differences may affect the meaning of words and behaviors (Zemke, Raines, & Filipczak, 2000). "Girls" or "hon" may be words commonly used by members of the World War II veteran generation to address women in the workplace, but may be viewed as highly derogatory by Baby Boomers or Generation X women. By the same token, the use of the phrases "you're so gay" (jerk, stupid) or "oh shut up" (I can't believe it) used by a Generation Y employee could be significantly misinterpreted by members of older generations.

Many differences in perception concerning the offensiveness of the behavior lies in people's ignorance about stereotyping and cultural oppression. In the example below, the person who was offended was able to educate the man making an offensive remark.

A partner in a law firm bragged to his colleagues that he had "jewed" a vendor down for services rendered. One of the two Jewish lawyers in the firm confronted his colleague and told him that the term was not appreciated. The partner was surprised and remarked "I always thought of it as an admirable business trait," to which the Jewish colleague replied "No, it is a term steeped in centuries of negative stereotyping, distrust, and violence toward Jews." The partner became very contrite, saying, "I'm sorry. I never knew. I just grew up with the term."

Differences Between Men and Women

Recent research shows that genders experience sexual harassment differently. For instance, men rarely experience unwanted sexual attention and sexual coercion, and they are typically not targeted by crude jokes, sexually explicit materials, or other sexist and sexually hostile behavior (Berdahl, Magley, & Waldo, 1996). Further, virtually every study during the last twenty years has shown that women are more likely to be offended by any sexual or gender-demeaning behavior in the workplace. However, men do experience a novel form of gender harassment that researchers label *enforcement of the heterosexual male gender role* when men behave in a gender-atypical or gay manner (Berdahl, Magley, & Waldo, 1996; Talbot, 2002).

John Ryan worked in a utility company. He was a new journeyman who had transferred from another company. When asked why he had transferred, he told his new co-workers that he wanted different hours to spend more time with his children. Two co-workers gradually began to harass John by making fun of his unwillingness to work overtime because he was a "mom" instead of a dad. They called him "Sally," his wife's name, and they gave him more meaningless chores that met the team's needs for water or equipment. They rubbed his head and called him frizzy. Finally, one day while fixing equipment in a forest area, they aimed their penises at him while they relieved themselves. When John complained, the co-workers and supervisor told Human Resources that he was just going through the normal initiation rites.

Men and women also differ in the impact of sexual harassment on them. Although men and women are similarly affected when they are victims of sexual coercion or other severe forms or great frequencies of sexual harassment, men appear to be much less anxious and affected at lower frequency and severity levels, particularly when the harassment is by a woman. For example, obscene phone calls in the workplace can terrify a woman who is concerned about her safety, whereas a man might feel annoyed or embarrassed. Even the slightest sexual innuendo from a boss to a woman may create a disrespectful atmosphere for women, where they perceive that they may not be judged by their competence. As one woman in an investigation remarked, "God, thank you for *not* sharing! I don't want to know his sexual, private thoughts. It makes me wonder if he is taking me seriously or just getting off on my being around."

Tips for Investigators

These are but a few examples of the role diversity can play in harassment investigations. These examples point out, however, how important it is for investigators to consider "diversity" factors when soliciting and interpreting evidence. Equally important, management *must* be well-educated in diversity so that they can determine the accurate level of severity and appropriate corrective action. Diversity factors are complex, but by always giving them consideration, investigators are less likely to misevaluate the harassing behaviors. To understand the role diversity might play in an investigation, investigators should:

- Always ask complainants about how they perceive the behaviors and the impact on them;

- Not rule out other types of harassment that may occur concurrently;

- Use "cultural informants" (trusted employees who are part of a particular culture or member of the "group") to help assess the behaviors; and

- Understand how their own cultural filters may be a hindrance or an advantage in the investigation by identifying their own strong biases and values.

Part Two

Prior to the Investigation

Chapter 5
Characteristics of Effective Investigators

IN THIS CHAPTER, WE WILL review the characteristics of a good investigator. If you are conducting investigations, this chapter will serve as a reminder of the skills that are most important. If you are not yet experienced, this chapter will allow you to determine whether you have the right skills to become a good investigator. Keep in mind that not every investigator is strong in every skill set listed here. However, being aware of the necessary skills will allow you to make sure that weaknesses do not hinder an effective investigation. Also, if you are weak in a particular area, pay close attention to the discussion concerning a team approach to investigations so that other members of the team can fill in skill gaps where necessary.

Unbiased Pursuit of the Facts

Investigators must be committed to the unbiased pursuit of the facts. An investigator must:

- Be comfortable with not being liked or having his or her work appreciated by everyone. No matter what the outcome of an investigation, someone will likely be unhappy or angry.

- Be able to approach the situation in a way that does not place him or her in the position of acting as an advocate for the complainant, the accused, or management.

- Be an effective advocate for a speedy resolution. An ideal speedy resolution is one that puts people back to work productively, provides appropriate remedies to injured individuals, takes action to correct and prevent inappropriate behaviors, and eliminates or diminishes the employer's liability. However, the investigator must do this in a way that does not prejudice current or future investigations.

- Be able to keep information learned during an investigation in strict confidence, reporting only to those with a need to know or act on the information.

Superior Communication Skills

An investigator must have superior communication skills, including the ability to relate to a wide variety of individuals. Investigators must often deal with distraught, angry, and sometimes emotionally troubled individuals. These skills must be developed before substantive training on investigative techniques and legal issues is provided. A person without these essential skills will be an ineffective investigator, regardless of investigative skills training.

Superior communication skills include these abilities:

- To listen accurately while simultaneously recording, processing, and analyzing the information;

- To empathize with the victims while maintaining neutrality and avoiding any judgment or conclusion until the investigation is complete;

- To ask open-ended questions about what may have happened without leading the witness and without foreclosing relevant information by prejudging the victim, the accused, or the relevant events; and

- To try new ways of obtaining and looking at potentially relevant information.

Ease with Difficult Behaviors and Emotions

An investigator must have the ability to ask questions and listen to responses about sexuality, deviant behavior, diversity, and other "difficult" issues without hesitancy, apparent embarrassment, or discomfort.

The investigator must be able to put the complainant, the accused, and witnesses at ease. This essential skill will allow the investigator to obtain as much relevant information as possible. Investigator behavior, either subtle or direct, that transmits a message of disapproval may prevent someone from providing any further information. Therefore, knowledge about, and experience with, the psychology of human behavior is absolutely necessary. The ability to portray neutrality while encouraging further discussion is also essential.

These specialized communication skills include:

- Knowledge of how individuals may feel about offensive, potentially harassing behaviors; coping mechanisms victims may use to deal with those feelings;

male and female sex roles; and other cultural factors that may influence feelings and perceptions; and

- Awareness of one's personal biases and comfort levels around these issues and the ability to set those aside while investigating.

Legal Knowledge

Investigators must have both broad and specialized knowledge of relevant legal cases, including the applicable criteria for evaluating allegations of discrimination, harassment, and retaliation.

Investigators do not need formal legal education to be effective. They must, however, have the theoretical and practical skills to identify and evaluate relevant evidence and reach well-reasoned conclusions about allegations of discrimination, harassment, and retaliation.

Recent court cases have made it clear that to avoid or minimize liability employers must (1) prevent sexual harassment from occurring, to the extent possible; (2) conduct prompt, full, and fair investigations on all allegations of potential discrimination, harassment, and retaliation; and (3) take prompt corrective action to remedy any harassment or retaliation that occurs. The standard against which these employer actions will be measured is that of a reasonable employer in similar circumstances.

Moreover, where an employer has facilities in more than one city, or in more than one state, the employer may be subject to different standards and different liability for the actions taken because of differences in state and/or local laws. In these cases, an investigator should consult with legal counsel to ensure that he or she is applying the correct standards to the particular investigation.

In this complex legal environment, an effective investigator must have:

- The time and commitment level necessary to become familiar with recent court cases and changes in the law so as to develop an expertise in the laws that apply to the cases she or he will investigate; and

- The knowledge of standards that apply in determining what constitutes relevant corroborating evidence to assess veracity, to evaluate the severity of the behavior, and to conclude what preventative, corrective, and remedial actions are appropriate under the circumstances.

Having a Law Enforcement Background

Often, the employee chosen for the role of investigator will have a law enforcement background. Many important skills that would be helpful to an investigator may result from law enforcement training. These include skills such as questioning, focusing, analyzing evidence, dealing with people, drawing out stories, and organizing reports and conclusions. However, some skills taught in a law enforcement setting may be a hindrance to effective investigations in the workplace setting. For example, a criminal investigator interviewing a suspect has one overriding goal: to get a confession. To accomplish this goal, law enforcement investigators have developed many "tricks" to try to garner the confession. These include well-known tricks such as "good cop/bad cop" or deception, threats to the witness or others, or outright accusations of lying. Such techniques are often counterproductive in the workplace setting. The goal in this setting is not to draw out a confession, but only to conduct a reasonable investigation, draw reasonable conclusions, and take prompt corrective action if any problem exists. Techniques that are abusive to the witnesses, such as those noted above, may increase the hostility in the workplace. Many times, the witnesses will have to continue to work with each other, along with the investigator. The aftermath of hostile feelings and a sense of divisiveness in the workgroup will often be much greater if such aggressive tactics are used. (See Chapter 9 for additional discussion of the differences between civil and criminal investigations.)

Excellent Relationship with Management

Investigators must have a clear and credible relationship with management. The investigator's role is to provide management with not only the facts, but also the technical expertise to interpret the facts and help management make appropriate and effective decisions about the alleged harassment and/or retaliation.

To do this, an investigator must:

- Be viewed as honest, expert, and unbiased and have a reputation for integrity and confidentiality;

- Be able to work as part of a management team to implement decisions effectively;

- Be able to balance the roles of "serving the organizational customer" with "representing the total organizational good," including advocating compliance with laws and proactive measures that ensure satisfied, motivated, and productive employees; and

- Be able to accept and support management's decision to modify or overrule recommendations.

Knowledge of Hierarchy and Culture

Investigators must also have knowledge of corporate/unit hierarchy and culture. They should understand enough about the culture to interpret information accurately in the organizational context, particularly when it is relevant to disparate treatment issues. Investigators should also be able to apply reasonable outside standards and distinguish between acceptable and unacceptable behaviors in any organizational culture.

An investigator must be aware of and able to understand:

- How the organization operates and the relevant reporting relationships;
- What documents are available to corroborate/dispute the allegations;
- Prior events, relationships, and other potentially relevant factors; and
- How to resist pressure that the organizational hierarchy may present (such as respect for superior officers who inquire as to the facts of the investigation, without a need to know, or political pressure from within or outside the organization).

Presentation Skills

In addition, an investigator must have effective written and oral presentation skills. Because "others" are not present during the interviews, the investigator becomes the conduit for both the emotional and factual data from which critical decisions are made.

An investigator must have:

- A good command of the English language, with a clear, concise writing style;
- The ability to organize and present evidence objectively and persuasively, with an understanding of the relevant factors and weight of particular facts;
- The ability to explain issues in "plain English," not jargon or "legalese"; and
- The ability to respond effectively to questions and apparent criticism without defensiveness or hostility.

Emotional Maturity and Detachment

The investigator must be able to deal with the emotional side of investigations. Many times, the investigator will be subjected to stories about horrid behavior of human beings. Many times, witnesses will display extreme emotions. Many times, the investigator will feel the anger, the sorrow, or the fear that the witnesses express.

The perpetrator of great harm to others may come across as someone who was genuinely just a victim of ignorance and circumstances and may elicit sympathy from the investigator. Thus, the investigator's emotions will come into play, and the investigator must be able to put these emotions into perspective. The investigator cannot let his or her own background and emotions inappropriately color the results of the investigation. Thus, the investigator must be capable of setting aside emotions and personal feelings, and reaching an objective conclusion.

Valuing and Understanding Diversity

Investigators must embody "diversity," both individually and as a group. They should be knowledgeable about their own cultural filters and about how ethnicity, gender, generation, and other cultural influences may affect perceptions and behavior.

Investigators within an organization should reflect, as a group, as much as possible, the diversity of the organization. At the very least, persons of both genders should be available to serve as investigators. As already noted, investigators should be knowledgeable about and open to issues of diversity that may affect the investigation. (See Chapter 4 for examples of the impact of diversity on investigations.)

Therefore, investigators must:

- Be aware of the different impact certain events may have on men and women, particularly where there also may be ethnic or other differences among individuals in the workplace;

- Understand the potential for different "truth telling" styles related to cultural differences, acknowledging that a storytelling style is no less credible than one that is linear and logical;

- Be aware of personal and organizational biases regarding behavior by culturally different employees; and

- Understand how diverse employees may approach a complaint or investigation, particularly when the investigator is significantly different from the complainant.

Choosing the Right Investigator

Each investigation should begin with an analysis of who the best person is to investigate the particular allegation. The answer for each allegation may be different; thus this step should not be overlooked.

In choosing the appropriate investigator for each investigation, the appropriate manager (or HR professional) should consider the following factors:

- Does the investigator have sufficient time to complete the investigation quickly?

- Does the investigator have a "clean" employment record, that is, there have been no allegations of misconduct against the investigator?

- Should the gender of the investigator be considered? In some situations, a female investigator may be able to win the trust and confidence of a female complainant more easily. A female complainant may also be more comfortable with a female if intimate details are discussed. Gender preference should not be assumed; however, the gender differences in the perception of sexual harassment, noted above and elsewhere in this manual, should be considered in choosing an investigator.

The Team Approach

Should one individual or a team investigate the allegation? Reasons for using a team may include (1) the problem of obtaining one investigator with all of the qualities noted above; (2) gender differences that may impact the investigation; (3) time and resources available to a team; and (4) the scope of the investigation. If a team is used, the plan must include a way to ensure that each investigator is fully informed about facts gathered by other members of the team.

Internal or External?

Should the investigator be an individual from outside the employer? Use of an outside investigator is sometimes necessary when the accused is a high-level manager. In addition, there may be reasons, such as the perception of bias, why no one from the employer would be an effective investigator.

Attorney as Investigator

Should the investigator be an attorney—either internal or outside? There may be excellent reasons why, under certain circumstances, an employer would like to have an attorney perform the investigation. One reason is the protection offered by attorney-client and work-product privileges. If litigation has already begun or an EEOC complaint has been filed, there may be a specific need for an attorney to conduct the investigation. However, for reasons explained later in this manual, this privilege is not absolute and may be no advantage if litigation results from the complaint. (See Chapter 8 for a discussion on attorney-client and work-product privileges.)

However, an attorney should not be the automatic choice as the investigator. Some attorneys do not make good internal investigators, as their styles may be too aggressive to be effective. The same theories that apply to a law enforcement background also apply to attorneys. In addition, you cannot assume that every attorney is familiar with the standards for harassment and discrimination, or with the techniques appropriate to such investigations. Not every attorney has been trained as an investigator. Thus, if an attorney is used, one should be chosen who has the same characteristics as noted earlier in this chapter. Finally, if an attorney is chosen, the organization must emphasize the appropriate focus of the investigation. Many times attorneys are trained to protect the organization from liability at all costs, and they may assume that means the organization cannot conclude that discrimination or harassment has occurred. In fact, if the evidence supports the fact that harassment or discrimination has occurred, the organization's best interests are in declaring that it did occur and in taking prompt corrective action.

Investigations should be conducted by skilled professionals who embody many characteristics and skills that are learned from experience as well as from formal education and reading. By understanding their own limits, strengths, and weaknesses, investigators can develop more of the characteristics. By understanding the necessary characteristics of key investigators, employers can make effective choices of who should investigate claims. By recognizing that some professionals may not have the appropriate background to run an effective investigation, organizations can confidently choose an investigator or team that best fits the needs of the case.

Chapter 6

Organizational Settings Conducive to Effective Investigations

WHILE INVESTIGATING IS A CRUCIAL ASPECT of preventing and resolving harassment in the workplace, it is not enough. There are many other components to diminishing harassment and creating respect. They include an organizational culture and leadership that project common values and respect; preventative policies, procedures, and training; resolution strategies that are in place; and resources available to develop the organization and heal the aftermath of harassment and discrimination. Because investigators advise organizations on how to fix the problems uncovered, they should be aware of all these components.

A Dynamic Organizational Model

Figure 6.1 shows the Culture of Respect Model, the elements of which will be further explained in the following section.

Organizational Values and Vision Leadership Practices

Harassment prevention programs often exist in a vacuum, not connected with the business or values of the organization. When that is true, organizations and their leaders often relegate harassment to the HR department and fail to articulate the "business case" for respect. These leaders fail to communicate why preventing and correcting harassment and discrimination are crucial to the creativity and success of the "business" of the organization. To create a culture of respect, leaders must:

- Articulate values that emphasize how people are treated and how they should interact;

- Communicate a vision that holds up the virtues of civility, diversity, and inclusiveness;

- Model professional and respectful behavior;

FIGURE 6.1

The Culture of Respect Model

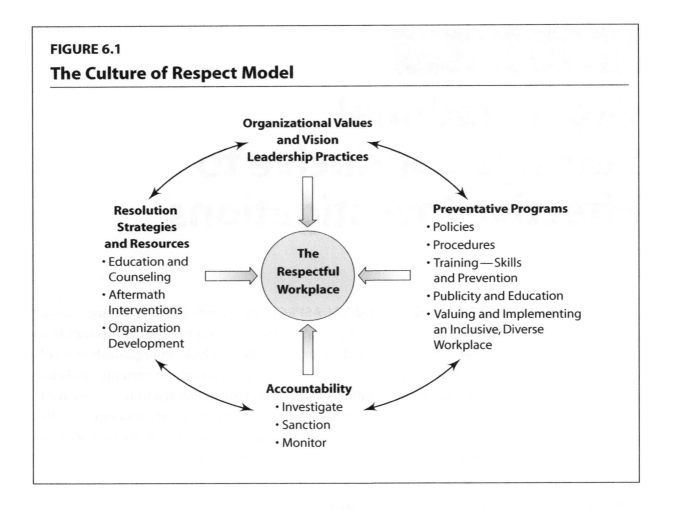

- Hold themselves and others accountable; and
- Support training and other programs that educate employees on how best to work respectfully together.

Preventative Programs

Preventative programs for harassment and discrimination include adequate policies and procedures, effective training programs, and continuous publicity and education. In addition, training programs in implementing, valuing, and capitalizing on diversity serve to create an integrated culture that is more unlikely to tolerate harassment (Fitzgerald, Hulin, and Drasgow, 1995). Finally, preventative programs provide tools for employees to work in a growing global community.

Accountability

The ability to investigate, deliver fair prompt sanctions, and hold everyone accountable means fewer people will harass. In addition, every level of the organization from management to employee should be empowered to speak up about violations of the policy. This manual creates standards for accountability and enforcement.

Resolution Strategies and Resources

A successful, respectful organization understands that once an investigation is complete and sanctions are administered, workplace interventions are likely to be needed. Employees who remain in the workplace need education and assistance to learn what behavior is appropriate and why. Harm and ill feelings created by the harassment require healing, and organizations will need to rebuild teams and change their cultures. (See Chapter 12 for more information on healing strategies.)

When all of the components of a culture of respect are in place, the culture works to eliminate harassment without any one aspect of the system working overtime. In a culture of respect, complaints diminish in frequency and severity, *every* type of training reinforces the values underlying respect, and healthy organizational life naturally regenerates itself after a problem or traumatic event. In a respectful culture, everyone cooperates together to create the respectful workplace, not just the Human Resources department. When all of these elements of a respectful culture exist, investigators can rely on the culture of respect to help resolve complaints and prevent further harassment.

Policies to Prevent Discrimination, Harassment, and Retaliation

A policy is one of the most effective tools to prevent harassment. However, to be most effective, a policy must contain several important elements and be distributed effectively.

Elements of an Effective Policy

The employer should have in place a legally sufficient, detailed policy prohibiting discrimination, harassment, and retaliation. The policy should be written in plain, non-legalistic words and be made available in alternate formats and in other languages, if appropriate. The goal is to communicate the policy clearly to every employee.

The employer's top manager should sign and introduce the policy. This introduction should focus on demonstrating genuine, firm, and enthusiastic management commitment and support for creating an environment that is professional and respectful toward all employees, at all times. The introduction should be followed by training that demonstrates in detail what the policy means and how the employees can follow it.

A policy should express an organization's values, commitment, and expectations by including:

- A prohibition against discrimination or harassment based on protected classes, such as sex, pregnancy, color, age, race, national origin, religion, and disability, as well as other protected classes that are covered by city, county, and state laws where the employer is doing business;

- Strong statements by top management that discrimination, harassment, and retaliation will not be tolerated;

- Specific expectations of management's behavior, particularly regarding implementing the policy;

- Clear, specific examples of what can constitute discrimination, harassment, and retaliation, with a separate section for and a detailed description of retaliation (It is particularly important to include examples of not only sexual harassment but also demeaning and derogatory conduct based on all protected classes.);

- A clear, prompt, discrete, and unbiased method for investigating and resolving allegations of discrimination, harassment, and retaliation; and

- The range of consequences for violating the policy and for filing a malicious or fabricated claim.

Employers should review related policies that may impact the ability to prevent discrimination and harassment complaints, such as dress codes, Internet or electronic mail usage, off-duty conduct, nepotism, romance, or dating policies. Employers should ensure that those policies are consistent with the goal of prevention of harassment.

General Harassment

Consider including a clause in your policy prohibiting any kind of behavior that is abusive, harassing, or disrespectful when it creates a hostile or demeaning environment for employees. Such policies enable management to address all types of destructive behavior without limiting the organization to those that focus on an employee's "protected class." Further, general harassment policies set a higher standard of behavior, thereby eliminating many behaviors that give rise to illegal discrimination and harassment. The organizations that have included a general harassment clause in their policy report that it is a very helpful tool for creating a respectful work environment and eliminating discriminatory harassment. An example is given below:

General workplace harassment is a form of offensive treatment or behavior, which, to a reasonable person, creates an intimidating, hostile or abusive work environment. Examples can include but are not limited to verbal or physical behavior that is derogatory, abusive, bullying, threatening, or disrespectful or ridiculing or undermining an individual with vindictive or humiliating words or acts. These behaviors can constitute harassment as defined by the company's policy, even if unrelated to a legally protected status.

How a Policy Should Be Distributed

Distribution is critical to implementing an effective policy. It doesn't help an organization to have a wonderful policy if employees are not aware of its existence or provisions. To that end:

- Make sure the policy or a poster representing your policy is posted conspicuously throughout the work environment;

- Have all employees, contractors, and vendors sign a statement showing they have received, reviewed, and understood the policy, but don't assume that the policy is fully understood until everyone is adequately trained; and

- Distribute the policy to all affected or potentially affected parties, including applicants for employment; new employees when they begin working; current employees on a regular basis; and contractors, customers, clients, and others who routinely enter the work environment.

The policy should be redistributed to employees on a regular basis, usually not less than once a year.

Procedures for Investigating Allegations

The employer should have in place an effective procedure to investigate and resolve allegations of discrimination, harassment, and retaliation promptly, fully, fairly, and as confidentially as possible.

The procedure should never require a formal written complaint. Even though the employer might prefer a written complaint, such a requirement may be a barrier to some people complaining and may also create the illusion that a written report is accurate and complete. In drafting a policy, make sure you do not create such artificial barriers. Other barriers to complaints could include requiring a rigid system of reporting, requiring reporting only to one individual who may not be available, or requiring that specific words be used (Gruber, 1998). (See Chapter 7 for a discussion about when you should do an investigation.)

Investigation procedures should:

1. If possible, give guidance on how individuals can obtain confidential advice and assistance in dealing with possible discrimination, harassment, and/or retaliation.

2. Identify how individuals can report concerns about possible discrimination, harassment and/or retaliation to the employer, including:

- To whom to report a concern. Identify multiple resources for communicating complaints, including diverse management and human resource representatives, that is, from various genders, ethnic backgrounds, and levels of the organization. Make sure there is no implication that an individual must first confront the accused or go through a rapid chain of command before complaining.

- Both a local reporting method and a national one, if the company is a nationally or internationally spread-out company

- A "Harassment Hot Line" or an 800 number that individuals can use to provide or receive information or support in connection with possible discrimination, harassment, or retaliation (Note that any identifying information received through this hot line should always be considered a complaint that requires follow-up.)

3. Include a process to ensure that, after a complaint has been filed, the complainant will be protected against further harassment or retaliation.

4. Provide mechanisms for keeping information developed during the complaint investigation as confidential as possible, only to be shared with others on a "need to know" basis.

5. Ensure that the complaint investigation will be performed by a neutral, credible investigator with a guarantee of basic "due process" rights for both the complainant and the accused. "Due process" is a legal concept and, as a constitutional right, applies only to public employers. However, all employers should have a plan in place for protecting the rights of both the accused and the complainant in the investigation process.

6. Indicate that all substantiated allegations will result in prompt, corrective action, including the possibility of "make whole" relief if appropriate for individuals impacted by the inappropriate conduct. (See Chapter 1 for an understanding of "make whole" relief and prompt corrective action.)

7. Provide a means by which relevant feedback on the proposed complaint findings will be communicated in summary form to both the complainant and the accused.

8. Publicize the company's procedures to all employees (for example, all employees should be told that any complaints will be promptly investigated).

Figure 6.2 is a flowchart depicting an overview of general harassment procedures.

FIGURE 6.2

General Harassment Procedures

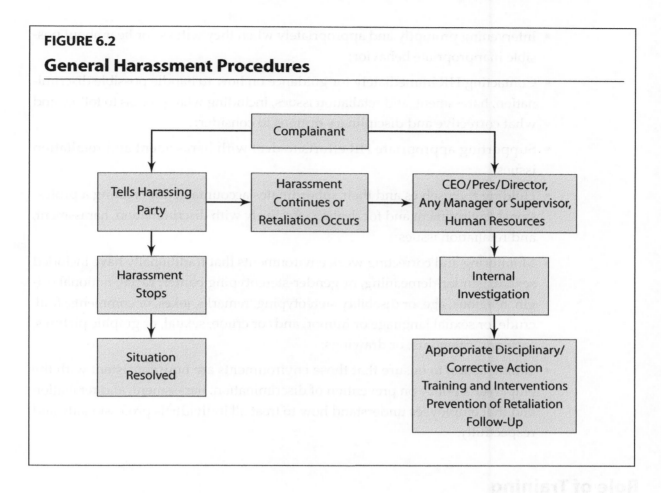

Role of Leadership

Managers and supervisors are critical to the success of the employer's discrimination and harassment prevention program. Recent research has shown that leaders who engage in a laissez-faire management style and who passively wait for situations to arise create an atmosphere in which harassment is more likely to flourish. In contrast, organizations with the least harassment tend to be managed by leaders who are actively engaged in preventative behaviors and who deliver clear sanctions when harassment occurs (Williams, Fitzgerald, & Drasgow, 1999).

Leaders can contribute most effectively by:

- Modeling respectful, appropriate workplace behavior with all individuals at all times;

- Raising the topic of discrimination, harassment, and retaliation regularly and appropriately, both in group settings and in one-on-one discussions, to ensure that all employees fully understand management's expectations and how they can raise and report possible discrimination, harassment, and retaliation concerns;

- Intervening promptly and appropriately when they witness or hear about possible inappropriate behavior;

- Contacting HR immediately for guidance on how to handle possible discrimination, harassment, and retaliation issues, including what process to follow and what corrective and disciplinary options to consider;

- Supporting appropriate HR efforts to deal with harassment and retaliation issues;

- Holding themselves and their subordinates accountable for creating a professional environment and for dealing effectively with discrimination, harassment, and retaliation issues;

- Monitoring and correcting work environments that traditionally have included sexual, gender-demeaning, or gender-stereotyping banter; racial, national origin, religious, age, or disability stereotyping, remarks, jokes, or comments; foul, crude, or sexual language or humor; and/or crude, sexual, or graphic pictures, cartoons, calendars, or drawings;

- Taking action to ensure that those environments are now consistent with the employer's policy on prevention of discrimination, harassment, and retaliation and that employees understand how to treat all individuals professionally and respectfully.

Role of Training

Effective and continuing training and education on discrimination, harassment, and retaliation prevention is essential for managers, supervisors, and non-supervisory personnel. Harassment and discrimination are complex and not easily understood by employees and managers. Effective training provides them with opportunities to ask questions, apply the concepts to situations, and form practical solutions to problems.

Effective Training

To be most effective, the training should be:

- Introduced professionally, enthusiastically, and personally by a credible member of top management who has already attended the training;

- Facilitated by a competent, experienced, interactive trainer (In the case of management training, organizations should consider using an outside expert, as outside experts can have the credibility and experience to challenge participants without risking their positions or relationships in the organization.); and

- Sufficiently long to allow the trainer and the participants to develop a rapport and to interact appropriately, including thorough discussions, role plays, question and answer, and problem-solving exercises.

The training should be held in separate groups for supervisory and non-supervisory employees so that all participants feel able to talk openly, and so that appropriate emphasis can be placed on the particular skills, duties, and responsibilities expected from each group.

Groups should be formed across organizational lines so individuals have an opportunity to exchange information and not be stifled by the "norms" of their specific workgroup. Employees may also be more likely to talk about harassing behaviors. The groups should include men, women, and ethnic groups in as representative numbers as possible so that participants can become more aware of how diversity may affect an individual's perceptions of behavior, including possible discrimination, harassment, and retaliation.

Groups should be small so that individuals have the time and opportunity to participate actively, ask questions, and have their particular concerns addressed.

How Often Training Should Occur

When a policy is first distributed or a new employee is hired, if employees cannot be trained immediately, conduct an in-person orientation that specifically covers the policy, emphasizes the protection against retaliation, and allows for a question-and-answer period. Training on elements of the policy should be conducted at least yearly.

Policies should be reinforced appropriately and regularly in staff meetings, safety meetings, and other places where important information regularly is discussed and disseminated. Follow up with training on relevant topics, including diversity, leadership, and communication skills.

Training that follows these guidelines will initially generate complaints, but can change attitudes (Magley, Salisbury, Zickar, & Fitzgerald, 1997). Complaints should be welcomed, because they give organizations an opportunity to resolve problems before they escalate into major incidents.

Role of HR and the Investigators

Human Resource (HR) experts and the complaint investigator are two of management's primary and most important tools for dealing effectively with harassment and retaliation issues.

HR staff (or staff designated to fill HR functions) must have the expertise to advise management on a day-to-day basis and to respond fully and promptly to potential issues that arise.

In addition, because HR will conduct or assist in discrimination, harassment, and retaliation investigations in most cases, the role of the complaint investigator is central to the HR function. In larger organizations, HR professionals can serve as intake coordinators for complaints, a sounding board for investigators in the field, advisors for management upon completion of the investigation, or as complaint investigators. In companies without a Human Resource department, those filling key positions should be trained on the basics of how to respond and investigate harassment claims and the company should know outside professionals who are competent and experienced and who can be retained to assist when necessary.

Competent investigations are only one element of creating a respectful workplace. Well-written and well-communicated policies and procedures, effective training for professionals at every level, and implementing follow-up and healing are also key to preventing and resolving harassment and discrimination. Finally, leadership that models appropriate behavior and drives the values and practices outlined in this book are so critical to creating a respectful workplace that without it organizations will fail to do so.

Part Three

The Investigation

Chapter 7

The Investigative Plan

When to Do an Investigation

WHEN DOES THE DUTY TO INVESTIGATE ARISE? According to federal cases, the duty to investigate arises when:

- A complaint is "known" to the employer;
- The employer should have known of a complaint; or
- The employer has constructive knowledge of a complaint.

This means that whenever an employee raises an issue about behavior that may violate the harassment or discrimination policy, then an investigation must be conducted. Keep in mind that, while an investigation may be conducted, it need not always be a "Columbo" investigation. If the complaint involves one alleged statement, the investigation may simply verify that the statement was made by talking with each party to the conversation. The tips included later in this chapter may help determine the scope of the investigation.

Also keep in mind that the complaint may be formal or informal. Avoid creating barriers to complaint resolution by requiring that a complaint be in writing or formalized prior to initiating an investigation. The goal is to resolve problems, not to ignore them until formalities are completed.

A duty to investigate is triggered *regardless* of the source of the complaint. The complaint can come from a co-worker of the affected employee or from a person outside the company, such as a spouse or friend of the affected employee. A complaint may come from the attorney for the affected employee. A complaint may also come from an outside agency such as the EEOC or the state human rights agency. A complaint can even come from a rumor or from a person in management who observes the behavior. Regardless of the source of a complaint, an investigation should be conducted when the employer first learns of the allegedly inappropriate conduct. The duty to investigate and take prompt corrective action is not suspended or eliminated because the complaint does not originate directly from the affected employee.

Intake of Complaints

Prior to a complaint being filed, the employer must set up an efficient system for receiving complaints. In the policy, the employer identifies who can receive complaints. Many times this includes any supervisor or manager, the EEO officer, or the HR department.

Organizations should train their managers to forward complaints to the appropriate person so that an investigator can be assigned. Generally, the responsibility for the intake of complaints and the assignment of an appropriate investigator falls to an individual in the HR Department or to the EEO officer. That person acts as the "intake coordinator." The intake coordinator takes responsibility for receiving a complaint and ensuring that it is assigned to an investigator immediately. In small organizations, the intake coordinator may also be the person assigned to conduct the investigation. In very small organizations, the manager may be responsible for every role in the investigative process.

During the intake of the complaint, the intake coordinator may gather available documentation, including the complaint if it is written, assign the appropriate investigator based on the criteria listed in Chapter 5, and contact the investigator to ensure availability. If the intake coordinator is not the one to actually complete the investigation, he or she must be diligent about forwarding the complaint to the appropriate person as soon as possible.

Developing an Investigative Plan

Once the investigator is assigned, he or she should develop a plan for how the investigation should proceed. The plan can be developed through the steps shown in Figure 7.1.

Gather the Preliminary Documents

First, gather preliminary documents that will assist in contacting and interviewing the complainant. These include:

- A copy of the relevant policy manual;
- A copy of any written complaint; and
- Any relevant organizational chart.

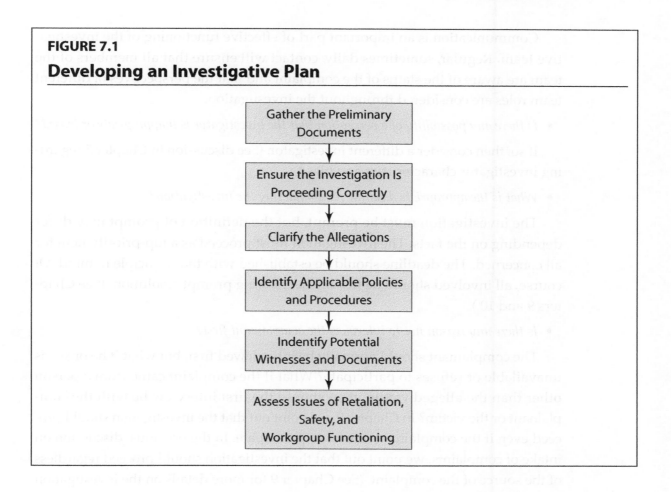

FIGURE 7.1

Developing an Investigative Plan

Gather the Preliminary Documents

↓

Ensure the Investigation Is Proceeding Correctly

↓

Clarify the Allegations

↓

Identify Applicable Policies and Procedures

↓

Indentify Potential Witnesses and Documents

↓

Assess Issues of Retaliation, Safety, and Workgroup Functioning

Ensure the Investigation Is Proceeding Correctly

During the development of the investigative plan, you, as the investigator, must ensure that the investigation is proceeding appropriately. Thus, the following questions may be helpful:

- *Should all or part of the investigation be protected by an attorney-client privilege?*

This may be desirable in circumstances where outside litigation has already begun, but it should not be the normal way of proceeding, since the employer will want to show it acted reasonably by proving that it conducted an appropriate investigation. (See the privilege discussion in Chapter 8 for more information on how the privilege applies to investigations.)

- *Who should be part of the investigative team?*

As noted in Chapter 5, a team of employees is necessary for fully effective investigations and prompt corrective action. This team may include the intake coordinator (noted previously), HR, corporate counsel, management representatives, and the investigator.

- *How will communication between management and HR be managed?*

Communication is an important part of effective functioning of the investigative team. Regular, sometimes daily, contact will ensure that all members of the team are aware of the status of the complaint and that the perspectives of different team roles are considered throughout the investigation.

- *Is there any possibility of a perception that the investigator is inappropriate or biased?*

If so, then consider a different investigator. (See discussion in Chapter 5 regarding investigator characteristics and bias.)

- *What is the appropriate deadline for completing the investigation?*

The investigation must be prompt, but the definition of prompt may differ depending on the facts. The investigation must proceed as a top-priority item for all concerned. The deadline should be established with that principle in mind. Of course, all involved should be flexible in ensuring prompt resolution. (See Chapters 9 and 10.)

- *Is there any reason not to interview the complainant first?*

The complainant should normally be interviewed first, but what if he or she is unavailable or refuses to participate? What if the complaint came from a person other than the alleged victim, then should the first interview be with the complainant or the victim? In Chapter 9, we point out that the investigation should proceed even if the complainant refuses to participate. In the previous discussion on intake of complaints, we point out that the investigation should proceed regardless of the source of the complaint. (See Chapter 9 for more details on the investigation stage.)

- *Should the accused be interviewed after the complainant or after all other witnesses?*

Generally, interviewing both the complainant and the accused first allows you to gather additional relevant information in one interview with other witnesses, without the need to retrace steps once information is received from the accused. (See Chapter 9 for more details on the investigation stage.)

- *Should any warnings be given because of due process concerns?*

Generally, in the investigation stage, warnings are not necessary. Due process warnings are necessary only in the public employer setting. Then the warnings must be given only when the employer is about to take corrective action that may include termination or significant reduction in pay. Consult your attorney if you think you may be required to give such warnings.

- *Should written statements be prepared for each witness, to be signed by them?*

This may inhibit some participation and diminish the candor of the accounts if there is any fear that the statements could be disclosed to others in the workplace. (See Chapter 8 for a full discussion.)

- *Should the interviews be tape recorded, or will they be memorialized by contemporaneous notes?*

Generally, the use of tape recorders can be intimidating to some witnesses and it is rarely necessary to obtain the information. Remember, the goal is to conduct a thorough and reasonable investigation. You will not be required to later prove in court that the alleged harasser "confessed." Thus, good notes show the thoroughness of the investigation.

- *How will the files be organized?*

You should have a consistent system established prior to completing the first investigation. Make sure that investigative files are kept confidential and separate from personnel files. The only entry in personnel files should be the disciplinary action taken or the corrective action taken on behalf of the complainant.

Clarify the Allegations

One of the first interviews will be with the complainant. A preliminary plan for the investigation may be set up prior to this interview, but the investigation plan cannot be finalized until after this interview is completed. In addition to the areas to cover with the complainant, addressed in the next chapter, you will want to gather information that will assist in refining the investigative plan. This includes the following:

1. Make sure you identify all of the complainant's issues by asking appropriate, non-leading questions. A claim that at first sounds like quid pro quo may in fact be one of a hostile work environment. The basis for the harassment may also involve more than the individual's sex, for example, "sex plus," where a woman or man of color or an older woman is harassed because of sex and color or age. In some cases, the conduct may violate other company policies or values, for example, job status or union affiliation.

2. Document what you think the complainant is alleging. If you are unsure, then have the complainant review, confirm, or correct your recollections. Some investigators like to have the complainant sign their documentation as accurately reflecting his or her concerns.

3. Determine how far back in time the claim goes. Incidents that are very old may provide background information that could show a pattern of behavior. Serious complaints about employees still in your workplace may also warrant an investigation, even if the complaints are several years old.

4. Decide whether you may have multiple complainants or targets. Investigate all complainants and all targets to determine the full scope of the issue.

Identify Applicable Policies and Procedures

Investigators must clearly understand the distinction between the legal burdens of proof and the ultimate goal of an investigation: to identify potential violations of policy. Don't become concerned about whether or not the conduct does or does not meet a legal definition of harassment and discrimination. Any behavior that includes disrespectful or offensive comments prohibited by your policy are enough to establish a policy violation. (See Chapter 10 on "Policy Violations vs. Violations of the Law.")

Be creative if your case doesn't fit squarely within a particular framework. Simply because the conduct does not meet a traditional definition of harassment does not mean it is not a violation of your policy. Consult appropriate legal materials and HR/legal if there are any questions about the legal implications.

Identify Potential Witnesses and Documents

Other parts of the investigative plan may be developed after an interview with both the complainant and the accused. Clearly, the investigative plan must be fluid and subject to change depending on the information discovered. Take the following steps to gather information that may change or alter the initial plan for the investigation:

- Ask the complainant and the accused what witnesses and documents may support her or his claim or defense;

- Identify individuals who could have been in a position to see or hear relevant information; useful sources of information include time cards, telephone logs, delivery invoices, e-mails, customer contact sheets, and personal observation;

- Talk with personnel, HR, and other administrative staff to determine what documents may have been available during the relevant time frame; review personnel files and any prior complaints involving the complainant or the harasser;

- Talk with uninvolved managers and supervisors about potential documents; and

- Don't overlook informal documentation, such as work or personal diaries, log books used for other purposes, workgroup meeting minutes, accident reports, and other unusual resources.

Assess Issues of Retaliation, Safety, and Workgroup Functioning

In developing the plan, you may need to alert management to issues that require immediate attention. The following points should be observed:

1. Ensure that you have questioned the complainant about retaliation and safety concerns and advised her or him that you want to hear about such concerns,

should they arise. (See Chapter 12 for a discussion about the need to check in with complainants during the investigation.)

> During the initial interview the investigator told the complainant that he should call her if any retaliation occurred. During the two weeks of the investigation, the investigator never heard from the complainant. However, when she went to debrief him following the investigation, he looked extremely upset. The complainant explained that he had found the word "bastard" scratched on his car one week before and that his safety equipment had been stolen the day before. "Why didn't you call me?" asked the investigator. "I am already being labeled a troublemaker; I don't want to make it worse," answered the complainant. The complainant will not always check in frequently, even if requested. Complaints of retaliation can often be discovered only by repeated checking, as the investigator here should have done.

2. Meet with responsible management to determine what effect the complaint is having on workgroup functioning and take steps with HR/personnel/legal to respond to issues through debriefing, team building, access to EAP, and so on.

3. If the workgroup is generally aware of the complaint, take immediate steps to short-circuit gossip and workgroup discussions that could undermine the validity of your investigation or create a more difficult work environment for the complainant or the accused. (See Chapter 12 for a discussion of how to address workgroup behavior.)

4. If safety and retaliation issues surface, meet with HR/legal and management to determine whether any individuals, including the accused and the complainant, may need to be removed from the work environment and how that can be done appropriately before the investigation is completed.

Setting Up Interviews

Location

Consider issues of safety and comfort, timing, and confidentiality by setting interviews in private, neutral locations. Also consider how witnesses will arrive at the interview site; it may not be desirable for witnesses to cross paths. Thus, you may want to set up a system where you will contact witnesses onsite to call them to the interview location, or have them wait in a neutral location where they will not intermingle.

Length

Set realistic time frames. An interview with the complainant and the accused will normally last longer than interviews with witnesses, and thus you must plan accordingly. The law requires prompt completion of the investigation.

Logistics

Personally schedule interviews to minimize the potential that others onsite may intentionally or inadvertently "leak" information.

Only when absolutely necessary or when the interview is a minor one should interviews be conducted over the telephone. Phone interviews are limited because they do not include the rich nonverbal feedback essential for understanding what is being communicated.

Size of the Investigation

Many investigators have a basic fear about investigations: How will they know when enough is enough? How will they know when to stop and when to continue? There is no clear-cut dividing line between gathering too much information and gathering too little. Instead, use the following questions as a checklist for determining when the investigation is complete:

- Have I asked the complainant and the harasser all of the relevant questions?

- Have I talked to people named by both the harasser and complainant as witnesses? If I have not, can I clearly articulate the reasons why I have not talked to certain people? (For example, many times a harasser will ask the investigator to talk to many witnesses who can vouch for his or her "character." While talking to some of these people may be helpful if they work in close vicinity to the harasser and complainant, very little would be gained by talking to the harasser's friends to determine whether they think he or she is a good person.) Determine whether additional interviews are necessary by asking whether potentially relevant information could be gathered from those individuals.

- Have I talked to those in the workgroup who could be potential targets for harassment? (For example, if the issue is sexual harassment of women, have I talked to all of the women in the workgroup? If the issue is national origin discrimination, have I talked to all potential victims?)

- Have I talked to former employees who are named as potential witnesses? Have I talked to potential victims who no longer work for the company? If not, is there a logical reason why their information would not be helpful?

- Is there a psychological need to be heard by witnesses whose information is tangential, but for whom participation in the investigation would be beneficial?

Try to avoid the urge to talk to every employee in the company. In many cases, it may not even be necessary to talk to everyone in the workgroup. Using common sense is the best way to narrow the scope, without missing important information. Using the checklists for the complainant, alleged harasser, and witnesses in the Appendix is also a helpful way to ensure that the investigation is as thorough as necessary. (See Chapter 10 also.)

Other Legal Issues to Consider

Federal Trade Commission Requirements for Notice

In 1996, amendments to the Fair Credit Reporting Act (FCRA) created notification and disclosure requirements for employers that use a "third party" to conduct any type of employee or applicant background checks. Many members of Congress apparently thought that the new requirements only pertained to credit checks. However, the language of the statute has been interpreted by the Federal Trade Commission (FTC) staff to apply to outside consultants who investigate alleged sexual harassment. If this is true, consultants and the employers using this information would be subject to the various notice and disclosure requirements associated with consumer reports. This ruling would require that an employer seek prior written permission from the accused before an investigation could proceed and provide that the accused should receive a copy of the investigation before any adverse action is taken.

The ruling, if binding, would make it much more difficult to obtain complete and accurate information in many harassment inquiries. Harassers would be placed in control of the decision over whether an investigation could proceed. This would thus conflict with the legal obligation that employers have to proceed with an investigation regardless of consent or permission of the harasser or the complainant. Recent cases have held that the FTC opinion is not valid and thus have eased some of employers' fears about whether to apply this reasoning. Many companies have chosen to ignore the FTC ruling. Consult with your attorney to ensure that you understand how your company should proceed.

Weingarten Rights for Non-Union Employees

Nonunion workers have so-called "Weingarten" rights. The name Weingarten is taken from a National Labor Relations Board (NLRB) decision addressing the right of unionized workers to request union representation in any employment interview with potential disciplinary consequences. By extending these rights to the non-union setting, employers without unionized workforces would be required to allow employee representatives in disciplinary meetings. A co-worker must be allowed to accompany targeted employees to investigatory interviews that may result in discipline.

The NLRB rulings leave many unanswered questions, including whether private employers must now advertise their workers' right to be accompanied by another employee when discipline is going to be administered. In addition, it is unclear whether this right would apply to the investigation of harassment complaints, because at the beginning of the investigation, discipline is uncertain. However, for now, employers would be well-advised that, when an employee requests that an employee representative be allowed to attend a disciplinary meeting, the employer should allow the practice or decline to hold the meeting. Consult with your attorney as to the precise rules your company will follow in applying Weingarten rights.

Developing an appropriate investigative plan serves several purposes. First, it allows you to approach the investigation in a logical, thorough manner. Second, it provides some assurance that the investigation is proceeding appropriately. Finally, it allows you to understand the issues and plan accordingly. A proper investigative plan is a valuable tool that should be well used as you prepare to launch the investigation.

Chapter 8

Documentation

MANY OF THE QUESTIONS that investigators have about their practices revolve around required record keeping. This chapter will discuss issues of (1) what records to keep; (2) what those records should contain; (3) whether any privileges should apply; and (4) how to write and disseminate a written report.

Record Keeping

Accurate, adequate record keeping is an important skill for investigators. Investigative records are discoverable during litigation or public disclosure requests, so it is important to retain materials relevant to the investigative findings. Investigators also need to be careful about collateral materials that could be collected, especially those containing unsubstantiated opinions, because such documents can be embarrassing and misleading and can suggest that evidence outside the investigative record was, or should have been, considered. During the investigation, take care to create notes and records that detail the proper course of the investigation, without extraneous material.

An investigator should keep the following points in mind when creating investigative records:

- A clear record of a well-conducted investigation helps communicate issues to management and supports the employer's response to the complaint;

- The absence of such thorough records significantly compromises the employer's ability to recall important details in the future; and

- Investigative records should be kept separate from personnel files and should be kept very confidential; disciplinary records and memos to the parties about the outcome of the investigation may be retained in the personnel file.

The Investigative File

Typical components of an investigative file include the following items:

1. A log of calls and actions by date of event. A sample log sheet is included in the Appendix. Each investigator should adjust the log to his or her personal style. The important thing is to keep track of the investigation in a way that ensures completeness of the file, but which also shows diligence and promptness of the investigative response.

2. Contemporaneous and final interview notes for each witness. Remember, each set of notes should include a reference to the dates of the interviews. It is not necessary in each case to create "final" interview notes if the contemporaneous notes are fairly complete. Some investigators prefer to keep only sketchy notes during the interview, then to create more complete notes later. While this may be your preference, keep in mind that it may lead the investigative subject to claim that the notes are fabricated when important information is added later.

3. All communications, e-mails, and letters to and from each witness.

4. All written witness statements, if any. Written statements are not necessary in most cases. The mechanics of meeting with witnesses several times simply to complete written statements that are accurate may impede the speedy progress of the investigation. In addition, written statements do not include the rich nonverbal feedback that a trained investigator can add to the information gathered. Finally, written statements rarely cover every point from an oral interview, and there is a danger that decision makers may rely too heavily on the written statement.

5. All written complaints. Note that in Chapter 6 we indicated that a written complaint should not be required in every case, but if there is one, keep a copy of it in the investigative file.

6. All relevant provisions of the policies considered.

7. All documents that were provided by witnesses or gathered by you. Each should have a notation of the date received.

8. Tape recordings, computer files, time cards, calendars, log notes, reports, telephone messages, e-mails, or any other document that might verify the allegations or refute them.

9. Your report, if any.

10. Documents reflecting follow-up meetings or communications with the accused or complainant.

Investigative Notes

Because investigative notes are potential exhibits in any future litigation, special care should be taken when creating them.

First, the attorney-client privilege should be considered and preserved at all times, if necessary.

Second, keep contemporaneous notes of what the witnesses say and the questions asked, but do not include in those notes any conclusions or impressions.

Avoid doodles or extraneous comments on the notes. However, notes about body language, emotional affect, and tone and other observations of behavior should be noted during the interview.

The notes should be reviewed immediately after the interview to correct any factual errors. Spelling and grammar can also be corrected at that point.

If you feel that the notes must be rewritten for clarity, do so, but the original notes should be retained. If the notes are rewritten, the new set of notes should be checked and rechecked for accuracy to ensure they remain consistent with the original notes. Items omitted or changed from the original to the recopied notes should be easy to explain.

Attorney-Client Privilege

Careful consideration of the role of attorney-client privilege should precede the investigation. Sometimes it is critical for the privilege to be preserved, such as when a public employer is bound by public records disclosure laws. In that situation, a public employer, to preserve morale in the workplace, may want to shield the investigative results from public disclosure until later. When that is true, protecting the confidentiality of investigative documents through a privilege is sometimes necessary and desirable. However, all employers should keep in mind that the privilege may be waived if litigation results, because the employer will want to introduce evidence of the investigation as part of its defense.

A clear understanding of the privilege is necessary. The privilege applies to communications between an attorney and those employed by the company only when the communications occur for the purpose of providing legal advice to the company. Thus, the privilege may only apply when an attorney is acting in the role of investigator or when he or she directs that the investigation be done so that he or she can provide advice on appropriate actions to take. However, it may not be in the client's best interest to have an investigator also serve as the attorney for the employer. This is because the witnesses may not perceive the investigator as a neutral third party, but instead as a person who is loyal to management. Care must be taken to clarify these roles and to disclose the roles to witnesses while assuring them of impartiality. When the privilege is sought, each witness must be informed of the existence of the privilege and its effect on the confidentiality of the conversation.

However, the employer must recognize that not everything in a harassment investigation may be shielded from disclosure by application of the privilege. For example, communications with lower level employees may not be covered by the privilege, since those communications may not occur for the purpose of providing legal advice. Some courts have held that the privilege applies only when discussions occur with higher level managers who will be making employment decisions.

Also note that the privilege can be waived. Also, if information gathered is shared beyond those with a need to know, then the privilege may be lost.

In seeking to preserve an attorney-client privilege, keep the following points in mind:

- Communications from the client to the attorney for the purpose of seeking legal advice are protected from disclosure;

- Communications from the attorney to the client giving legal advice are protected from disclosure;

- The label "Confidential Attorney-Client Communication" is recommended for use on all privileged communications between attorney and client; and

- The privilege protects only the *content* of the confidential communications and does not mean that the documents discovered or the facts uncovered are protected from disclosure.

Attorney Work Product Doctrine

Work performed at the direction of the attorney for use by the attorney "in anticipation of litigation" may be protected from disclosure. Thus, even when the attorney is not the investigator, some protection from disclosure may be provided when the attorney is directing the investigation. The work must be done "in anticipation of litigation." If the investigation involves merely an internal complaint that must be investigated in the regular course of business, this privilege may not apply. This protection is not absolute and disclosure may be required in limited circumstances.

Waiver of Attorney-Client and Work Product Privileges

The protections associated with the attorney-client and attorney work product privileges may be intentionally or inadvertently waived. An example of waiver is disclosure of privileged information to third parties. Thus, in seeking to preserve the privileges, care must be taken to ensure that only those with a need to know are provided with the information. Employees involved in the investigation must be instructed not to talk about it in stronger terms than in a normal investigation.

Internal Document Management

Even if investigation documents do not bear a legal privilege, they should be treated with a high degree of confidentiality. Disclosure of documents should be on a need-to-know basis only. This may include disclosure to government agencies investigating discrimination complaints or in response to subpoena or discovery requests.

Writing an Investigative Report

A report is the formal documentation of the investigation. (A sample report is included in the Appendix.) Therefore, it should include all that is necessary, but no more.

When a Report Is Necessary

The first question to ask is whether a report is necessary. You can deliver the summary orally if management is comfortable with that option. For public employers, due process may require a written investigative report that will be provided to the complainant and the accused.

Even if a written report is provided, the management team responsible for the decision on prompt corrective action should review the entire investigative file. If they do not, then they must be able to state, with accuracy, that the summary they review contains all the relevant factors.

Clear and Concise Language

Employers expect investigative reports to include clear, concise statements of relevant facts, along with supporting evidence. *Use plain English.* Throughout the report, state facts and conclusions in neutral, objective, precise, and thorough language. Generally speaking, conclusions that use legal terms are inappropriate and may not always be accurate or in the employer's best interests. Therefore, it may be more appropriate to simply recognize whether the facts show a violation of company policy. A sample investigative report is included in the Appendix.

Making Recommendations

Management should decide whether, and what kind of, recommendations will be included in the report. Some employers expect a report to include recommended findings on whether the allegations have been substantiated and recommendations on what corrective action to take in response to any substantiated misconduct. Since these are matters of individual choice, an investigator should consult with management before issuing a report with findings and recommendations.

The obvious disadvantage of including recommendations will be when the managers decide *not* to follow the recommendations. Then there must be a clear and cogent reason for not following your recommendations. In most cases, it is better for your conclusions to be focused on the determination of the facts and for the recommendations on prompt corrective action to be reported to management orally, if at all. Sometimes Human Resource professionals and investigators are in a better position to judge whether the proposed action is consistent with how the employer has treated similar cases in the past and can make recommendations to management on prompt corrective action.

If the report will include recommendations or conclusions regarding prompt corrective action, the final report generally should be written only after management, legal counsel, and investigators have met to review the information and all understand the outcome of investigation and the options for resolution.

Referencing the Policy

A report should always set out the policies at issue and relevant evidence applicable to each issue. Conclusions should be centered around whether a violation of policy occurred, and not around whether the law was broken.

Issues to Avoid

Extraneous or irrelevant information should not be included. That material is best relegated to a side file. Examples might include the accused's status as a popular member of the community who leads several charitable organizations or the fact that the complainant has a child born out of wedlock. If there is a question of relevance, the evidence should be identified with an explanation of why it is or is not relevant to or probative of the issues.

Avoid any mention of the content of any communication with legal counsel to preserve the attorney-client privilege.

In the report, do not list the names of witnesses as attributed to statements they made, except that you may, depending on the circumstances, list the names of the complainant and the accused. You may, if requested, include a list of the individuals interviewed; however, if the confidentiality of the witnesses is critical, you may want to eliminate names completely. For public employers, if the written report will be provided to the accused, names should be listed for due process reasons.

Organizing the Report Effectively

It may be helpful to break the report into the following sections:

- Allegation (List the allegation considered)

- Policy at Issue (Quote the relevant policy)

- Facts Found (List the facts relevant to this allegation, including corroboration, documents reviewed, credibility issues resolved, and so forth)

- Conclusion (Indicate whether the allegation is sustained, not sustained, or inconclusive)

Here is what a report should include:

- Begin the report by focusing on the precise nature of the complaint alleged. It may be helpful to break the complaint into separate allegations and follow each part of the complaint with a listing of the facts found to support or refute each allegation.

- The report should address each allegation separately and provide a conclusion, if asked for. The conclusion should incorporate information on allegations not originally made, but discovered during the investigation. This ensures that no issue is overlooked or overshadowed by other factors.

- Also provide a summary of any injury alleged.

- If there are findings in the report, the report should state what evidence supports particular findings. If the evidence is insufficient to make a finding, this should be explained.

- Discuss your conclusions on credibility or list any reasons why a conflict in the evidence cannot be resolved.

- If names of witnesses are included, a list of names of those contacted should be included at the beginning of the report.

- As discussed previously, attach to the report a log showing the timetable of the investigation.

- Identify any interim relief provided to the complainant during the investigation, such as administrative leave, counseling, and reassignment of duties.

- If recommendations are included in the report, the recommendations should address what relief, if any, is applicable; what discipline, if any, is appropriate; and what organizational follow-up, if any, should be planned.

If the report is extensive, it is appropriate to include an executive summary. Generally it is not advisable to prepare an extensive report. If an executive summary is prepared, however, this summary also could serve as the documentation provided to the parties. A sample report is included in the Appendix.

Documenting Follow-Up Activities

To the extent that you are involved in activities subsequent to the investigation, log all such involvement and keep appropriate records. These records might include notes pertaining to:

- Discussions about prompt corrective action;

- Follow-up discussion with the complainant and accused to relay the results of the investigation; and/or

- Additional activity taken in response to the complaint, including policy changes, discipline administered, and so on.

Disseminating the Written Report

Many times, you, as the investigator, or the employer will be asked for a copy of the written report. Employers should resist any attempts to obtain copies, unless required to do so because litigation has begun or a public records request has been made. Copies of the written report should not be given to the complainant, the alleged harasser, other employees, or the media. Many times, information included in the report may be harmful to repairing the relationships among co-workers. The complainant can be told the results of the investigation, that is, that a violation of policy was or was not found and that corrective action was taken. The alleged harasser can be told the results of the investigation. Other employees may be told the results of the investigation in an appropriate aftermath process. (See Chapter 12 for a discussion of the aftermath process.) However, the employer should treat the report itself as a confidential personnel document that can be released only to those who are involved in the decision-making process. Copies distributed should then be collected and stored in a confidential file concerning the investigation.

Careful documentation of an investigation is absolutely essential. Yet, the skills involved in creating such documentation are often ignored. Following the tips in this chapter will help the investigator become skillful in this important component of the investigation.

Chapter 9

Tips and Techniques for Conducting the Investigation

IN THIS CHAPTER WE WILL ANALYZE the entire course of the investigation from beginning to end. Once the investigative plan is complete and prior to actually beginning the investigation, you as the investigator must consider issues such as confidentiality, the style of the investigation, and the questioning process. In conducting the investigation, you may seek information on how to handle difficult situations that you have never encountered before. Finally, investigators need guidance on what questions to ask of each witness and how to gather necessary information.

Confidentiality

In any investigation, confidentiality is critical to a successful outcome. Rumors about what is or is not involved in an investigation can kill the morale and effectiveness of a workgroup. (See Chapter 12 for a discussion of the aftermath of a complaint.) Thus, there are guidelines for (1) when to share information; (2) how much to share; and (3) what you can do to control the amount of discussion about the incident occurring in the workplace.

Sharing Information

You need to be very careful about sharing information during the investigation. Here are some tips:

- Share information on a "need-to-know" basis. Provide a reasonable boundary where only those management and HR people who have input into managing the situation and are involved in decision making are given the detailed facts discovered during the investigation.

- Limit yourself to getting the facts and share with those interviewed the amount of information they need to give in response to relevant questions and allegations.

- Restrict the amount of information revealed by reminding witnesses about the guidelines for confidentiality and making sure they model appropriate boundaries for sharing information.

- If you need to vent or debrief, use designated investigators or Human Resource management.

What You Can't Do

Absolute confidentiality should never be promised, because such a promise is impossible to keep. For example, the following promises should not be made:

- *Promises to hide the identity of the complainant/alleged harasser.* It is not difficult for most people to identify the major parties to an investigation from the questions asked, the information they hear from others, and the events they have witnessed, so remind the complainant and alleged harasser of the organization's natural limits in keeping the complaint anonymous. This way they are less likely to blame management for perceived "information leaks." Also remind the complainant that if he or she shares information with co-workers, that will contribute to his or her being identified as the complainant.

- *Promises to control the grapevine.* Warnings about retaliation charges, rights to privacy, defamation, respect, and organization policy may not be enough to stop employees from sharing information. Be alert to workplace gossip and intervene promptly to curtail it as much as possible. Remind each witness that confidentiality is requested and that they should refrain from discussing the interview or the events in question with other employees.

Ways to Ask Witnesses Not to Share Information

Generally, asking the witnesses to consider how they would feel if everyone were talking about them is an effective way to make them understand why talking about the interview is not a good idea. In addition, you can explain to them that no one really knows the full picture, and so repeating part of the story might be harmful. You can also explain to witnesses how stories, once repeated, can be blown out of proportion or misinterpreted, and thus how even false stories can be spread and have a detrimental effect on the workplace. Sometimes reminding employees of the "telephone" game they played when they were children is illustrative. In this game one person starts the game by whispering a common phrase in one child's ear, and the phrase is then passed from child to child until the last child announces what he or she hears. The phrase is always mangled at the end, with comical results. The analogy helps employees understand that they may not hear things exactly the way they are, and that repeating them can only result in false rumors.

Civil vs. Criminal Investigations

There are a number of significant differences between civil and criminal investigations. Thus, an investigator experienced in criminal investigations may have to adjust his or her thinking and style to adapt to the civil setting. Here are some of the major differences and how they impact style or technique.

Assumptions

In beginning a criminal investigation, certain assumptions govern the gathering of evidence. First, the target of a criminal probe is considered to be either guilty or innocent. In harassment investigations, the assumption is completely different. Establishing guilt or innocence is not the goal of the investigation. Instead, the goal is to conduct a reasonable investigation and reach a reasonable conclusion. The focus is on the anti-harassment policy and determining whether the policy has been violated in any way. The employer should not care whether the alleged harasser is "guilty" of harassment as legally defined. Instead, if the policy is violated, prompt corrective action will be taken, regardless of whether harassment legally occurred.

Burden of Proof

The burden of proof is very different in criminal cases. Criminal conduct must be proven beyond a reasonable doubt. In harassment law, harassment must be proven by a preponderance of the evidence, which means that it is more likely than not that the harassment occurred. This is a much lower burden. Thus, while the criminal investigator is intent on getting a "confession" so that the allegation can be proven beyond a reasonable doubt, the harassment investigator must merely conduct a reasonable investigation and reach a reasonable conclusion, based on the evidence gathered. As long as the investigation is reasonable, missing a piece of information is not critical to the employer's position. In addition, you are not seeking to prove that the harassment meets the legal definition, but merely that some behavior occurred that was a violation of policy. This is much different and allows a less confrontational approach to investigations.

Evidence

Evidence in a criminal case must be gathered according to strict "chain of custody" rules. Thus, when a criminal investigator gathers a blood sample, it must be preserved in a way that he or she will be able to testify authoritatively that the blood introduced in evidence is exactly the same blood that was collected at the scene of the crime. The evidence in a harassment investigation rarely needs to be identified in such a precise manner. Most of the evidence will be oral statements from the witnesses. Documents obtained will generally be organization documents, unless the complainant or witnesses kept notes or diaries. In any event, it is very easy to prove what was discovered, and thus what information was used. No strict chain of custody rules apply. Instead, the focus is on whether the employer was reasonable in gathering the appropriate information and documents.

Warnings

We are all familiar with Miranda warnings, even if we don't know them by that name. In a criminal investigation, before questioning a suspect, the police must say: "You have a right to remain silent, . . . your statement can be used against you in a court of law. . . ." No such warnings must be given to witnesses in a harassment investigation. In criminal investigations, witnesses can simply refuse to speak to the police, but in a harassment investigation, the organization can require cooperation (it may not always happen, but it can be required) as a condition of employment. While some public entities investigating harassment that may involve a criminal charge may have to give a separate type of warning called the Garrity warning, most employers need not worry that their investigation will be tainted without particular types of warnings.

Time Limits

In the criminal setting, a crime may have a particular statute of limitations, and thus the investigation must be completed within that time frame, usually years. Because the limitation periods are long, an investigation can drag on for months until the police feel comfortable that they have sealed a case they can prove beyond a reasonable doubt. However, in the harassment setting, employers cannot continue an investigation in the hope of uncovering the decisive bit of proof that they are missing. Instead, a decision on corrective action must be reached as soon as possible so efforts must be made to complete the investigation as quickly as is reasonably possible.

Interview Techniques

Many times, police officers use interview techniques that are harsh and manipulative. That style of investigation is not well-suited to a harassment investigation. Often, all of those involved in the investigation will continue to be employed and must work together. Do not use a style of questioning that damages the workplace. Remember, a confession is not necessary; only a reasonable investigation is needed. Using gentler but still probing techniques is more appropriate. Treating employees like criminals will increase the likelihood that interventions are necessary in the aftermath of a complaint. (See Chapter 12 for more information.)

Questioning Techniques

The following are good "tips" to keep in mind as you conduct the investigation:

- Don't offer a lot of information; don't "educate" the person.

- Don't reveal unnecessary information in the course of forming your questions.

- Do ask open-ended questions about how the person was involved.

- Don't discuss your investigative plan.

- Do tell witnesses the investigation will be completed as quickly as possible and you will interview any person who seems to have relevant information.

Many witnesses will ask questions like: "Have you interviewed Mary?" or "How many people have you talked to?" or "How much longer will this take?" If they ask about a specific person, respond with: "What information do you think Mary would have that would be helpful?" You can respond in this way even if you have already interviewed Mary, simply to check to make sure you have talked to witnesses about all of their relevant information.

- Don't discuss your personal opinions.

- Don't form conclusions before you have completed your investigation and don't offer an opinion on the merits of the investigation.

- Don't believe any story until you get the "other side." If you do, you will be accused by the alleged harasser of being biased and having formed your conclusion before all of the facts were gathered.

Sometimes a witness will ask: "Don't you believe me?" or will ask you to comment on what you have concluded thus far. Avoid these questions. Respond to the former question with something like: "You appear to be sincere and cooperative, and I appreciate that," without expressing an opinion on credibility. Sometimes very challenging witnesses will require you to go further and indicate that you are not drawing any conclusions until all the facts are gathered.

- Don't try to counsel the person on personal or emotional problems. Discover all of the facts surrounding these personal or emotional issues, but you must remain detached from the individual.

- Do acknowledge people's feelings by saying something like: "I can tell you are really upset by this."

- Don't let the emotion and your response to it become the focus of the investigation.

- Don't be tempted to become an advocate. Refer the person to appropriate counseling resources if necessary.

- Don't assume every case is the same or become over-reliant on checklists.

- Do use checklists to keep track of your investigation, but don't be afraid to vary from the list in each investigation.

- Don't demean anyone during an interview or offer advice about what the complainant or the alleged harasser should have done during the incident.

- Don't automatically discount credibility because an individual has disciplinary problems, has been flirtatious or inappropriate with others, delayed reporting, or has apparent psychological problems. Use this information as a factor that you use to judge credibility or corroboration, but treat these facts with caution and do not make assumptions based on your own history or personality.

- Do keep the parties informed during the investigation.

- Don't avoid questions because they involve embarrassing information. If you need to know, ask the question.

- Even if you must use words that you would never utter otherwise, don't avoid asking questions because it seems impolite or indelicate. Using explicit language is sometimes necessary for thorough questioning. It is your job to ask the questions.

- Don't fail to consider the quality of the information. Distinguish between hearsay and first-hand knowledge by following up with questions that clarify whether the person was present for the event or conversation or simply heard about it from someone else.

> Many times a witness will recount that Joe hit Mary, but when pressed for exactly what the witness saw, the witness will indicate that he was not present for the incident but only "heard about it" from Mary, or he did not see Joe hit Mary, but only saw Mary crying and heard her say Joe hit her. Precise facts are necessary to sort out credibility issues.

Questioning Style

How you both organize your questions and follow up with the witness will determine whether or not your investigation is thorough. Follow up with questions that will give you more information than the bare facts. Sample follow-up questions include: "What gave you that impression?" "I wonder why she did that?" "What makes you angry?" "Why do you think she left?" "What would you say if . . . ?" "What words were used?" Try to cover events in chronological order, and ask detailed questions about each time period. With respect to each event, remember to ask if this was an isolated event or part of a pattern of behavior. Many times a witness will focus on one traumatic event and forget to tell the interviewer about other smaller incidents that occurred earlier.

However, it may also be effective with a particular witness to let him or her jump around and tell the story in his or her own way. Different witnesses have different styles of relating information. If the witness is not telling the story in chronological order, it may be best to not interrupt the flow of storytelling. You must take care to keep the chronology straight in your head, so ask follow-up questions to make sure the timing is correct. Another strategy is to let the witness tell the whole story, then go back to a chronological review of the story to fill in the gaps.

Ask open-ended questions that help the person describe what he or she saw, heard, or experienced. You can follow open-ended questions with more specific questions to cover all topics. Obtain clear and detailed descriptions of physical behavior, the context in which the harassment occurred, and relationships of the people involved.

Don't frame questions that assume guilt or innocence. For example, don't ask the alleged harasser why he or she was sexually harassing the complainant. Don't use words like "harassment" or "discrimination" in questions, because those words imply that you have already reached a conclusion. Also, research has shown that women who experience sexually harassing behaviors only label them as sexual harassment about one fifth of the time (Fitzgerald, Swan, & Magley, 1997). It may be appropriate to use words like "inappropriate," if used carefully, especially toward the end of the interview, to summarize. You can ask a witness, "Was there anything else that happened that *you thought* was inappropriate [intimidating, disrespectful, offensive]?" In this way you are asking the witness to make the characterization, but still getting information about other types of behaviors and the witness's reaction to behaviors, which are important to the conclusions to be drawn.

Summarize the witness's testimony to ensure you are hearing the person accurately and to allow the person an opportunity to close gaps, add detail, and verify the evidence. You can also reassure the person that you are listening by providing comments that reflect that you are listening without expressing an opinion.

Examples of summarizing and reassuring include: "I see how that could happen," "Sounds like that was surprising," "It seems like that affected you emotionally," "Sounds like you were not happy with how that went," "Your experience with your boss was positive until that day," and "You felt like people were avoiding you."

Be certain to ask about information you have that conflicts with what the person is telling you, without informing the witness of the conflict. Do not be afraid to use silence as a questioning technique. If you can avoid filling dead air with another question, particularly at critical moments, sometimes the witness will succumb to the urge to fill in the silence by giving more information. During these periods of silence, you can appear to be contemplating the previous answer, nodding appreciatively at their cooperation, expressing a confused or questioning look, or in some way showing the witness that continuing to discuss the issue is appropriate.

Setting Atmosphere: Manner and Tone

Communication is about 75 percent nonverbal, and your manner and tone will often communicate more than the words that you use. Keep the following points in mind when conducting an interview:

- Always be courteous, respectful, and professional.
- Be flexible—follow the style of the interviewee while making certain you cover the points you must to meet legal and policy standards.
- Never argue with the person—do not be accusatory or judgmental.
- Be welcoming and inviting. Indicate that you are concerned, but at the same time genuinely interested in what the person has to say.

We have witnessed some interviewers in class settings revert to questioning that might be labeled as "good cop, bad cop" styles, where the interviewer becomes accusatory, raises his or her voice, or accuses the witness of lying. We have never seen this technique used successfully. While it may work well in criminal settings, it is inappropriate for a workplace setting.

Keep in mind that, after the investigation, all of these individuals may remain organization employees. Avoid using a style that adds to the divisiveness of the issues and casts doubt on your impartiality.

Body Language

There are many schools of thought about body language. Many classes that teach interviewing techniques also teach that you can make assumptions based on the body language of the individual. For example, a person who crosses his arms across his chest has something to hide, or if a witness does not make direct eye contact, then she must be lying. Don't read too much into such body language or draw conclusions based on it. Instead, make observations about behavior and habits during an interview, but do not rely heavily on any preconceived notions of what the behavior means.

You can use reflective questioning techniques to test your perceptions of body language. For example, if a witness is fidgeting in his or her seat, you can say, "You seem to be moving around a lot; are you uncomfortable in that seat?" The witness may respond that he has a back condition that makes it difficult to sit in a hard chair, telling you that the movement was not related to discomfort with your questions. Establishing a rapport with the witness at the beginning of the interview, to establish a baseline of gestures used when he or she is comfortable, will also allow you to judge when the witness becomes uncomfortable by changing those gestures.

For example, in some cultures, it may be considered rude to make direct eye contact. A person raised in such a culture may avoid eye contact during the interview because the interviewer is in a position of authority. In traditional U.S. culture, lack of eye contact is often interpreted as evasive, disrespectful, or dishonest, which may be an incorrect assumption. Another example is that some witnesses may express extreme stress by becoming very quiet and showing little feeling or modulation in their verbal tone. In these cases, it would be erroneous to conclude that the lack of visible emotion reflects what the person really feels.

Questions to Avoid

Some common questions that investigators ask or want to ask may create problematic perceptions from those being interviewed. There are ways to discover the information without alienating the interviewees. Here are some examples of poor questions.

What do you want the organization to do? It is not up to the witnesses or the complainant to decide what the organization should do. By asking this question, you may give the complainant the impression that whatever outcome he or she desires is the outcome that will result. You could raise expectations that, when not met, would create more anger with the organization. The complainant is not responsible for the outcome; the organization is. Some complainants will be angry if this question is asked, interpreting it as the organization's shirking of its responsibility to decide on appropriate action. You should inquire as to the complainant's goals, but do so by asking what he or she would like to get out of the investigation. You can also make sure he or she understands that no decision on what will happen will be made until all the evidence is gathered, and that the final decision will be made by management.

What did you do to encourage this behavior? This question implies that the complainant is somehow at fault for the behavior. This may invoke very angry responses from the complainant. Instead, ask what the complainant was doing prior to the event, what was said, and then how the complainant reacted. This will help you obtain the same information without implications of responsibility.

Did you tell the harasser to stop? This typically implies that there was some duty to tell the harasser to stop. The law does not impose such a duty. Instead, the law requires avenues of complaint that do not involve the harasser, because it may be very difficult to directly confront a harasser. Instead, ask the complainant what he or she said to the harasser each time the harassment occurred.

Why didn't you come forward earlier? This implies that the complainant may not be telling the truth or has some other motivation for coming forward now. It also assesses blame for not reporting the events earlier. Instead, the focus should be on why the complainant chose to come forward at this point. You can also ask questions about who the complainant told about the behavior earlier. It could be that the complainant thought she was complaining to other managers, but nothing happened.

Dealing with Distressed Employees

Because of the inherent stress of investigations, it is common for employees to project their feelings on the investigator. Responding to these feelings can be one of the most challenging aspects of investigating. Use your communication skills to respond nondefensively. In other words, don't take it personally.

Strategies to use when the interviewee is angry and defensive include the following:

- Document the behavior and set limits if behavior is abusive, disrespectful, or in violation of company policy.

- Feed back the person's behavior by saying, "Are you aware you are [raising your voice; banging your fist]?"

- If you are feeling threatened or if the behavior is clearly over the line, order him or her to leave, or you leave. Always be aware of your own rights to dignity and respect.

- If you feel unsafe or need another set of ears or eyes, invite a respected professional to sit in the interview with you.

- When employees resist cooperating with the investigation, remind them of their ethical and corporate responsibility to participate. If you can, show them the part of the policy that requires them to participate. As a last resort, describe the penalty for non-participation.

Strategies when the interviewee is distraught and upset include the following:

- Slow down your pace and explain the information many times. People who are emotionally upset must process feelings before information can be stored and you will help by slowing down the process and asking them to feed back what they have heard.

- Be supportive and always practice active listening, but know your role. When you are listening 90 percent of the time and not getting to your need for information, be aware that you may have transitioned to the role of counselor and emotional advocate. This can be a dangerous role conflict for you! Take a step back and stop the interview or refocus.

- Include another professional. Another HR consultant in the room may help to split the role of supporter and investigator.

- When you believe the emotions and trauma are significant and will extend beyond the interview room, be prepared to refer and/or get professional help for the person. A larger than normal percentage of complainants and those accused have significant emotional problems, including personality disorders, multiple personality disorders, post-traumatic stress disorder, addiction issues, and so on. These employees need careful and sure-footed guidance to competent EAP or other referral sources. In very rare cases, the interviews may be conducted in the presence of a therapist (for the victim) because the person "decomposes" during the interview. Sometimes facts cannot be ascertained fully until professional help aids the person in recalling significant events and details.

Order of Interviews

Generally, the complainant should be interviewed first. If there is more than one complainant, then the additional complainants should be interviewed next. Many times other witnesses will also be interviewed before the alleged harasser. However, depending on circumstances, the investigation could also take the following order: (1) complainant, (2) alleged harasser, and (3) witnesses. However, in this case additional interviews with both the complainant and alleged harasser may follow to clarify any additional information learned from witnesses. Even if the alleged harasser is interviewed last, a follow-up meeting with the complainant may be necessary to clarify information learned from the alleged harasser.

Conducting the Investigation

In many ways, actually conducting the investigation is the easiest part of complying with the employer's obligation to investigate. Once an investigator develops skills in questioning witnesses, the investigation itself is often the most interesting part of the process. In this section, we provide tips and suggestions for conducting the investigation.

Ten Most Common Mistakes

1. **Failure to Obtain Input from the Accused** The person accused of harassment or discrimination *must* be interviewed. There are two sides to every story. Even if you believe the complainant and have witnesses to the behavior, the alleged harasser could offer a different perspective and have reason to believe that the complainant solicited the behavior. In addition, the alleged harasser's account is relevant to issues such as appropriate corrective action.

2. **Failure to Obtain Input from the Complainant** The person who was subjected to unlawful discrimination or harassment *must* be interviewed. If the person has submitted a detailed written account of the facts, the temptation is to avoid this step in the process. It is rare that a written account includes *all* the relevant information. In addition, the emotional impact of the harassment is lost without a personal interview. Sometimes the person who submitted the complaint is not the target of the harassment, or not the only target. All targets or potential targets must be interviewed.

3. **Shortcutting the Investigation** When extremely serious allegations are made, some investigators are tempted to skip the investigation completely. For example, when rape is alleged and police are involved, the temptation is to allow the police to make conclusions. However, even those serious cases should be investigated, because the obligation to investigate belongs to the employer, not to an outside agency. The allegations could be refuted by other evidence found by doing a full investigation. Investigations have revealed that a consensual sexual relationship was involved, although rape was alleged. In addition, as noted above, the criterion for evaluating evidence is different in criminal and civil investigations. Finally, an investigation should never be viewed simply as an effort to "cover a base." While the law requires a prompt investigation, the purpose of the investigation is to uncover any potential problem and resolve it.

4. **Dragging Out the Investigation** Often, employers will unintentionally drag out an investigation. Perhaps they are hoping a bolt of lightening will strike and a decision will not have to be made. Sometimes the investigator or manager involved is simply too busy. If this happens, the courts may deny the affirmative defense because the investigation was not completed in a timely manner.

5. **Terminate Now, Investigate Later** This mistake is similar to number 3. The alleged harasser should never be terminated until after the investigation. However, he or she can be placed on administrative leave pending completion of the investigation.

6. **Failure to Close the Loop** Sometimes an investigation will reveal additional types of discrimination or harassment. For example, an investigation that begins with a complaint of national origin discrimination could reveal harassment based on race or religion. Follow through to ensure that *all* allegations made during the investigation are explored, without regard to artificial limitations like the scope of the original complaint. In addition, any necessary rebuttal interviews must be conducted, where the complainant or the alleged harasser is given the opportunity to respond to what other employees said in order to provide a full picture of the problem.

7. **No Second Set of Eyes** The investigation should be done by a person different from the final decision maker, if at all possible (see Chapter 7 for a full discussion). This allows the investigation to be reviewed with a critical eye if necessary. Differentiating between the roles of the investigator and the decision maker serves as a check against mistaken or hasty decisions based on an incomplete investigation. (See Chapter 6 for a discussion of the organizational structure ideal for appropriate investigations.)

8. **Inadequate or Flawed Documentation** Documentation is critical not only for keeping records of what transpired during the investigation, but also to prove what was done if litigation arises. (Chapter 8 contains a detailed discussion of the types of documentation necessary.)

9. **Failure to Protect Privacy** Leakage of information about the investigation could spawn rumors and destroy the reputation of the alleged harasser, the complainant, or witnesses. If the rumors started by the investigator are untrue, defamation liability could result. In addition, there is intangible damage from ruined reputations, especially where all of the employees must perform as a team once the investigation is completed.

10. **Requiring Face-to-Face Confrontation** Following the common model for conflict resolution, some employers believed the harassment complaint can be resolved by bringing together the complainant and the accused. The assumption is that the complaint is about an interpersonal conflict where there is mutual responsibility. However, harassment is most often an assertion of power and a potential civil rights violation. A meeting between the accused

and the complainant could have disastrous results and, at the very least, add to the complainant's psychological trauma. Thus, harassment complaints should *never* be handled by facilitating a conversation between the accused and the complainant. Following an investigation and a formal outcome, there are rare occasions where the complainant may want to speak to the accused. This type of meeting should never be attempted without expert assistance and careful facilitation.

Employers who use a "teaming" management philosophy may believe that the best way to address a complaint of harassment is to pull the "team" together to let them work out their differences. This approach also has the potential of polarizing the work group and creating an explosive climate. It sends a message to the complainant that the complaints must be amended or "compromised" for the sake of the team. Bringing the whole team together to hash out harassment issues is even more dangerous, because there is more pressure on the complainant to drop the complaints for the sake of team unity.

Common Problems That May Arise

Investigators often encounter difficult problems in the course of an investigation. If you are not prepared for these situations and they take you by surprise, mistakes can result. We have listed below some of the situations that we have encountered and offer guidance on how to handle those situations.

The Complainant Says "I Will Handle It Myself"

There is sometimes an underlying feeling among employees that a complaint should be "worked out" without going to management to intervene. In addition, some managers would rather avoid a confrontation or investigation if possible. They also believe that handling problems at the lowest level is appropriate.

As a result, when the complainant asks a manager not to start an investigation because he or she would like to handle the problem alone, the manager is inclined to honor that request. However, the law does not allow a manager who has knowledge of discrimination to do nothing. If such a request is received, the manager should tell the complainant that the organization has an obligation to investigate the matter and will try to respect privacy and confidentiality, but at the same time management is responsible for ensuring a harassment-free environment.

It Has Been a Long Time Since the Events

Regardless of when the alleged harassment occurred, you must complete an investigation at the point when you first learn of it. The length of time that has passed may be relevant when determining credibility, but the mere passage of time does not mean that the events did not happen, or that corrective action is not necessary.

Instead, the passage of time may mean that the complainant feared retaliation or was otherwise prevented from bringing the complaint forward.

The Complainant Fears That Retaliation Will Follow

The organization must still act on the complaint, even if the complainant fears retaliation. In fact, there is an even greater obligation to prevent retaliation if the fear is expressed. Thus, the organization should assure the complainant that retaliation is prohibited and will be punished. The complainant should be invited to disclose any retaliatory behavior that occurs. A strong message should be sent to the alleged harasser(s) that any behavior that might be viewed as retaliation is unacceptable.

The Complainant Wants to Remain Anonymous

Promises of anonymity should never be made, because they can rarely be kept. Instead, assurances of confidentiality to the extent possible and no retaliation should be reiterated (see the section on confidentiality at the beginning of this chapter).

The Complainant Will Not Cooperate

Make sure that the complainant knows that the investigation will continue and that his or her cooperation is important. Assure the complainant that the investigation is an attempt to be fair to all, to hear the complete story, and to do a thorough investigation. Assure the complainant that no retaliation will follow. Sometimes it may be helpful to have a letter or some assurance from the highest levels of management that no retaliation will be tolerated and that the cooperation of the complainant is required. Non-cooperation most often happens, though, when the complainant is no longer employed; in this case, all the employer can do is request the cooperation. If it does not happen, do the most thorough investigation possible despite this limitation.

If the complainant refuses to meet with you, a letter like the one the investigator wrote in *Duviella v. Counseling Service of the Eastern District of New York* (2001) might help. This particular letter impressed the court so much that it was a factor in finding no liability for the employer. The investigator wrote to the complainant urging her to meet with him and promising to meet any time she was available. The investigator wrote that the organization "takes her allegation of sexual harassment very seriously" and that he was "committed to carefully, thoroughly, and expeditiously investigating [her] allegations." The investigator explained that a face-to-face meeting "would greatly enhance [his] ability to fairly complete the investigation and recommend appropriate action." He also explained that the organization "does not and will not tolerate any retaliation." When the complainant scheduled but then cancelled a meeting, the investigator again wrote her urging cooperation and told her she could bring her attorney to the meeting. The investigation proceeded without the complainant's input.

The Complainant Quits in the Middle of the Investigation

Attempt to find out the reasons why the complainant quit. If the reason is in any way related to the harassment or retaliation, try to convince management to intervene. Perhaps administrative leave with pay could be offered, to allow the complainant to remain an employee while the investigation and prompt corrective action proceeds. Never fire a complainant during an investigation. The chances that firing the complainant could be perceived as retaliation are great. Wait until all the facts are discovered and you have made every attempt to contact and meet with the complainant about the results of the investigation.

The Alleged Harasser Will Not Cooperate

As with complainants, when the alleged harasser refuses to cooperate, try to obtain requests for cooperation in writing from the highest levels of management. Assure the alleged harasser that the investigation is an attempt to be fair to all involved and to hear the complete story, and explain that it would be a better investigation if he or she would offer information. However, make sure that the alleged harasser knows that the investigation will proceed despite a refusal to cooperate.

A Witness Refuses to Be Interviewed

Try to obtain cooperation from an uncooperative witness using the same techniques as noted above. If you are not successful, assure the witness that he or she can contact you at any time. Some witnesses also fear retaliation, so an assurance of non-retaliation from a top manager may help. Check back more than once if you feel it might be helpful.

Witnesses Do Not Speak English

Find a person to assist in the investigation who speaks the native language of the people involved.

Witnesses No Longer Work for the Organization

This should not deter you from attempting to secure witnesses' information. Many times a witness who saw an injustice occur is eager to provide information so that the injustice is corrected. Often, these individuals make the best witnesses because their testimony is not emotionally tied to retention of their jobs.

A Witness Insists That His or Her Attorney Be Present

If the witness insists on attending with private counsel, consult with your own legal counsel before proceeding. Generally, third parties not employed by the organization should not be allowed to participate in organization investigations.

Sometimes, a witness who is no longer employed will insist on attending only with his or her own counsel. In that situation, you may choose to proceed, but only after first cautioning the lawyer that his or her role is that of advisor to the witness and that role does not allow him or her to interfere with the investigation. Note the presence of the attorney in your investigation notes. Also note whether the presence of the outside party hampered your ability to gather the facts. You should not allow the attorney to ask questions or in any way interfere with your process of gathering information. In addition, you should instruct the attorney that if he or she wishes to consult with the client, that consultation should occur only during breaks from the interview and not while the interview is in progress.

The Employee Insists on Attending with a Union Representative

The union contract may allow an employee the right to bring a union representative to the interview. In addition, as noted in Chapter 7, there may be times when an employee has a legal right to representation, such as when the interview is for the purpose of imposing discipline. Generally, use the same strategy as when the employee requests an attorney and simply make sure that the presence of an additional party does not hamper the investigation.

A Criminal Act Is Alleged

Do not call the police unless the complainant requests that you do so. Whether the activities are prosecuted criminally is not determinative of your investigation. As noted earlier, the burdens of proof and interests of the criminal system are different. In addition, sometimes a person who is accusing another of criminal conduct may not want to report the crime because he or she fears the court system and becoming embroiled in a more public controversy. To inflict these burdens on a complainant without consent may cause more emotional damage. However, you can call the police when the criminal act is against the organization itself, such as when a person destroys organization property or brings a gun to work and threatens to shoot employees.

A Lawsuit or Administrative Complaint Is Filed
Before an Investigation Is Finished

The employer has an obligation to complete an investigation and decide on prompt corrective action, regardless of the existence of a lawsuit or administrative complaint. Many times, if the employer's first notice of a problem is the lawsuit, it is the first opportunity to resolve the problem. In addition, taking prompt corrective action at that point may decrease the plaintiff's damages. The employer should never rely solely on the outcome of an external investigation in determining prompt corrective action, as an outside investigation can take many months. For example, an EEOC complaint must be filed within 180 (or 300 in most states) days of the last discriminatory action. Then, the EEOC can take as long as necessary to complete the investigation because, while the claim is pending at the EEOC, the complainant retains the right to bring legal action. EEOC and related state agency investigations can sometimes take years to complete. Meanwhile, the workplace needs the healing that may take place if corrective action is taken promptly. Also, the duty to resolve workplace harassment is placed on the employer, not the outside agency. Investigate each complaint even if an outside agency is also looking at the issue.

Defining Prompt and Thorough

There is no legal definition of "prompt." Some investigations have been deemed "prompt" when they were completed within two weeks. Others may have taken longer, but interim relief may have been provided. Some investigations may not be prompt if they take more than a week. The important thing is to set aside less-pressing matters and attend promptly to the investigation. It is also important that, once the investigation is completed, management decide quickly on prompt corrective action. If the employer can show that immediate attention was given to the problem until its logical conclusion, then the law should find that investigation to be "prompt."

The law does not define "thorough," but following the guidelines included throughout this manual should help the employer to conduct a "thorough" investigation.

Copies of the Report

The general rule is that the report is a confidential personnel document and no one should be given a copy except those in management with a need to know to make prompt corrective action decisions. (This issue was discussed in Chapter 8.)

The Interviewing Process

Before beginning any interview, determine what process you want to use. Here are some tips.

Interview Notes Your interview notes will be critical later, so ensure that they are neat and organized. Start a new page for each witness and do not combine notes for different witnesses. At the top of each page indicate the date, the witness interviewed, and those present. Note that, while you may not include the names of witnesses in the written report (see Chapter 8), you do need to keep track of which notes are attributable to each witness. If there are multiple pages, this will help keep pages together. It is generally better to take detailed notes, as verbatim as possible. The paper you are using and the style of notes you take should not detract from this goal.

Management Endorsement of the Investigation In serious or highly complex cases, it is sometimes helpful to have a letter from the top leader asking for the employee's full and honest participation and reiterating the retaliation policy.

Developing Rapport At the beginning of each interview, spend time establishing rapport, but do not become so friendly with a witness that you undermine your impartial role. Pay attention to styles of communication and how you and the interviewee process information.

Written Statements If you believe there may be a later challenge to the accuracy of your notes (such as when you know a witness allegedly denies and refutes any statements made about her), you may want to immediately show your notes to the witness and have him or her sign them. Some companies have the witnesses sign written statements. This is not necessary, but can be done if desired. If a witness refuses to sign a written statement, this should not hamper your investigation. There may be times when a witness will repeat a story orally, but will not want to put it in writing for fear of who might see the information or that a permanent record may come back to haunt him. As you can see, asking for a written statement may create problems that would not be present if you simply gathered the information and kept good notes. Remember, you need only conduct a reasonable investigation, not prove any specific fact later in court. Many times, the documents gathered in an investigation are not admissible later in court because of problems with their hearsay nature or other perceived deficiencies. Focus on getting the information needed to make an informed decision.

Preparation Prepare thoroughly for each interview. Determine the issues to be addressed with each witness. Ensure that you understand the facts you already know, but be prepared to keep an open mind in learning new facts. You may want to write out the questions you intend to ask as a way to record the questions. However, be prepared to deviate from your list if new items are raised.

Terminating Each Interview End each interview with a clear statement about what will happen next and what is expected (confidentiality, respectful behavior, and so forth).

Review for Accuracy and Completeness After each interview, review your notes for accuracy and completeness.

Retain All Notes Keep in mind that all notes are potentially discoverable in litigation. Never destroy any notes. If you wish to write a new set of notes more neatly, keep the old set of notes in the file. (See Chapter 8 discussion regarding documentation.)

Universal Interviewing Issues to Cover with Each Witness

- Explore each person's role/job as it relates to knowledge of the parties and the incident. This will assist you in determining credibility later.

- Assess the relationship of each witness to the complainant and alleged harasser (personal and work). This is an important factor in determining bias when you are judging the truthfulness of statements.

- Inquire about the competence of each witness to observe what happened (proximity, physical or visual ability, and so on). The ability of a person to repeat what he or she sees and hears is critical when there are conflicting stories.

- Ask each witness who was present at each event. You will learn the names of other witnesses you may want to contact during the investigation. Ask each witness to identify others who might have relevant information. Be sure to ask why the witness thinks the others may know something so that you can decide whether they must be interviewed.

- Ask each witness if he or she has any documents that might shed light on the issue, such as memos, e-mails, notes, calendars, or diaries.

- Explain to each witness that it may be necessary to interview him or her again as new information comes to light.

- Never give the impression that you disbelieve anything a witness is saying.

- Ask if there are any other questions the witness thinks should have been asked that were not. Let the witnesses know where they can reach you if they think of additional information.

- Ask if the witness has any reason to fear retaliation for speaking with you, and follow up with appropriate management if the answer is positive.

- Ask every witness what else happened, what else he or she would like you to know.

- Ask questions that imply that the witness may have something else to share ("What else have you heard?" "What else happened that made you feel . . . ?" "What else would you like me to know?" "And then what happened?"). These questions are frequently asked throughout the interview because they allow the witness to remember *all* that may have happened, even if the witness could not recall it earlier.

Introductory Remarks with Each Witness

Introductory remarks should be addressed to each witness at the beginning of each interview. Cover the following topics.

Confidentiality Explain to each witness that you are treating the information you obtain as confidential. You should explain the confidentiality parameters as noted earlier. Ask each witness to treat the interview as confidentially as you will and to show respect for everyone in the process. Ask each witness not to discuss any part of the interview with anyone else to avoid undermining the investigation.

Retaliation Each witness should be assured of the freedom from retaliation for participating in the inquiry. Point to the employer's policy against retaliation. Answer any questions the witness may have about retaliation. Many times this discussion will result in a question about who will learn that the witness has cooperated in the investigation. You can at that point repeat that you will not tell other witnesses what is said and you will report the information gathered only to the team deciding on appropriate corrective action.

Fairness Each witness should be assured that the employer seeks fairness, balanced against the needs of each employee and the needs of the organization. Cooperation from witnesses is one way to achieve fairness, because all sides of the story are heard. In addition, those who are not the subject of the investigation can be assured that they are not the target.

Complaint Process Each witness should be reminded that the employer has a complaint process, allowing each employee to bring forward concerns and have the organization look at them objectively and resolve them. This is part of the complaint process that ensures everyone in the organization is treated fairly.

Policy   Explain the organization's policy against harassment and the requirement to promptly and thoroughly investigate each complaint.

Organizational Desire   Explain the organization's desire to resolve the matter promptly and reasonably.

Your Role   Explain your role in the process.

Interviewing the Complainant

Preliminary Issues

Inform the complainant of his or her rights (for example, rights to representation), your role, the organization's policy against retaliation, confidentiality expectations, and what you hope to accomplish during your interview.

Give him or her an opportunity to ask questions or express how he or she is feeling. Ask if the complainant feels there is any reason why you cannot be fair or objective.

Ask questions during the interview about when the complainant learned of the organization policy against harassment, and what the complainant knows about it. If there was a long interval between the incident and the complaint, try to find out what was happening to the complainant during the interval. For example, you can learn why the complainant waited by asking whether she told her friends or co-workers of the harassment during this interim. You can also ask what the complainant was telling the harasser during this time frame. Most often, such questions will lead naturally to a discussion of the complainant's state of mind and provide explanations of why the complainant did not report the behavior immediately (i.e., "I thought if I avoided him it would stop" or "He stopped for awhile, but then started up again"). You can follow up those statements with more questions, without blaming the complainant for waiting too long to report.

Learning the Facts

Solicit the complainant's story, including when he or she told management or any one else. ("Did you speak with anyone else about this behavior? Who? When? What did he say about it?") Get specifics, such as the nature of the behavior and the complainant's reaction to the behavior, including any emotional reaction. Ask what the complainant said to the harasser. Ask how the complainant responded to the harassment (internally, within the organization, and externally, outside the organization). For example, you should ask the complainant what he or she did in response to the behavior at work (i.e., avoided the harasser), as well as what he or she did outside of work (i.e., sought counseling).

Verify who, what, where, when, and how often each behavior occurred, and continually elicit what else made the complainant feel demeaned, harassed, discriminated against, or whatever the complaint is.

Ask the complainant what he or she did in response to the offensive behavior. In asking these types of questions, make sure that you do not imply that the complainant should have reacted in a particular way or should have objected. You can ask, "When that happened, what did you do?" "Did you say anything to him when he did that?" You may need to ask if the complainant and harasser ever had a social or dating relationship. You may even need to ask whether they ever had a sexual relationship. Treat these latter issues very sensitively, and address them toward the end of the interview to avoid an abrupt end to the discussion before most of the facts are discovered.

Document the impacts of the alleged behaviors, including feelings, emotional reactions, physical reactions, behavioral reactions, and economic consequences, inside and outside the workplace. Ask if the complainant sought medical attention for any emotional reaction.

Document all potential witnesses to events and those the complainant has told about the events, including reactions to them. Obtain copies of any relevant journals or notes kept by the complainant or other witnesses. Solicit any documents that might support the complainant's claim.

Document if a complainant is reluctant to divulge names and details and offer other opportunities for disclosure. Document any comments that complainant makes that appear to support retaliation, and note any concerns raised about potential retaliation.

Be certain to ask about information you have that conflicts with what the witness has said, without revealing the conflict. Ask about, assess, and document information related to credibility issues.

It may be helpful to use the checklist for the complainant's interview included in the Appendix. However, do not become overly reliant on checklists; use them simply as a tool to get started. You must add your own inquiries based on the facts and the areas you want to explore.

Interview Closure

Find out what the complainant wants from the investigation, but never promise that the organization can deliver it. ("What do you want to get out of this process?") This provides you with some sense of the complainant's expectations. It also begins the healing process for complainants because their personal needs are being elicited. Listen intently to the complainant's needs, and respond by telling the complainant that once the facts are gathered, the organization will make a decision and meet with the complainant to discuss that decision.

Ask if the complainant can return to work with the harasser. ("Can you return to work with the harasser? If so, is there anything the organization can do to assist you in resuming a positive working relationship? If not, why do you believe you cannot work with the harasser?") If a negative response is received, follow up with management and inquire about administrative leave to ensure that any damage is not continuing during the investigation. Sometimes the complainant will see no problem with working with the alleged harasser, but the allegations are so serious that the employer will make an independent decision to remove the alleged harasser from the workgroup during the interim or grant voluntary administrative leave to the complainant.

Explain what will happen next and make certain the complainant knows how to contact you if he or she needs to talk or has further information. Let the complainant know how she or he will learn of the results of the investigation.

Reassure the complainant about the organization's policy on retaliation, and ask him or her to contact you if retaliation occurs. Always thank the complainant for coming forward.

Interviewing the Alleged Harasser

Preliminary Issues

Explain why you are talking to the person. For example, say that the organization has become aware of allegations of misconduct/violation of policy, or whatever the case is. Inform the alleged harasser of his or her rights and the organization's policy relevant to investigation. Emphasize the prohibition against any form of retaliation and give examples of what could be perceived as retaliatory conduct.

Caution the person regarding sharing information with anyone during investigation. Provide an opportunity for the alleged harasser to ask questions and share reactions to the meeting. Be sure to reiterate that no conclusion has been reached as to the veracity of the complaints.

Hearing the Facts

Explain the allegations in enough detail for the alleged harasser to be able to respond fully to the claim. You need not reveal the sources for your information. Go from general questions to specific claims, and do not stop at general denials. If the alleged harasser says the complainant is lying, question him or her about the complainant's motivation. Ask if anything has happened between the two or them that might lead to untruthfulness.

If the alleged harasser contends alleged acts were welcome, ask for all facts supporting that contention. Ask detailed questions about the nature of the complainant's participation in the behavior. Ask for a detailed account of the time, place, and circumstances of each incident, as well as for information about relevant witnesses and documents. If the alleged harasser denies being present, ask for information that might verify where she or he was at the time.

Ask the alleged harasser to identify witnesses or other sources of relevant information, and why they are relevant.

If you have specific information that conflicts with the alleged harasser's version of events, ask for an explanation without revealing the conflict. Assess and document credibility.

If there is a question of whether the alleged harasser is a supervisor, ask questions about his or her job duties and responsibilities so management has the information it needs to make this determination.

Interview Closure

If the alleged harasser refuses to participate, advise him or her that the organization will have to take action based on the information gathered in the investigation, with or without his or her participation, and that it is in his or her best interests to participate to ensure a fair and accurate gathering of facts.

Explain what will happen next and make certain the alleged harasser knows how to contact you if she or he needs to talk or has further information.

Ask the alleged harasser what steps she or he thinks should be taken to ensure a complete and thorough investigation. Note that this is not the same as asking what the organization should do to resolve the complaint, but instead focuses specifically on the investigation. By asking this question, you are inviting the alleged harasser to share information on whom the alleged harasser thinks you should interview and what documents he or she thinks you should review.

Interviewing Witnesses

Preliminary Issues

Explain the scope of the investigation in general terms. Solicit all information that may be relevant. Don't reveal confidential data or discuss other interviews unless you must do so to elicit relevant information.

Respond directly to any hesitancy to cooperate with empathy and reiterate that the organization expects employees to cooperate and prohibits retaliation against those who participate in any EEO investigation.

Explain the importance of receiving factual, truthful information, without threatening the witness.

If the employee is a member of the union and requests to attend with a union representative, you must not proceed until that union representation is provided.

Obtaining the Facts

Find out specifically what this witness saw or heard. Use an open-ended questioning technique.

Ask the witness if he or she knows of other first-hand witnesses. Be sure to ask for information on what the witness thinks the others know. Distinguish between character witnesses and those who observed the events in question.

Interview Closure

Explain what will happen next and make certain the witness knows how to contact you if he or she needs to talk or has further information. Make certain all witnesses understand that you will be seeking corroboration of all relevant information, including their testimony.

Advise each witness of the possibility that he or she may be interviewed again if new "facts" make that appropriate.

Caution each witness about discussing the investigation or the information provided with others in the workforce.

Completing the Process

Don't interview additional witnesses when facts become so clear that additional interviews would be redundant. However, do interview every person who was allegedly subjected to the behavior so that you can identify the full scope of the conduct. Once you believe you have completed the investigation, begin to consider how to make a determination, which will be discussed in the next chapter.

Gathering Factual Documentation

Many times the factual documentation that you gather will provide the most important corroboration and allow you to draw appropriate conclusions. With every issue, consider whether there are any documents that may help to gather the appropriate information. These include:

- *Personnel files.* Performance evaluations, reprimands, and other documents provide a picture of how the complainant's work performance has been judged and how the alleged harasser has performed.

- *Payroll records.* These records will show promotions, pay raises, and leaves taken.

- *Calendars.* These provide information to help establish dates that an event occurred. Computer calendars may show appointments and times when the witnesses were together.

- *Electronic communications.* These are becoming more important. In tracking an office romance, it would be important to check e-mails between the individuals involved to determine whether the relationship was consensual. Don't forget to check to see if deleted e-mails and computer information can be recovered.

- *Time sheets.* These will tell you when the witnesses worked on the same day (see box). If a complainant alleges that she had to take a lot of time off because of the harassment, time records will verify this.

In one investigation, the complainant alleged that the harassment happened daily, but time records showed that she worked with the harasser only two days in the previous two months. In another investigation, the witnesses claimed five people were present and saw an event, when time records showed that the five had never worked the same shift in the previous year.

- *Organization memos.* Many times information will be recorded in a memo showing times and dates.

- *Supervisor files.* Many times supervisors will keep their own notes and records of information relating to their subordinates. Be sure to ask if these files exist, and check them for relevant information.

- *Diaries.* Many times a complainant will keep a diary of what occurred. Be sure to ask for a copy.

- *Pictures.* If any of the events were recorded by pictures, ask for copies.

- *Computer records.* If any of the events involve Internet activity or computer documents, check computer history records to show what might have been accessed at what times and when certain documents might have been created.

- *Organizational charts.* These may be helpful in understanding the chain of command.

Implementing an investigation requires you to carefully plan what questions need to be asked, how to approach each witness, and what topics should be covered in the interview. This chapter has provided guidelines for conducting a thorough investigation.

Chapter 10

Making the Determination

Deciding When You Are Finished

SOMETIMES, THE HARDEST PART of the investigation is to know when you are finished. Here are some questions to ask yourself:

- Have you addressed each and every complaint of harassment, discrimination, or retaliation?
- Have you interviewed both the complainant and the alleged harasser?
- Have you conducted rebuttal interviews to clarify any new information?
- Have you interviewed any other possible victims of the harassment?
- Have you interviewed all witnesses that the complainant and the harasser identified? If not, have you articulated a logical reason why that information would be redundant or irrelevant?
- Have you used every means possible to determine the true facts, especially when the charges are severe?
- Have you reviewed all documents that might be relevant?

If you answer affirmatively to the above questions, then you are likely finished. If while drafting your report you identify gaps in your critical knowledge, then you should close that gap. Otherwise, don't be tempted to continue to investigate when the investigation may be over. Accept the possibility that you may never know exactly what happened. You can only draw logical conclusions and make a reasonable decision. (See also the section in Chapter 7 on Size of the Investigation.)

Policy Violations vs. Violations of the Law

The primary purpose of an internal investigation is to discover the facts about a complaint to determine whether or not the behavior is a violation of an organization's policy to prevent harassment or another policy.

It is not necessary to try to determine whether the facts also show a violation of any EEO laws. Organizational policy is designed not only to comply with EEO laws but, more important, to address less severe behaviors that can lead to EEO violations and create a disrespectful work environment. The behaviors investigated may or may not ultimately be established in a court of law as unlawful harassment.

For this reason, it is more appropriate for management to label behavior as inappropriate, unprofessional, disrespectful, and as a violation of the organization's policies. Decisions about whether the behavior also violates EEO laws are better left to the courts.

Determining Credibility

Often, making a determination involves testing the credibility of the participants in the harassment events. Courts and administrative fact-finders have identified various factors that can be used in determining credibility, including those shown in Figure 10.1 and described below.

Opportunity and Capacity to Observe

To be credible, a witness must have been in the relevant place, at the relevant time (which could include immediately preceding or following an event), and close enough to the event to have been able to observe it. In addition, the witness must have the ability to understand what she or he saw and to narrate it intelligently. Credibility will be at issue if the witness:

- Had a view of events that was obscured, for example, by a partition or by other people);

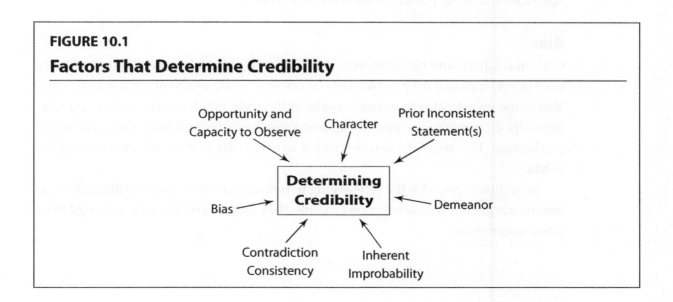

FIGURE 10.1

Factors That Determine Credibility

- Could not hear the event accurately, for example, because of a hearing impairment or the intrusion of outside noise;

- Had his or her attention focused on something else at the time;

- Was not fluent in the language overheard, or lacked sufficient cultural understanding to be able to accurately interpret the events; and/or

- Could not coherently tell what she or he saw because of a disability, the effects of medication, or some other impediment.

To assess these possibilities, it may be critical to visit the environment where the alleged event occurred. You must understand what the scene looked like at the time of the alleged event and meet personally with the witnesses.

Character

A poor reputation for truthfulness will diminish a witness's credibility, but morals or values generally will not be relevant. For example, the fact that a witness previously perjured himself or herself, or has been caught in other lies, would be relevant. The fact that a witness is committing adultery generally would not be relevant.

Prior Inconsistent Statement(s)

The problem with a prior inconsistent statement is not that the present statement is false. Rather, the fact that there is an inconsistency raises doubt as to the truthfulness of both statements.

The form of the inconsistency (oral, written, conduct) is immaterial, and the inconsistent statement(s) or conduct need not be in direct conflict. Also, where the inconsistencies are merely inadvertent, there is no need to declare that the inconsistencies make the present testimony non-credible.

Bias

Certain relations and circumstances may impair a witness's impartiality. A witness who is not impartial may consciously or unconsciously shade his or her testimony. You as the investigator therefore must be sufficiently familiar with underlying relationship, circumstances, and influences among parties and witnesses and in the workgroup. This will help you determine whether bias in the testimony reasonably exists.

In addition, consider the self-serving nature of some statements. Although these statements are not necessarily non-credible, they may be entitled to less weight than other statements.

Contradiction and Consistency

Contradiction of testimony provided by one witness by the testimony of another witness is irrelevant unless the conflicting evidence is believable. The issue in contradiction is the inference that a witness who is mistaken about one fact may be mistaken about more facts and, therefore, may not be a trustworthy witness. Discrediting a witness on one issue does not mean that she or he must be discredited on all issues. However, the mere fact that testimony is not contradicted does not mean that it should be credited.

Where the witnesses contradict each other, further investigation of the contradicted facts will often be necessary. Draw appropriate conclusions about credibility based on the number of contradictions and consistencies.

Inherent Improbability

This factor requires you to evaluate the likelihood that the event occurred as described by witnesses. For example, is it improbable that a person would risk fabricating a memorandum that must clear two levels of supervision? It is more likely that a person would risk fabricating a self-serving memorandum that she or he has produced for his or her own use, because it is not subject to contemporaneous supervisory review.

Demeanor

Demeanor refers to the carriage, manner, behavior, and appearance of a witness during testimony. Demeanor can only be judged through direct observation. The validity of demeanor evidence can be affected, however, by cultural differences and changed circumstances. For example, a person who avoids eye contact may be trying to hide something, but she or he also may be embarrassed, shy, intimidated, or respectful. Similarly, a "victim" who was intimidated during the event may now feel more empowered and will appear different than at the time of the incident.

Note: Never consider a third party's view of a witness's credibility unless you have some credible factual support for the opinion. Never let anyone who is not a witness in the investigation (for example, a colleague) influence your judgment about a witness with "outside evidence," such as "Everyone knows that X exaggerates." If the witness and the "evidence" will not appear in your report, do not consider them.

Finally, remember that most credibility factors involve some degree of subjectivity, especially when many different factors come into play. To avoid making mistakes, try to find as many objective facts as possible, and rely on purely subjective assessments only when absolutely necessary.

Deciding What Is Relevant

Evidence is not relevant if it does not illuminate the issues to be decided, including the elements of proof. Thus, the fact that one of the parties has been "sleeping around" is relevant only if the "sleeping around" included the other party. The fact that someone has "slept around" does not mean that she or he welcomes sexual advances from everyone, or that she or he "deserves" what she or he gets. Also, just because two members of an ethnic group use "terms" for each other and tell jokes about their heritage doesn't mean that they shouldn't be offended when someone outside their ethnic heritage uses the same terms. While no one in the workgroup should use such terms, the fact that an employee is not offended when another employee uses it does not exclude that same employee from taking offense in another context. These terms can have very different meanings within the "safer" group.

When in doubt about what you can consider relevant, talk with HR/legal to ensure that you are not making decisions based on irrelevant factors.

Corroborating Evidence

Any credible evidence that tends to support one party's version of the facts is corroborating evidence. The weight of the evidence varies with the relevance of the evidence and with its objectivity. For example, if three independent witnesses support the complainant's allegation that the accused used derogatory religious terms to describe the complainant, there is strong corroboration. The corroboration is significantly less if the three witnesses are family members or close friends of the complainant.

Courts have accepted as corroborating evidence the following:

- The complainant told someone about the incident(s) at about the time they occurred and said that she or he did not welcome the behavior;

- The complainant took steps to avoid the accused by seeking a transfer, staying out of a particular work area, passing up overtime opportunities;

- The complainant's performance, attendance, attitude, or health deteriorated;

- Other individuals experienced similar behavior from the accused;

- Other individuals witnessed all or part of the offensive behavior;

- Other individuals witnessed the effects of the behavior on the complainant;

- The complainant documented* significant incidents or events in a diary, journal, or work log;

- The complainant tape-recorded the incidents; and/or

- The accused admitted part or all of the behavior, but said she or he was "just kidding."

*Recording anything without the consent of all parties is illegal in some states, unless the person recording has a court order.

If the complainant told no one about the harassment for six months, but independent witnesses verify that the complainant was edgy, moody, and difficult to work with during that period, when she or he formerly was easygoing, then those observations may serve to corroborate the complainant's statement that something has happened. If there are other personal or work reasons for the changes in demeanor, for example, the complainant was going through a divorce or was caring for a terminally ill relative, the corroboration is weaker.

Boorish Behavior and Bad Management

As previously stated, the law on harassment does not cover boorish or "jerk" behavior, unfairness, nepotism, personality conflicts, or bad management. In fact, many complainants who come forward under an anti-harassment or respectful workplace policy are complaining about activity that is not illegal. However, every complaint that is a legitimate problem of an employee should be solved by the organization. Doing so creates trust in the complaint system, rights a wrong that affects someone's work, and helps prevent other behaviors, including unlawful harassment.

Risk Factors

In resolving complaints of harassment, discrimination, and retaliation, employers must be aware that handling the investigation poorly and resolving a complaint inappropriately greatly increases the risk of reaching the litigation stage. A number of reasons exist for avoiding litigation:

- The jury system is favorable to plaintiffs. A recent survey in Washington State showed that juries favor plaintiffs more than twice as often as judges do. If the complainant is sympathetic, a jury is likely to believe him or her. Similarly, many managers and/or management decisions may appear cavalier or insensitive to juries, who then may attribute discriminatory motives to them.

- When an environment has been shown to have negative behavior in it, such as favoritism or a loose, crude, or nonexistent code of conduct, these factors may influence a jury to reach other conclusions, or they may aggregate the effects of the environment and the alleged harassment.

- When an employer is unpopular with residents of a particular area for whatever reason, the employer takes a risk that by going to court its unpopularity will overshadow the facts.

- When there are other dissatisfied individuals at work, whether because of harassment or other factors, the employer takes a risk by going to court that others may bring claims forward as well.

- When the employer unreasonably investigates and/or remedies known problems, the employer risks increased compensatory and punitive damages in court.

These and other risk factors should be weighed carefully in making a determination on how claims of harassment and retaliation should be resolved.

Making a Determination

Once all of the information has been gathered, and not before, you can make a determination about (1) which version of the facts is correct and (2) whether the employer's policy has been violated.

Chapter 8 discusses which, if any, of the above conclusions should be included in a written report. Ideally, before any conclusions are reduced to writing, the employer's legal counsel will be consulted and a determination will be made as to the risks and benefits of placing one's conclusions in writing.

Concluding the investigation, and making a determination, are often the most critical parts of the investigative process. Following the tips included in this chapter will ensure that no steps are overlooked.

Part Four

Beyond the Investigation

Chapter 11

Prompt, Corrective Action

YOU AS THE INVESTIGATOR PLAY AN IMPORTANT ROLE in determining prompt, corrective action. First, your conclusions and findings form the parameters of possible corrective action. Thus, you must gather sufficient information on the nature and scope of the problems so that the appropriate prompt, corrective action can be taken. Second, you may be asked for your recommendations for corrective action. Managers may want oral recommendations so that they can make the most informed decision. Often, you are the person with the most knowledge about the people involved and know what it will take to stop the harassment and prevent it from happening again.

As you read through this chapter you will notice that we now use the terms "victim" and "harasser," rather than complainant and accused. For the purpose of this chapter and others that follow, we are making the assumption that the investigation found that harassment did occur.

A Working Definition of Zero Tolerance

Many companies indicate that they have "zero tolerance" for harassment and discrimination. That is a laudable policy, but the use of the term "zero tolerance" often creates confusion in the minds of management and employees alike. Zero tolerance for the behavior does not mean that every person who violates a policy will be automatically terminated. Instead, zero tolerance means that the employer will *take appropriate steps to ensure that the behavior does not continue.* Employees who understand this concept are less likely to be offended if an alleged harasser is not terminated and less fearful that if they say anything wrong they will be terminated.

Presenting the Issues to Top Management

Generally, you will not make a final decision on prompt, corrective action. However, you will play a vital role in presenting the information gathered in the investigation to top management and in making a recommendation on appropriate action, if necessary.

When presenting the results of the investigation, follow these guidelines:

- Ensure that you have an excellent grasp of the issues and facts so that you are prepared to answer any questions that arise;

- Make your presentation calmly, succinctly, and clearly, using visuals if they could help;

- Start your presentation by identifying the issues to help people focus, as it is not helpful to talk about facts before your audience knows the issues;

- Help managers understand why you reached certain conclusions, if that is not apparent from the evidence;

- If more than one conclusion is possible, explain why you believe that your conclusion is appropriate;

- When discussing remedies, help managers see why the solutions work;

- In order to transmit the impact and severity of the behaviors, it may be necessary to share specific phrases, pictures, and behaviors with management to avoid minimizing the harassment and its impact;

- Help managers understand why your disciplinary recommendations are appropriate and consistent with past practice and good business and if some inconsistencies exist, explain why and how they should be resolved; and

- If questions arise that reveal holes in the facts or investigation, immediately offer to follow up and do so promptly. Do not try to defend an investigation that arguably will benefit from additional work.

Judging the Severity of the Behavior

One of the most challenging tasks for management is to assess the severity of the misconduct. The severity must be assessed before discipline is determined. Table 11.1 provides some examples to illustrate two different levels of severity.

The items in the table were pulled from an analysis of the legal and psychological literature. Recently, these factors have been tested (Schneider, Swan, & Fitzgerald, 1997) and found to accurately predict psychological and work-related outcomes for harassment victims. It is best to regard these factors as indicators of

TABLE 11.1

Two Levels of Severity

Less Serious	More Serious
A Single Incident Verbal Comments "Complimentary" or "Welcoming"	A Repeated Incident Physical Contact/Proposition Threatening, Intimidating, Demeaning, or Derogatory
One Aggressor Physical Threat Not an Issue Directed at a Group	Many Aggressors Physical Threat Possible Directed at an Individual
Escape Possible One Victim Minimal Power Factors Used Otherwise Good Environment	Escape Restricted Multiple Victims Multiple Power Factors Presence of Other Harassment or Threats in the Environment
Rehabilitation of Aggressor Possible/Remorse Evident	Aggressor Denies Conduct or Is Defiant/Recidivism Potential High

how severe the harassment might be. Use these factors to help management reach a more objective and informed decision. Management may also apply their own experience and knowledge, but every case should be decided on its own facts.

Disciplinary Considerations

Discipline is often appropriate for harassment, discrimination, or retaliation incidents. Although your role as the investigator is to provide input, rarely should you be the person who decides on the appropriate discipline. Nevertheless, you should be aware of factors used in determining what discipline may be appropriate for the harasser. The employer should select discipline that is sufficient to stop the harassment, prevent retaliation, and deter future harassment.

In determining whether, and how much, discipline may be appropriate, you may help the employer to consider the following factors:

- Did the harasser have notice that his/her conduct was prohibited? That is, did the harasser receive:

  - A copy of the employer's harassment prevention policy?

  - Guidance from a manager or supervisor about what constitutes inappropriate conduct under the policy?

  - Management modeling of appropriate conduct?

  - Effective harassment prevention training?

- Information from the employer about how it will deal with substantiated harassment incidents?

This information does not excuse the behavior, but if the harasser was unaware that the behavior was inappropriate, it may affect the discipline. If training did occur, the discipline may be harsher.

- Was the substantiated misconduct severe (see Table 11.1)?

- Is the offender in a leadership position? For example, supervisors who engage in lesser offenses may be more severely disciplined or removed from a position because they are in a leadership position and set the tone for the workplace.

- The culture and context of the workplace may make some behaviors more or less severe as well.

- Notoriety, that is, whether the misconduct was sufficient to negatively affect the employer and/or the work group, is important.

- The harasser's overall work record: On balance, how does the offense compare to the individual's overall work record, including work performance, length of service, prior misconduct (or absence thereof)?

Note: A good employment record does not mean that the harassment was not serious or that the harasser should be retained. The lesser the severity the more a good employment record may be relevant to discipline or whether the behavior is likely to reoccur.

- Was the complainant's conduct ambiguous? Could the harasser reasonably have believed that the conduct was not offensive?

- Has the employer recently strengthened its policy on harassment, provided employee training, and/or clarified its workplace expectations? If so, the employer could impose a more severe sanction for conduct the employee knew or reasonably should have known was inappropriate.

- Should managers in the chain of command be disciplined also? Did management's behavior contribute to the harassment by ignoring a complaint, discounting the complaint or complainant, and/or failing to investigate or take appropriate action?

- To what extent did other managers have knowledge of what was expected of them (conveyed through training and/or policy)?

- To what extent did management's failure to respond exacerbate the situation, increase liability for the organization, or allow harm to continue to employees?

- To what extent did abusive or poor management practices contributed to inappropriate behaviors?

> If management contributed to the problem, then failure to extend discipline to management communicates to line workers that management is "above the law."

- If you discover that a manager or employee has deliberately lied about important facts concerning an investigation, this is a significant ethical issue that requires a strong, immediate response, including discipline. Failure to actively address lying as a serious violation of company ethics serves to undermine the entire investigative process and company policies. This is true regardless of the outcome of the investigation.

Types of Discipline

An employer can consider many different types of discipline as part of a prompt, corrective action. Descriptions of some follow.

Reprimands

A reprimand may be sufficient if the alleged misconduct is on the mild end of the offensiveness scale. As one court has said, Title VII does not require the most serious sanction available for the first documented offense. However, reprimands probably should *not* be used when the complaint is a second offense, because whatever action the employer took on the first offense was obviously ineffective. If a reprimand is chosen, the employer must monitor the situation closely to ensure that no retaliation occurs and to ensure that the reprimand is effective in stopping the harassment.

Even if no violation of policy is discovered, corrective action of some kind may still be appropriate. For example, the incident could highlight the need for a change in policy. In addition, the organization could still caution the employees involved about appropriate workplace behavior, even if no violation of policy is discovered. This should contain a reminder about the policy, a reprimand about recurrence of any behavior that might violate the policy, and a warning about retaliation.

Suspension

A suspension may be appropriate if it stops the harassment. The length of the suspension will depend on the severity of the conduct.

Demotions

Demotions are a strong form of discipline, particularly appropriately when a supervisor or manager engages in harassment. Depriving the harasser of his or her power helps prevent harassment from reoccurring.

Transfers and Reassignments

Transfers and reassignments should not be considered as disciplinary, but as corrective action. However, the employer must be sure that the harassment will *stop*, not simply transfer the harassment to new victims in another area. In addition, if the transfer or other action leaves the offender in contact with the victim, then it likely will not be deemed an effective disciplinary measure.

Transferring or reassigning the complainant should never be considered as corrective action. A transfer can help a complainant begin anew with co-workers and be assured a safe work environment. However, a transfer may be appropriate when it is completely voluntary on the part of the complainant and is not detrimental to him or her.

Termination

This is the last option on the spectrum, but also the most appropriate one for severe or repeated harassment. When considering termination, it is sometimes appropriate to assess the sincerity of the harasser's remorse and his or her ability to change.

Other corrective actions to consider:

- Additional training for workforce and supervisors
- Team building or interventions
- Organization development consultation
- Reductions in pay
- Reemphasis of the policy
- Changes to the policy if necessary
- Discipline for supervisors who handled a complaint inappropriately

---

Training for Workgroups

It is common for organizations to suggest that the entire workgroup, department, or even division receive harassment training after a complaint. They believe that training will lessen their liability and teach people not to engage in the behaviors identified in the complaint. This approach to corrective action is wrong-headed and often dangerous. In Chapter 3 we discussed the impact of harassment on the workgroup. The last thing a stressed, alienated workgroup needs is structured training that, in effect, communicates that their behavior may also be inappropriate. What workgroups really need is an opportunity to discuss the situation and deal with their feelings (see Chapter 12). Also, it is rare that every member of the workgroup is responsible for the disrespectful or harassing behavior. As a result, workgroups view training with hostility and resentment, because they feel that they are being punished for the offensive behavior of others.

We find that allowing the workgroup time to heal and conducting training as part of a general training effort or at a later date is more likely to be viewed positively by the group (Salisbury, 1996).

Training for Individual Harassers

When the organization has decided to keep an employee, it is important that the employee fully understand why his or her behavior violated policy. Sometimes that is accomplished with a brief session with the employee's manager and the HR professional. However, especially with high-level managers, it is sometimes necessary to spend the time and money on individual training with an expert who understands the psychological and legal aspects of harassment (Salisbury & Jaffe, 1996). Regular group training alone is rarely effective, many times because the harasser does not see his or her exact circumstances reflected in the training—in fact, he or she might come out of the training believing that his or her own behaviors were not nearly as egregious as those talked about in the training. Thus, the employee may use group training to minimize the behavior.

Individual training is not counseling. It is an educational model designed to address the specific behaviors identified in the complaint and requires the employee to read, talk about, and write about the harassing behavior. The counseling model for helping harassers change tends to be ineffective because of the lack of legal and specialized knowledge of mental health therapists. In addition, the counseling model is driven by the client and emphasizes confidentiality. Training is not confidential, rather is an educational approach to changing behavior. It helps to hold the harasser accountable for his or her behavior. The training can last from two to ten hours, depending on the individual issues. The culmination of the training is an oral and/or written presentation by the trainee about what he or she has learned.

Even if the organization does not have access to experts, they can use knowledgeable Human Resource staff to do the training. Individual training is an important tool for organizations if they want to help the harasser be successful and ensure that the behavior does not reoccur.

Prompt corrective action involves a variety of actions that the organization must take to end the harassment and prevent it from reoccurring. Present the facts to management in a way that promotes understanding and helps guide the organization toward appropriate discipline and other methods of correcting the behavior. This stage of the investigation must be completed before the organization can bring closure and begin the process of healing.

Chapter 12

Remedies, Healing, and Follow-Up

MANY TIMES YOUR ROLE as the investigator is over once the facts are gathered and a determination has been made as to the veracity of the complaint. However, one of the most important goals of an investigation is to provide information to management to enable individuals and groups to heal and become successful and effective. Based on hundreds of investigations and situations, this chapter is a guide to determining how to follow up and remedy harassment.

Remedies for Aggrieved Employees

Under the EEOC Guidelines, prompt corrective action requires that the aggrieved individual be made "whole." This includes all of the following:

- Corrective action to right the wrong;

- Remedial action to remedy the harm caused by the wrong; and

- Preventative action to ensure that the wrong does not recur.

In the last chapter we discussed prompt, corrective action. In this chapter we will address another aspect of the EEOC Guidelines, remedial actions. The EEOC Guidelines identify the following components as part of remedial action to remedy the harm caused by a substantiated discrimination claim, including harassment and retaliation:

- Mandatory, nondiscriminatory placement, which requires putting the aggrieved individual in the position she or he would have occupied without the discrimination;

- As appropriate, back pay, benefits, non-competitive promotions, shift differentials, annual and sick leave, training, details, travel, overtime, expunging of employment records and so forth;

- Removal of discriminatory influences;
- Management/employee training and/or discipline;
- The employer's commitment that there will be no further discriminatory conduct; and
- As appropriate, attorney fees, costs, back pay, interest on money lost, medical/psychological care, changed work schedules, and so on.

In appropriate cases involving harassment, an employer also should consider providing the aggrieved individual with compensatory damages for pain, suffering, humiliation, and emotional distress. An employer also should work with the aggrieved individual to plan how that individual will reenter the organization or function effectively. This plan could include workgroup debriefing, ongoing monitoring of the work environment, team building, and other support services.

An employer also should consider working with the aggrieved individual to help her or him realize some positive outcomes from the harassment experience (for example, an improved work environment generally, an employer policy statement on harassment, an enhanced process for dealing with issues, more effective and comprehensive prevention of harassment training, an employee committee to monitor how these issues are handled, and so on). It is well known that victims of a traumatic situation can recover better if they are involved in activities that prevent the same trauma from happening again. Finally, employers should develop a plan to follow up with the individual on an ongoing basis to ensure that her or his ability to function in the workplace has not been compromised as a result of the complaint (Salisbury, 1996).

The Need for Debriefing

In the early years of harassment complaints and investigations, organizations and their attorneys were very concerned that, if they told complainants and others the outcomes of the complaint, they would create more problems. They feared that sharing information would not only breach confidentiality, but potentially create liability for the organization that, by sharing information, has "admitted" that illegal activity has occurred. These assumptions, however, backfired. Complainants who were not debriefed were not convinced that their complaints had been acted on and, as a result, sought out attorneys. Witnesses and the workgroup already knew most of the so-called "confidential information" and were left with anxious, hostile feelings about the process and the complainant, thereby laying the groundwork for retaliation. Finally, as more harassment cases were litigated, it became clear that if the organization did not remedy the harm that harassment created, the court system would (Salisbury, 1996).

Maria and Joan have both brought forward complaints about their manager's abusive behavior and demeaning comments about their religion. They were assured that "the organization" would respond immediately. Other employees were interviewed and the workgroup began to gossip among themselves as the investigation dragged on for weeks. The manager became withdrawn and hostile to the workgroup. The atmosphere became tense and co-workers seemed to blame the complainants for the change. Maria and Joan were concerned that, despite reassurances to the contrary, they could not trust their manager to be fair and not to retaliate. They went to the HR department to find out what had happened to the complaint and received the curt reply: "As you know, we have investigated and have taken action." "What action?" asked the complainants. "We can't tell you," responded the HR manager. "That's private." Frustrated and feeling threatened, the two women sought out an attorney who wrote a letter accusing the company of not responding to their complaint and threatening to file a lawsuit asserting that her clients had experienced retaliation.

Leading the Debriefing

Whoever does any of the individual debriefings should be *very* familiar with the details of the complaint. Usually there is an HR person and/or an investigator, and sometimes management is present, particularly when discipline is going to be communicated.

Debriefing the Complainant

The well-being and the needs of the complainant are a primary concern during the aftermath from a complaint. From the first moment of contact, whether with a manager, supervisor, or HR professional, the complainant is sensitive to whether the complaint is being taken seriously and to whether the response is thorough and respectful. The strategies listed below go a long way to meet these expectations and ensure a credible and meaningful outcome for the complaint.

Maintain Communication and Trust During the Investigation Keep the complainant informed about progress and make certain he or she knows how to reach you immediately if he or she has questions, concerns, or more information to share if there is retaliation. *Note:* Managers who are accused of wrongdoing should not be involved in this process.

Debrief the Outcome After management decides on the final outcome, sit down with the complainant and go through management's decision and the basis for that decision, including what you did (include how many interviews you conducted, corroboration and credibility issues, conclusions, and plans for resolution). Do not compromise the confidentiality of any witnesses. If the complainant does not agree with the outcome of the complaint, ask the complainant what else could have been done to ensure a fair and thorough outcome. If there is reasonable evidence that should be reconsidered or sought (such as other witnesses), you should immediately reopen the investigation. If there is no reasonable additional evidence to seek, it is helpful to steer the complainant toward what he or she needs at the moment.

In talking with the complainant, it may also be helpful to share the discipline* given to the accused but ask the complainant not to share it with others in the workplace. Remember that discipline does not always help achieve closure for the complainant because the discipline may be, according to the complainant, too much or too little. Other remedies described in this chapter may be equally or more valuable to the complainant.

Communicate Remedies and Recovery Plans If appropriate, explore with the complainant any remedies you wish to offer, including counseling, retraining, debriefing the workgroup, team building, administrative leave, expunging employment records, reimbursing for sick/vacation leave, and so forth.

Explore Next Steps in Detail Carefully go through what will happen next and communicate management's and HR's roles in the next steps. Explore timelines. Identify the management and HR people who will continue to facilitate outcomes.

Continue to Communicate Regarding Retaliation Continue to provide active protection and support for the employee, including thorough periodic check-ins about how things are going in the workplace. Remember, simply telling the complainant to contact you if retaliation should occur is *not* always adequate, as complainants are already feeling the effects of filing a complaint and are sometimes reluctant to say anything more that will make them more visible or vulnerable in the workplace.

Record Points Covered Keep written documentation of what you have discussed with the complainant. Sometimes a follow-up letter will help the complainant

---

*The ability to share such disciplinary information may be limited by law, policy, or union agreements.

understand and respond to your resolution strategies. (Always consult with your attorney about any such letter before sending it.)

Evaluate Remedies When Cause Is Found When cause is found, the employer should consider offering appropriate remedies that make the person whole and help to return the person to his or her position successfully. In other words, the employer should make a good faith effort to ameliorate the impact of the harassment and communicate to the employee that everything reasonable is being done. The costs of these remedies are small compared to the costs of constructive discharge (see Chapter 2) and other legal consequences of serious discriminatory harassment. Also, in many cases a legal process has begun either through a private attorney or through the EEOC and has resulted in a small settlement because the employer has done all that could reasonably be done to resolve and heal the situation.

Administrative leave may be offered to reduce the opportunity (if evaluated at moderate to high) for retaliation or for escalation of workplace tensions during the investigation. It may also be offered after the investigation to allow appropriate healing and/or training before reintegrating the complainant into the workplace. This remedy should not be imposed unilaterally on the complainant. It is helpful to discuss the case with the complainant and his or her treating physician or therapist. For some complainants, being "removed" from their jobs is very threatening and negative because they fear losing their jobs or that colleagues will view them as weak or problem employees. Also, administrative leave that is not mutually planned and discussed could result in the complainant's perception that it is retaliation and that the employer has no intention of returning him or her to work.

Appropriate *counseling* should be offered when the degree of harassment is at a moderate to severe level and/or when the complainant shows visible effects; whether to accept this service should always be the choice of the complainant. The employer cannot force a particular EAP service or counselor on an employee. A minimum of five to ten sessions can be offered initially, but the amount should be geared to the particular situation. The employer can request counselor input for continuation of counseling when counseling exceeds the initial approved sessions. Remember, the impact of discrimination can widely affect a person's life outside of work, and those issues may need counseling as well. For example, the complainant may need to resolve historical issues of abuse that are triggered by the harassment, or the family of the complainant may need professional help to deal with the impact of the events on the family.

The organization should also consider covering *medical costs* associated with the effects of harassment (medication, doctor exams, TMJ dental treatment, and others), paying the complainant's out-of-pocket expenses that are not covered by insurance.

Debriefing the Accused

The organization has many of the same obligations to the accused as it does to the complainant. Whether or not the alleged behaviors occurred, the organization will, more often than not, also have to reintegrate the accused back into the workplace. By following the suggestions below, you can help make a very difficult and stressful process respectful and fair for the accused.

Maintain Communication and Trust During the Investigation Keep the accused informed about the investigation's progress and make certain he or she knows how to reach you immediately if he or she has questions, concerns, or more information.

Debrief the Outcome When management decides on the final outcome, sit down with the accused and go through management's decision and what you have done (including how many witnesses identified, interviewed, corroboration and credibility issues, conclusions, discipline, and plans for further resolution). *Do not* compromise the confidentiality of witnesses.

Plan More Than One Debriefing It often takes one or two hours for the first feedback session. You may want to plan subsequent meetings as well, because people rarely hear everything or are able to communicate their questions and feelings the first time.

Debrief the Discipline Once you have debriefed the factual outcome, management must communicate any discipline or other employment consequences that result from the findings of the investigation. We recommend that management be involved in all debriefing of discipline since it is their responsibility. It is very important to explain *why* (in terms of discipline factors) management has decided on the particular consequences.

Review Policy and Laws Briefly reference the company's policy as well as explaining legal ramifications if appropriate. Remind the accused of the prohibition against retaliation and what you expect in terms of behavior toward the complainant.

Provide a Counseling Option If you believe there are personal issues (alcoholism, personal crisis) that have had an impact on the person's behavior, then, with management's approval, provide specific referrals for the person.

Consider Training If management has chosen to retain the employee, evaluate the need for individual or group training. This may include the accused spending time with a trained professional outside the company or participating in group training the next time it is scheduled. Both types of training should have a follow-up that includes a report back to management about what the person learned with regard to his or her behaviors. This training, however, should be done soon after the debriefing to increase its impact (see Chapter 11 for more details).

Lay Out Expectations and How Progress Will Be Evaluated There should be a brief but formal plan for someone in the employee's management chain to evaluate his or her progress over an appropriate period of time. The more serious the behavior, the longer the scrutiny. A record should be made of the employee's progress to validate the organization's corrective action.

Debriefing Workgroups

As noted in Chapter 3, workgroups can also be severely affected by harassment and an investigation. They can become severely dysfunctional or, at the very least, can spend countless hours privately processing the complaint and not engaged in their work. Debriefing workgroups can be one of the most important interventions to promote healing and create a workplace where both the complainant and the accused can work successfully. The hundreds of workgroup debriefings conducted by the authors of this manual have never resulted in adverse legal action and have been extraordinarily successful in addressing the damage done by harassment and investigations (Salisbury, 1996).

That said, however, it is not always necessary to debrief workgroups. Many times, when the harassment is limited to the parties involved and the behavior is low in severity, it is not appropriate. Following are some of the factors that indicate when the organization should consider debriefing the workgroup(s) involved in the investigation:

- There are many witnesses, complainants, and accused. As the number of those affected who have knowledge increases and as stress increases, so does the need for group interventions.

- The harassment is at a moderate/severe harassment level (see Chapter 11). More severe harassment has more fallout for people and therefore may indicate that entire workgroups need attention.

- There is high emotion in the workgroup and members are polarized. Workgroups can feed off each other and create a high-risk environment for retaliation.

- The person being accused is in management or is a high-status employee. Employees are more likely to involve themselves emotionally in a harassment complaint that affects someone that is a leader in the organization. What happens to that person also affects their lives.

- Rumors, gossip, or publicity are affecting the workplace and productivity. Workgroups who don't know the truth tend to make it up. Sharing the basics of what happened helps minimize negative gossip and allows the workgroup to achieve closure.

Stages of Debriefing

Stage One—Getting Together The first stage is to bring those involved in different aspects of the investigation, including key HR professionals, the investigator, and management, together to talk about what happened and to plan how to debrief the workgroup. It is important to be absolutely honest with each other about the mistakes and faults in the investigation or in the complaint system. A consultant familiar with this type of debriefing* should be used to train others or deal with particularly difficult situations.

Plan your debriefing by starting with the most affected group first. Bring together small groups of no more than six to fifteen. Try to mix groups to avoid the divisive effect of cliques. Do not leave out affected employees. Attendance at debriefings should be required. Even those who may not have knowledge and want no part of the situation should be debriefed.

Stage Two—Introductions The debriefing should be introduced and led by management. In their introduction, management should state the purpose of the meeting, including why the organization decided to share the information. Management should stress that the meeting is a "no fault" meeting in that everyone is encouraged to speak his or her mind, ask questions, and share needs.

Stage Three—Creating Ground Rules Management should set the ground rules, including keeping the information confidential, explaining that anyone who needs to know will be given the information by the debriefing team; respecting others' experience and feelings; speaking for oneself and letting others speak for themselves. One person on the debriefing team should be assigned to facilitate the group's process.

---

*Critical incidents debriefing after violent or other workplace traumas is very different from the debriefings described here.

Stage Four—The Presentation Usually you or an HR professional will begin by presenting the basic allegations investigated. Share the timeline of what happened and when, how many witnesses were interviewed, and generally what kinds of corroboration existed. Depending on the situation, the names of the complainant and accused may or may not be shared during the debriefing. Next, management shares its interpretation of the data and what decisions it has made and why.

Stage Five—Critique of the Process and the Organization After the facts have been shared, management should open up the forum for people to share their reactions, concerns, and questions. The debriefing team facilitate and direct this part of the process by saying things like: "We would like to hear any criticisms or reactions so that we can improve our processes." "What is your general reaction to what we just shared?" "How could we have done this better?"

Stage Six—Setting Limits and Retaliation Toward the end of the debriefing it is important to help the workgroup understand appropriate and inappropriate ways to respond to the complainant and other affected employees. One way to introduce this topic is to ask the workgroup members how they would like to be treated if they returned to work after an investigation. Reiterate that disrespectful and unprofessional behaviors will not be tolerated at any time.

Stage Seven—Expectations and Follow-Up Designated supervisors and managers may need to follow up with particularly resistant or distraught employees, maintain checks on group climate, and respond to other concerns and issues during the weeks and months that follow.

During the debriefing, the debriefing team should be ready to discuss why stress and bad feelings result from harassment situations and provide education about legal, policy, and other issues when relevant. The team should also be ready to provide lists of confidential support services for employees who may be particularly affected by the situation and want additional support.

As the debriefing progresses, the debriefing team should supportively listen and respond to other group concerns about the workplace and the work team. Workgroups often move off of the investigation and harassment and begin to talk about other organizational issues. If this occurs, management should listen, responding briefly and writing the concerns down. They should always follow up on these issues and, if necessary, schedule additional time to discuss these issues.

The debriefing team should paraphrase (restate what you hear to allow clarification and acknowledge that you are hearing what is being said) what is said and respond to criticism without defensiveness. Management and employees sometimes agree on action steps during the debriefing, and management should follow up on the agreements.

All debriefing sessions are different, even within the same workgroup and investigation. This example, however, is fairly typical of what can happen.

The harassment complaint against the manager was serious. It included sexually suggestive remarks, physical touching, and abusive retaliatory behavior toward a female subordinate. The manager was well-liked and the woman was not. As a result of the investigation, the manager was fired and the woman was on administrative leave to recover. The debriefing of the workgroup began with a tense, hostile environment created by the workgroup. When the investigator shared the information, she gave specific examples of the behaviors, including the manager's asking about the woman's sex life, coming up behind her and rubbing her shoulders without her permission, telling her explicit stories about his own sex life, and screaming and yelling at her repeatedly after she had told him to stop. The workgroup was in disbelief at what happened. They questioned the corroboration for the complainant's story; the investigator was able to point to their own testimony and admissions by the manager.

Their questioning and hostile remarks about the complainant went on for over an hour. The workgroup criticized the organization for taking two months to investigate the problem and for not conducting training for management during the last five years. Management listened, acknowledged its mistakes, and described organization remedies that were being planned. While the division manager and the HR investigator empathized with the loss to the workgroup, they worked hard to also acknowledge the harm done by the fired manager. They educated the group about the policy. They asked the workgroup how they would like to be treated if they were the complainant, then built on their answers to explain the expectations of the organization regarding retaliation by anyone in the organization.

Although the workgroup was still upset about what had occurred, some of them thanked management for the debriefing, and the hostility from the group lessened considerably.

Debriefing Checklist

- Basic Time Issues (Investigator)

  When was the complaint received and completed?

  How many people were interviewed?

  How long did it take and why?

  How many investigators were involved and why?

- Initial Complaint Description (Investigator)

  Describe the general behaviors complained about.

  Describe other behaviors discovered during complaint.

- Describe the Specific Outcomes (Management)

  What evidence you used to draw conclusions (physical, witnesses, corroboration, admissions, and so forth).

  What management did and why.

- Describe the General Outcomes (Management)

  Training, other awareness interventions.

  Policy, procedure, and other system changes.

  Other organizational interventions and changes.

Debriefing Employees and Witnesses

- Debrief in groups or individually those witnesses who were highly involved in the investigation, for example, people who personally witnessed the harassment.

- Allow questioning and venting (as appropriate) by those involved so that their feelings may have less impact on their work and on others.

- Refer to EAP (in a helpful, not punishing way) when appropriate.

Debriefing and healing the aftermath is an important step in creating a respectful workplace, resolving the harassment, and preventing retaliation. Management and Human Resource professionals need to think through the harm that is done to employees as a result of the harassment and investigation and implement actions to address it. Only by their doing so, can organizations and their employees learn from the complaint and be emotionally prepared to work together again.

Chapter 13

The Investigator as Witness

WHEN AN EMPLOYER IS SUED after you have conducted an investigation, you, as the investigator, may be called to testify as a witness. You may be asked to respond to questions like the following:

- What evidence did you gather during the investigation?
- What instructions were you given by the company on how to conduct your investigation?
- Who did you interview?
- How quickly did you do the investigation?
- To whom did you report your results?
- What knowledge do you have about how the company responded with prompt corrective action?
- What is your opinion of the witness's credibility?
- What training have you had in conducting investigations?
- What books and resources did you use in conducting your investigation?
- What other investigations have you conducted prior to this one?
- What notes did you keep regarding the investigation?
- Did you write a report, and if so, did you keep a copy and any previous drafts of the report?
- Who received the report?
- What conclusions did you reach and why?

Whether you will be allowed to testify about any of these things may depend on whether your testimony is offered at trial or during pretrial proceedings known as "depositions."

The U.S. judicial system allows people to sue if they believe any of an employer's conduct violated the law. Once they sue, our system allows them to be heard, first by a judge, and then possibly by a jury. These proceedings require witnesses, including those who have direct knowledge of what happened. If you do not testify voluntarily, the court can order you to appear by issuing you a "subpoena." A subpoena is an order issued by a court commanding a witness to appear and testify or be held in contempt of court.

In the U.S. system of justice, the parties can prepare for a jury trial by finding out what witnesses know through a process called discovery. While there are various types of discovery, the process that you should be familiar with is known as a deposition, a method of recording a witness's testimony under oath prior to the actual trial.

Depositions allow a party to know in advance what a witness will say at the trial. Depositions can also be taken to obtain the testimony of important witnesses who cannot appear during the trial. In that case, the transcript will be read into evidence at the trial.

If you are called to testify in a deposition, the rules allow you to be asked virtually any question, regardless of whether you believe it is relevant, and regardless of whether the evidence may be admissible in front of a jury. For example, you may be asked personal questions about your employment experience and whether you have been reprimanded or disciplined. Generally, a deposition is taken before a court reporter in a conference room, with the plaintiff's attorney and the defense attorney present. If you are a witness for the employer, the plaintiff's attorney will ask you questions. You are placed under oath and are required to answer every question asked, unless your attorney objects and instructs you not to answer.

Generally, the attorney for the company will meet with you to discuss your testimony prior to the deposition. That way, you can ask questions about things you are unsure about before you are placed under oath.

The basic rules about testifying as a witness at a deposition are as follows:

- Listen carefully to each question, and answer only the question asked. Do not volunteer information that is not responsive to the question.

- Many times the question is awkward and does not make sense. Do not answer what you think the attorney *may* be asking. Instead, ask the attorney to clarify the information being requested. You can always ask to have the question repeated or rephrased if you do not understand it.

- Many times a question will include more than one question. Either ask to have the question broken into separate questions, or clarify in your answer which question you are answering.

- It is perfectly okay to say, "I don't know." That answer is preferable to trying to please the questioner by volunteering information when you are not really sure. *Never* guess, even if you feel like you should know the answer.

- It is perfectly okay to say, "I don't remember." That is preferable to volunteering information that later appears to be contrary to the written documents or your own notes.

- It is perfectly okay to ask if you can refer to your notes before you answer. (Make sure that your attorney is not planning to claim an attorney-client privilege for your notes prior to using them. It is best to ask the attorney during pre-deposition preparation what documents you may bring and what documents will be present in the deposition room.)

- Listen to what the company attorney says. Attorneys have the opportunity during depositions to object to a question if they think it is ambiguous or not understandable. If there is an objection, think carefully about whether you clearly understand the question before you answer.

- It is okay to ask to take a break to use the restroom, get a drink of water, or speak with your attorney. Simply ask for a break when needed.

- The best way to make sure you do not make mistakes is to be very well prepared for your deposition. Good notes taken during the investigation will help refresh your memory on exactly how you conducted the investigation and what information you learned. Review all your notes and your report and make sure you are very familiar with the facts. Pay attention to all of the facts and the appropriate answers.

- Always tell the truth. Many times a witness will be tempted to fudge just a little to make the case look better. Lies will almost always be exposed, so it is simply better to tell the truth; let the attorneys decide what to do with the facts.

- Never lose your temper, no matter how rude the other attorney seems! Losing your temper only causes you to lose focus, and once you lose focus it is hard to concentrate on answering the questions appropriately.

Keep in mind that your testimony will be recorded, and that it is under oath. Often a witness's deposition will be taken by the opposing side and used to discredit the witness at trial if the trial testimony varies from the testimony given during the deposition. (A lawyer might ask a witness at trial, "Are you lying now or were you lying then?")

Testifying During Trial

When you appear at trial, the process is different. The lawyer who calls you to testify will ask you questions designed to bring out the facts you know. This is called *direct examination.* After this is completed, the lawyer for the opposing side will be given an opportunity to ask you questions about the same information, through questioning called *cross-examination.*

Witnesses may testify to matters of fact and, in some instances, provide opinions. They also may be called to identify documents, pictures, or other items introduced into evidence. Generally, witnesses cannot state opinions or give conclusions unless they are experts or are especially qualified to do so. Witnesses qualified in a particular field as expert witnesses may give their opinions based on the facts in evidence and may give the reason for those opinions. If you are an experienced Human Resources professional with a great deal of experience in investigation of harassment claims, an attorney may ask you to testify to an expert opinion. Generally, your attorney would have discussed this with you prior to trial. Most of the time, you will be called to provide "fact" testimony, that is, knowledge of the facts of the investigation.

Objections may be made by the opposing counsel for many reasons under the rules of evidence, such as leading questions, questions that call for an opinion or conclusion by a witness, or questions that require an answer based on hearsay. Most courts require that a specific legal reason be given for an objection. Usually, the judge will immediately either sustain or overrule the objection. If the objection is sustained, the lawyer must ask the question in a different way or ask a different question. If the objection is overruled, you may answer the question. When there is an objection, wait for the judge's ruling prior to answering.

Surviving Cross-Examination

Cross-examination is where the attorney for the plaintiff asks questions to try to support the plaintiff's case. Don't be afraid of cross-examination. You may think the opposing lawyer is trying to pin you down on details or trick you into saying the wrong thing, but the opposition has the right to test your recollection to find out how your memory of facts compares with the memories of others. Just as you must be well-prepared for your deposition testimony, you must be very well-prepared to testify at trial in both your direct testimony and your cross-examination.

The rules on cross-examination are very similar to the rules noted previously for depositions:

- The cross-examiner may ask you leading questions—questions that suggest only one answer. Make sure you understand the question; then answer it as accurately as you can. If you do not know the answer or cannot remember, say, "I don't know" or "I don't remember."

- You are generally testifying for your employer, and you want to make a good impression on the jury. Therefore, you must speak clearly enough to be heard, in a confident manner. An inaudible voice detracts from the value of your testimony and tends to make the court and jury think that you are not certain of what you are saying.

- As in depositions, if you do not understand a question that has been asked, do not try to answer it anyway. Ask for clarification. Never volunteer information. If you can, answer the question with a "yes" or "no."

- Don't guess or speculate! The only thing you will be permitted to testify to is what you know personally. What you know is important; what you think about the people or the events that happened is not important.

Needless to say, if you and the company do a great job investigating the claim and taking prompt corrective action, it is unlikely that you will go to court. But if you do, following these guidelines will help you be prepared and effective.

Conclusion

Investigation of harassment and discrimination complaints has become a focal point of the prevention and correction tools available to employers. It is a crucial part of ensuring that adequate information is available to employers who are making important decisions about remedies for harassment and discrimination and prompt correction of problems in the workplace. This manual provides investigators with the tools needed for ensuring that the investigation is done promptly and thoroughly.

Training Internal Investigators

Program Overview

REGARDLESS OF THE LEVEL OF EXPERIENCE, few investigators have the full spectrum of knowledge and skills contained in this book. In addition, courts are increasingly critical of investigations performed by those without specific investigator training (see, for example, *Bennett v. Progressive Corporation*). Training internal investigators has many other advantages: It ensures adequate and consistent investigations; it creates a team of investigators who can work more effectively together; it helps the organization identify weaknesses in the investigating process; and it helps keep investigator skills up-to-date in an ever-changing legal environment.

This program is designed for anyone in the organization who may be entrusted to investigate harassment and discrimination complaints. It may also be useful for those managers and Human Resource professionals who may make decisions about prompt corrective action. Participants will develop an understanding of the psychological and legal elements of an investigation, practice using investigator skills, and apply strategies for healing the outcomes of harassment.

This training should be facilitated by experienced and knowledgeable workshop leaders. Their credentials should include experience investigating many complaints, attendance at investigation workshops, in-depth knowledge about the legal and psychological aspects of investigating, and workshop training skills. This training is highly content-focused. The training will follow much of the book and the trainer(s) will need to refer back to the manual for some of the specific content referred to in the training guide. For this reason, the training cannot be effective unless each participant has a copy of this book.

Training Goals

Some of the goals of training are

1. To understand the characteristics of effective investigators and assess the strengths and weaknesses of participants;

2. To understand and apply the legal and psychological underpinnings of investigations;

3. To develop and strengthen investigative skills;

4. To understand the role diversity plays in effective investigations; and

5. To develop skills for healing the aftermath of complaints and investigations.

Program Outline

Activity	Time	Method	Handouts Used
I. Opening Activity: Goals, Fears, and Motivations	30 minutes	Icebreaker	
II. Characteristics of the Effective Investigator	20 minutes	Discussion and Self-Evaluation	A
III. Introduction to the Law of Harassment and Discrimination	55 minutes		
A. Introduction to the Law of Sexual Harassment	20 minutes	Lecturette and Group Discussion	
B. Other Types of Harassment	10 minutes	Group Discussion	
C. Retaliation	15 minutes	Group Discussion	
D. Other Important Concepts Surrounding Harassment	10 minutes	Lecturette	
IV. Elements of an Effective Policy	20 minutes	Group Discussion & Small Group Activity	B and C
V. The Psychology of Investigating	45 minutes	Lecturette and Group Discussion	
A. Introduction to the Psychology of Harassment			
B. The Different Kinds of Sexual Harassment			
C. Harassment as Incivility			
D. Coping with Harassment			
E. The Impact of Harassment on Individuals and Groups			
F. The Psychology of Harassers			
G. Conclusion			
VI. Diversity Issues in Investigating	55 minutes		
A. The Four Layers of Diversity	15 minutes	Small Group Exercises	D
B. Stereotypes and Generalizations	10 minutes	Small Group Exercises	E
C. Cultural Map Exercise	30 minutes	Small Group Exercises	F
VII. Documenting the Investigation	30 minutes	Large Group Discussion	
A. Record Keeping			
B. Attorney-Client Privilege			
C. Writing a Report			

Activity	Time	Method	Handouts Used
VIII. Triad Role Play	60 minutes	Role Play	G
A. Prearranged Role Play			
B. Triad Role Play			
IX. Forming an Investigative Plan	60 minutes	Discussion and Small Group Skill Practice	H
X. Questioning Skills	30 minutes	Lecturette	
XI. Role Play	4 hours	Skill Practice	I and J
XII. Reaching a Conclusion	30 minutes	Lecturette and Large Group Activity	
A. Deciding What Is Relevant			
B. Drawing Conclusions			
C. Recommendations			
XIII. Prompt, Corrective Action	30 minutes	Large Group Discussion	K
A. Discipline			
B. Remedial Actions			
XIV. Healing the Aftermath	60 minutes	Lecturette and Large Group Discussion	K and L
A. Debriefing the Complainant, the Accused, and the Witnesses			
B. Debriefing the Workgroup			
XV. Conclusion	20 minutes	Small Group Discussion	M

Program Instructions

> *Note to Trainer:* This training will require one or more flip charts or an overhead projector and markers. Copies of the book should be available for all participants. Additional materials will be noted as needed in the workshop outline.

I. Opening Activity: Goals, Fears, and Motivations (Icebreaker)

Materials needed: one index card per participant

Time: 30 minutes

1. Review the trainer's workshop goals on a flip chart or overhead.

2. Split the group into triads (three-person groups) and have each person write the following on an index card.

   - Their personal goal for the workshop

   - Their greatest fear regarding investigating

   - Their greatest motivation for investigating

3. Ask participants to share their answers with their groups.

4. After they appear to be finished, reconvene the entire group and ask one member of each group to report out each member's response. Write their answers in different columns on the flip chart.

5. Share any fears mentioned in the book that are not on the chart.

6. Emphasize that the workshop will address many of the fears they have mentioned.

7. Use their goals to help guide the workshop content.

II. Characteristics of the Effective Investigator (Discussion and Self-Evaluation)

Materials: Handout A

(*Note to Trainer:* Review Chapter 5)

Time: 20 minutes

1. Give copies of Handout A to the participants.

2. On a flip chart or overhead review the characteristics of the effective investigator from Chapter 5. Give participants a moment to evaluate whether each characteristic is a possible strength or weakness for them.

3. Then ask participants to list their greatest strengths and their greatest weaknesses on Handout A. Emphasize that the knowledge and skills take many years to fully develop.

4. Encourage participants to focus on developing and improving these characteristics in the workshop.

III. Introduction to the Law of Harassment and Discrimination

(*Note to Trainer:* Review Chapter 2)

A. Introduction to the Law of Sexual Harassment (Lecturette and Group Discussion)

   Time: 20 minutes

   1. Provide an overview of the development of the law on sexual harassment, using the information in Chapter 2.

   2. In discussing the affirmative defense developed in *Faragher* and *Ellerth*, point out the portion of the affirmative defense that requires employers to prevent harassment. Ask participants to call out ways they think an employer can prevent harassment. List those ways on the flip chart.

   3. Summarize the different ideas after participants are finished, adding any that they have missed. Explain that Chapter 6 outlines many different actions that an employer can take to prevent harassment.

   4. Point out the portion of the affirmative defense that requires employers to promptly correct harassment. Ask participants to call out ways they think an employer can correct harassment. List those ways on the flip chart.

   5. Summarize the different ideas after participants are finished, adding any that they have missed. Explain that Chapters 11 and 12 outline many different corrective and remedial ideas for employers to use, and that you will be addressing those later in the training.

B. Other Types of Harassment (Group Discussion)

   Time: 10 minutes

   1. Begin discussing the other types of harassment, pointing out that they are all subject to the affirmative defense analysis. Explain race/color, national origin, religious, age, and disability harassment.

   2. Ask participants to share their ideas of what type of behavior might fall into each category.

C. Retaliation (Group Discussion)

   Time: 15 minutes

   1. Explain the legal concept of retaliation.

   2. Ask participants to name the types of actions taken by an employer that might be deemed retaliation.

   3. Explain the important things to remember about retaliation.

4. Point out the investigator's obligation to be vigilant to signs of retaliation as the investigation progresses.

D. Other Important Concepts Surrounding Harassment (Lecturette)

Time: 10 minutes

1. Explain the concepts described in Chapter 2, including:

    - Third-Party Harassment

    - Sexual Favoritism

    - Workplace Dating

    - Temporary Workers

    - Nontarget Harassment

    - Same Sex Harassment

    - Off-Duty Conduct

    - Illegal Aliens

2. Ask participants to think of examples they might encounter in each category.

IV. Elements of an Effective Policy (Group Discussion and Small Group Activity)

(*Note to Trainer:* Review Chapter 6)

Materials Needed: Handouts B and C

Time: 20 minutes

1. Explain the organizational model that effectively prevents harassment. Describe how the policy plays a role in the prevention of harassment. (This is described in Chapter 6.)

2. Ask participants to call out elements they think should appear in an effective policy. Then compare those elements to those recommended by:

    - The EEOC (make sure participants understand that this is a minimal requirement).

    - The sample policy for Microcosm in Handout B and accompanying explanation in Chapter 6.

3. Break the group into five small groups and ask participants to compare their policy to the Microcosm policy and determine whether any elements are missing. Have them prepare a list of the missing elements. Set that list aside for later in the training.

4. Discuss the best practices for distributing a policy. Discuss some of the cases cited in the Appendix where the plaintiff in litigation claimed that she or he never received a copy of the policy. Have the participants brainstorm about ways that they could make the policy available to every employee, often.

5. Divide the participants into even groups, to the extent possible. (*Note:* these may not be the same groups as previously.) Assign a case study from Handout C to each group. Ask the participants to answer the questions posed at the end of the list of case studies.

6. After 10 minutes, reconvene the large group and have each group appoint a spokesperson to provide answers to the questions aloud to the whole group.

7. As each group is explaining its answers, record answers on the flip chart and point out to the whole group how the answers are consistent.

8. Ask other members of the whole group whether they disagree with any conclusions reached by the small group and why.

9. Remind the group about any legal considerations that affect their decisions.

V. The Psychology of Investigating (Lecturette and Group Discussion)

(*Note to Trainer:* Review Chapter 3)

Time: 45 minutes

A. Introduction to the Psychology of Harassment

1. On an overhead or flip chart, list the following headings. Briefly describe them for the participants.

   • Kinds of Sexual Harassment

   • Coping with Harassment

   • The Impact of Harassment on Employees and Work Groups

   • Understanding Harassers

   • Environmental Factors in Harassment

2. Emphasize the importance of the psychological aspects of investigating. Share an example from your own experience where understanding the information contained in Chapter 3 was key to effective investigating.

B. The Different Kinds of Sexual Harassment

1. On a flip chart, write the different kinds of sexual harassment: coercive harassment, unwelcome sexual attention, and gender harassment. Also share examples from your own experience and from Chapter 3.

2. Share the general terms and definitions of types of harassment.

- Talk about the percentage of each type usually found in workplaces.

- Talk about the differences in same sex harassment between men and women.

- Ask for questions and comments.

C. Harassment as Incivility

1. Share the definition of incivility and make the following points:

- Many complaints contain these behaviors.

- These behaviors are as harmful as discriminating harassment.

- They should also be addressed in the organization as part of corrective action.

2. Invite them to share some of their experiences with these behaviors.

D. Coping with Harassment

1. Read the list of questions at the beginning of Chapter 3. Ask participants: Have you ever asked yourself these questions about victims of harassment?

2. Write the five categories of coping on a flip chart. Discuss and give examples of each.

3. Explain that racial harassment is different, because recipients rarely minimize or view the behavior as benign. Ask them why that might be the case (the lifetime experiences that people of color have had with racism).

4. Share how organizational procedures affect whether or not employees report harassment and that retaliation is the number one fear of complainants.

5. Ask them what impact this research has on interpreting victim behavior during an investigation? Record their responses on the flip chart. Add any that might be missing.

E. The Impact of Harassment on Individuals and Groups

1. Ask the group, from their experience, what they perceive as being the impact of harassment on employees. Add effects they do not describe that are in the chapter or from your own experience.

2. Ask the group, from their experience, what they perceive as being the impact of harassment on workgroups. Add effects they do not describe that are in the chapter or from your own experience.

3. Ask what they think the implications of these effects are for conducting harassment investigations. Be sure that the following points are covered:

- Judging the severity of the harassment
- Healing the aftermath of the complaint
- Dealing with employees during the investigation

F. The Psychology of Harassers

1. Share the example in Chapter 3 of the harasser who did not understand why his behavior was so offensive to others or share an example of your own.

2. Ask the participants why they thought this person said inappropriate things. Use their comments to segue into the following points, writing them on the flip chart.

- The characteristics of men who are likely to commit quid pro quo harassment based on John Pryor's research as cited in Chapter 3.
- The individual's reasons for harassment.

Give your own examples or seek examples from your participants for each one.

G. Conclusion

1. End this part of the workshop by summarizing the points at the end of Chapter 3 on the relationship of the psychology of harassers to investigating. Elaborate briefly on each.

VI. Diversity Issues in Investigating (Small Group Exercises)

Materials: Handouts D, E, and F
(*Note to Trainer:* Review Chapter 4)
Time: 55 minutes
A. The Four Layers of Diversity

1. Distribute copies of Handout D.

2. Briefly explain each kind of diversity (and the category) and relate the differences to how people are treated or the kind of cultural influence that is present in that kind of diversity. For example, sexual orientation is an internal form of diversity and many people who are not heterosexual do

not feel free to share anything about their personal lives, such as pictures or events at work because they are afraid of judgments and hostile behavior from their co-workers.

3. Give meaningful examples based on your organization, the region where you live, or personal examples from your life.

B. Stereotypes and Generalizations

1. Distribute copies of Handout E.

2. Define "stereotype" by using examples other than race or gender related to participants (geography, business, people from the south, and others).

   • Emphasize that the problem with stereotypes is that they are applied to everyone in a group and are often not accurate and have a negative impact on interactions with people.

   • Also ask the group what happens when they meet someone who doesn't match their stereotype—we say they are the exception, we do not change the stereotype.

3. Define generalization by eliciting examples of their experiences with different cultures or groups. Emphasize that individuals in a group can be very different, but generalizations allow us to talk about diversity between groups.

   • Ask the group about a recent place they have traveled to that is very different. What would they like others to know about the culture or people of that region that would be helpful and accurate most of the time? You may also give your own examples.

   • Close by saying that generalizations allow us to talk about differences between groups without assuming that everyone is the same.

C. The Cultural Map Exercise

1. Distribute copies of Handout F.

2. Explain to participants that this exercise helps the investigator look at himself or herself as a cultural being who has values and behaviors that come from many influences.

3. Using the four layers of diversity, ask participants to consider the current influences in their lives (work, parenting, hobby, religion, or whatever). Ask them to think about the percentage of their life that each part represents. Then direct them to map and label their cultural influences on Handout F.

4. When everyone has finished, ask participants to form pairs and to share their maps and answer the questions at the bottom of the handout.

5. After they have all shared, ask them what they have learned about themselves and ask for examples of how their cultural maps may affect their investigations.

6. Using the information in Chapter 4, summarize the following points and share an example of each.

   • Research on how Hispanic women respond to harassment

   • The experiences of African-American women and how they respond to harassment

   • Studies about the differences between men and women when they are harassed

7. Summarize the four points at the end of Chapter 4 that apply diversity research to investigating.

VII. Documenting the Investigation (Large Group Discussion)

(*Note to Trainer:* Review Chapter 8)
Time: 30 minutes
A. Record Keeping

   1. Talk about the investigative file. Have the participants, as a large group, brainstorm about the types of things that will be kept in an investigative file. Write the responses on the flip chart.

   2. Point out the investigative log and checklists in the Appendix that will help in keeping an accurate record of the investigation.

   3. Explain to the participants the importance of keeping accurate and dated records of the progress of the investigation.

B. Attorney-Client Privilege

   1. Explain the concepts of attorney-client privilege.

C. Writing a Report

   1. Point out the sample report in the Appendix. Discuss the rules for writing a report covered in Chapter 8.

   2. Have the participants share their ideas about how investigators can produce a concise and effective report.

3. Explain the problems with including recommendations in the report, as noted in Chapter 8.

4. Have the participants discuss ways that they can effectively deliver the information to management without including a recommendation in the report.

5. Discuss the dangers of disseminating the written report to the complainant and the accused.

6. Have the participants discuss how the reports will be distributed and how the information in the reports will be communicated.

VIII. Triad Role Play (Role Play)

Materials: Handout G

Time: 60 minutes

A. Prearranged Role Play

1. Ask someone in the class to think of a harassment situation.

2. Before the role play, ask the class to observe both the content of what you say and the techniques you use.

3. Conduct the role play with the volunteer complaining to you, the investigator.

4. After the role play, ask the participants for feedback and ask what you might have done differently.

B. Triad Role Play

1. Pass out copies of Handout G and ask participants to read through it.

2. Divide the group into triads (if necessary, a group of four can be used). Explain that they will be participating in a role play that will provide some practice with interviewing skills and that each person will have the opportunity to play each role. Explain that the roles are that of the investigator (here the investigator is a Human Resource person taking the complaint), the complainant, and a neutral observer. In this particular role play, the "complainant" is not necessarily a person who has filed a complaint; instead, she has indicated in an exit form that she is leaving because of a particular supervisor. The participants should be instructed to treat her like a complainant.

3. Explain that the observer does not say anything during the interview, but simply fills in the observation sheet with examples of good interviewing skills and helpful suggestions.

4. Explain that the person playing the investigator will try to use questioning skills to discover the necessary information.

5. Explain that the person playing the role of the complainant will try to place himself or herself into the role of a person who is complaining about harassment and will offer answers that are consistent with that role.

6. Ask the group to quickly decide who will be playing the different roles. Instruct complainants to be realistic and emotional if necessary.

7. Allow the group 15 minutes per role play and feedback session. After 10 minutes, ask them to stop the role play and share the feedback in their group.

8. Once the first role play and feedback session is completed, ask the participants to switch roles and assign the interviewers to the complainant role. The observers will now be the interviewers.

9. Repeat the role play and feedback process.

10. After the participants have completed the second role play, have them repeat the exercise one more time so that each person in the group has had an opportunity to play the interviewer.

11. Debrief the exercise with the whole group, asking participants to offer comments on what they learned about different interviewing styles and questioning techniques. Be sure to elicit information about demeanor of the interviewer and techniques that did not work well. Ask them to share what they thought was the most difficult part of interviewing.

12. Conclude by telling the participants that the information learned in this first interview will form the basis for the investigation that will be conducted in the larger role play.

IX. Forming an Investigative Plan (Discussion and Small Group Skill Practice)

Materials needed: Handout H

Time: 60 minutes

1. Explain to the participants the elements of the investigative plan, as explained in Chapter 7. Explain how to formulate an investigative plan.

2. Break the group into five teams (because there are five witnesses to interview in this role play). These teams work best when there are no more than three people in each, but the class size will determine the number on a team. Try to compose groups with a mix of experienced and inexperienced investigators.

3. Once they are divided into groups, explain to the participants that they are a team of investigators working together to investigate the complaint from the role play activity.

4. Distribute copies of Handout H and tell the teams to plan their investigations by completing the handout.

X. Questioning Skills (Lecturette)

(*Note to Trainer:* Review Chapter 9)

Time: 30 minutes

1. Outline for the participants the questioning skills necessary for a good investigation. Discuss open-ended questions, follow-up questions, and so on, described in Chapter 9.

2. Discuss with the participants the questioning techniques you recommend, based on a review of Chapter 9.

XI. Role Play (Skill Practice)

Materials needed: Handouts I-1 through I-5; Handouts J-1 and J-2

Time: 4 hours

1. Before the training, arrange for five employees who are not part of the training session to play a role in this activity. Assign each of them one of the witness roles described in Handouts I-1 through I-5. Provide the witnesses only with their roles and no other information. Formulate strategies for the "actors" on how you would like them to portray themselves. Feel free to add facts to each witness role as appropriate. Provide some challenges for the participants by instructing witnesses on their style of answering questions (for example, the busy executive who looks at his watch and answers his cell phone; the witness who wants to know what is going on before answering; the shy witness who answers with yes or no; the rambling witness who talks about everything except what is relevant; the reluctant witness who is a friend of the harasser and doesn't want to get him in trouble; the suspicious witness who thinks you are out to get him; the witness who pulls out a tape recorder and wants to record the session; the witness who thinks this harassment stuff is all a way to get people illegitimately fired; or any other scenario you have come across in your experience!).

2. Ask the training participants to re-form the five teams used in the Investigative Plan exercise.

3. Explain to the groups that they will be putting their plans into action by interviewing witnesses involved in the harassment scenario used in the triad role play.

4. Briefly introduce each of the people playing characters in the role play, giving their names, their roles within the organization, and their roles in the harassment scenario. (The role players generally are not present for any interview other than their own and are not introduced by their real names.)

5. Explain that each team will have a chance to interview one of the five role players. As the role play progresses, each team should act as though it has been the investigative team throughout the investigation. Each team has all of the knowledge that has been gathered so far in the role play. Thus, during interviews that the team is not conducting, the team members will have to listen carefully to learn important information about the situation so that they can assist in assessing the information at the conclusion of the investigation.

6. Decide on the order you want the witnesses interviewed in, and assign each of the role players to a team. Assign times to the role players so that they are aware of when their interviews are scheduled.

7. Tell the teams that they will have a maximum of 30 minutes to conduct the interview. Give the teams a few minutes to plan how they will handle the interview, including who will cover what subjects and how members will "hand off" to the next team member.

8. Distribute copies of Handouts J-1 and J-2 to the participants. Instruct them that they can use this form to take notes of their observations when other teams are interviewing.

9. Bring forward the first role player to be interviewed. Allow the team members to greet the role player as though he or she were an actual witness and then conduct the interview.

10. During the interview, feel free to whisper instructions to the team members, such as "ask about . . ." or "hand off to the next member." Your role during the role play is to guide the interviewers on the right path. At times, you may need to step in and role model the interview for the team, but do this only if the team seems to be struggling and cannot complete the interview properly. In most cases, allow the team to make mistakes, because that is the best learning experience.

11. After each interview, ask the entire group to share what techniques they saw that worked well and what could have been better. Remind the group that they are learning from each other. Write their tips on a flip chart, and post the tips around the room for all to use in later interviews.

12. After each interview, review and chart what evidence the interview has discovered. Then ask the group what else they might have done to elicit information. Finally, to prepare for the next role play, elicit from the group what facts they still need to know from succeeding witnesses.

13. Give the next group no more than 10 minutes to prepare for its role play.

14. Continue in this manner until all five interviews have been completed. Remind participants that in an actual investigation, they likely would have interviewed many more people. Ask the participants to brainstorm additional witnesses they would have interviewed and additional information they would have sought.

XII. Reaching a Conclusion (Lecturette and Large Group Activity)

(*Note to Trainer:* Review Chapter 10)

Time: 30 minutes

A. Deciding What Is Relevant

1. Present the principles from Chapter 10 for deciding what is relevant.

2. Have the participants determine, based on the case they have just investigated, what evidence is relevant and what is not. Record their answers on the flip chart.

B. Drawing Conclusions

1. Discuss the concepts of corroboration and credibility from Chapter 10.

2. Have the participants decide what evidence from their investigation is corroboration for the complaint and what credibility issues exist. Record their answers on the flip chart.

C. Recommendations

1. Discuss the concept of the investigator making recommendations. Distinguish between recommendations about credibility, violations of pol-

icy, and prompt corrective action. Discuss the way your company would like investigators to make recommendations.

2. Have the participants determine, as part of a large group discussion, what recommendations they would make on the case they investigated, regarding: (1) credibility of the complaint and (2) whether a policy was violated.

XIII. Prompt, Corrective Action (Large Group Discussion)

Materials Needed: Handout K

Time: 30 minutes

A. Discipline

1. Explain the concept of prompt corrective action as defined by the EEOC.

2. Have the participants brainstorm the types of discipline that are available, distinguishing between those that are disciplinary (termination) and those that may not be (transfer).

3. Have the participants identify the type of discipline they would impose, and on which parties, in the role play case they have investigated. Ask them to record their thoughts on Handout K.

B. Remedial Actions

1. Explain the concept of remedial action.

2. Have the participants brainstorm on the different types of remedies that might be available to the employer.

3. Have the participants identify the type of remedial action they would recommend for the role play they have investigated. Ask them to record their thoughts on Handout K.

4. In the large group discuss the appropriate remedies and record them on the flip chart.

5. Make sure that the participants discuss possible discipline for supervisors in the chain who did not take action.

XIV. Healing the Aftermath (Lecturette and Large Group Discussion)

Materials Needed: Handouts K and L

(*Note to Trainer:* Review Chapter 12)

Time: 60 minutes

A. Debriefing the Complainant, the Accused, and the Witnesses

1. Share the importance of healing the aftermath of harassment complaints as it relates to work productivity, preventing further harmful behavior and retaliation, and emotional healing for those involved.

2. Discuss the remedies listed in Chapter 12 for the complainant.

3. Review and share the rationale contained in Chapter 12 for debriefing those involved in the investigation.

4. Emphasize that these debriefings must be accomplished every time and should be documented by the investigator.

5. Ask the participants what should be shared with witnesses and what should not.

6. Ask participants to complete the rest of Handout K.

7. If you have time, you can role play either or both of the debriefings for the investigation you have just finished. Ask participants for volunteers to play the roles of the complainant and the accused.

B. Debriefing the Workgroup

1. Briefly review the discussion on effects of the harassment on the workgroup from Chapter 3 and share the rationale for debriefing workgroups.

2. Describe what factors may indicate the need for debriefing and review them.

3. Prepare a flip chart with each stage of debriefing on it. Describe the stages of debriefing from Chapter 12.

4. Ask the group what sort of workgroup debriefing they would do for the workshop investigation example. Use Handout L to organize the information that should be shared at a debriefing. Record their answers on the flip chart. Add to or correct their input, if necessary.

5. If you wish to extend the time of the workshop, you can ask participants to "play" a workgroup from the complaint used in the role play while you and others role play the debriefing team.

6. Emphasize to participants that each group is different, even within the same department.

7. Discuss with the group how important it is to be nondefensive but prepared for group debriefing. Also discuss the importance of management following up on any suggestions or concerns that emerge during these sessions.

XV. Conclusion (Small Group Discussion)

Materials Needed: Handout M

Time: 20 minutes

1. Have the participants share what they have learned.

2. Using Handout M, have the group brainstorm ideas for improving your organization's policy, procedures, and investigative process.

3. Record the suggestions on a flip chart and pass them on to your management. As an alternative, you can divide the group into their investigative teams and have them record their suggestions on Handout M, to be turned in to the trainer at the end of the training for transmittal to management.

4. Ask the participants to complete an evaluation of the training session.

HANDOUT A

Self-Evaluation Form

Review your experience and knowledge and compare it with the characteristics described in the manual.

1. What is your greatest strength?

2. What areas need development?

3. What would you like to work on specifically in this workshop?

HANDOUT B

Microcosm Respectful Workplace Anti-Harassment Policy

Microcosm is an equal employment opportunity employer. We value our diverse employees and clients, and we strive to create a professional and respectful workplace. Bias, prejudice, harassment, and disrespectful behaviors are not tolerated at Microcosm, Inc.

Harassment based on race, color, sex or sexual orientation, religion, national origin, age, disability, veteran or marital status, or retaliation, including opposition to prohibited discrimination, will not be tolerated. Appropriate preventative measures shall be used to promote respect for the rights of co-workers. Remedial measures and/or corrective actions, up to and including dismissal, shall be utilized when acts of harassment occur. Each employee has an affirmative duty to maintain a workplace free of harassment and intimidation.

This policy applies to anyone who does business with Microcosm (contractors, vendors, clients, and any others). All harassment complaints, regardless of where reported or from whom, shall be taken seriously and resolved.

Roles and Responsibilities of Management

All of our leaders (supervisors and managers), through their actions, shall model respectful behavior by:

- Encouraging reporting of harassment and/or discrimination incidents;

- Taking remedial measures to stop harassing behavior whenever reported or observed;

- Notifying management or Human Resources of all allegations or incidences of harassment in the workplace; and

- Ensuring that retaliatory behavior is not allowed.

Harassing Behavior

Harassment is any conduct that:

- Degrades or shows hostility toward an individual because of race, color, sex or sexual orientation, religion, national origin, age, disability, veteran or marital status, or because of retaliation for opposition to prohibited discrimination or

- Creates an intimidating, hostile, or offensive working environment through written (e-mail, computer), graphic, or verbal communications (voice mail, oral, or otherwise), including comments, jokes, slurs, or negative stereotyping; or interferes with an individual's ability to do his or her work.

Additionally, sexual harassment is also specifically prohibited and defined as unwelcome sexual advances, requests for sexual favors, or other verbal or physical conduct of a sexual nature when the sexual conduct has the purpose or effect of unreasonably interfering with an individual's work performance or creating an intimidating, hostile, or offensive work environment.

Examples of sexual harassment include, but are not limited to:

(continued)

- Demeaning and/or derogatory harassment toward one's gender;
- Demeaning behavior, staring, pinching, touching and other physical contact, or blocking the movements of another person;
- Unwelcome sexual comments, innuendoes, jokes, or abusive personal remarks;
- Sexually explicit displays or distribution of pictures, materials, or objects in the work area;
- Offering or implying a reward or threat concerning work assignments, performance review, discipline, promotions, or other terms or conditions of employment in exchange for sexual favors;
- Unwelcome amorous advances or propositions, physical conduct, obscene gestures;
- Obscene letters, phone calls, e-mails, or unwelcome words or comments with sexual or other discriminatory meanings;
- Unwelcome requests for sexual favors or repeated social contact; sexual assault; or other unwelcome sexual contact.

General Harassment

General workplace harassment is a form of offensive treatment or behavior that, to a reasonable person, creates an intimidating, hostile, or abusive work environment. Examples can include but are not limited to verbal or physical behavior that is derogatory, abusive, bullying, threatening, or disrespectful or ridiculing or undermining an individual with vindictive or humiliating words or acts.

Retaliation Prohibited

Employees who complain of harassment or discrimination, who provide information related to such complaints, or who oppose harassing and/or discriminating behavior shall be protected against retaliation. Retaliation is considered as serious as prohibited harassment, and immediate and appropriate disciplinary action, up to and including dismissal, shall be instituted. During the complaint investigation, all parties shall be reminded that retaliation is prohibited.

Examples of retaliation can include negative actions such as, but not limited to, unwarranted poor performance evaluations; change in job duties as a consequence of reporting harassing behavior; other negative employment decisions; laughing at, ignoring, or failing to take seriously reports/complaints of harassment; or continuing/escalating harassing behavior after the employee objects.

Addressing Harassment

If you feel you are being harassed or retaliated against, you are encouraged to notify any supervisor, manager, member of the Human Resources staff, or Paul Johnson, the president of Microcosm.

Complaint Investigation

Whenever we become aware of harassment, immediate remedial measures shall be taken to stop the behavior.

(continued)

HANDOUT B *(continued)*

All allegations, regardless of where reported, shall be forwarded to any supervisor, manager, or plant manager, Human Resources, or directly to the corporate offices. The complaint shall be reviewed to determine whether a detailed fact-finding investigation is appropriate.

If a fact-finding investigation is necessary, the investigation shall begin immediately. An investigator shall be appointed to gather and consider the relevant facts. Employees are expected to be ethical and honest throughout all proceedings. The confidentiality of all parties who are interviewed or present information about the harassment allegation shall be maintained as much as possible, with the information being disseminated only on a need-to-know basis.

The alleged harasser shall not have supervisory authority over the individual who conducts the investigation and shall not have any direct or indirect control over the investigation.

Corrective Actions

If the findings of the investigation indicate that a violation of the harassment policy has occurred, immediate and appropriate corrective and/or disciplinary action, up to and including dismissal, shall be administered. Corrective actions shall be proportional to the seriousness or repetitiveness of the offense. (An oral or written warning, training or counseling, monitoring the harasser, transfer or reassignment, demotion, reduction of wages, suspension, or dismissal may all be appropriate.)

Policy Distribution

Every employee shall be supplied with a copy of this policy each time it is updated. Additionally, the complaint reporting procedures and other information about harassment shall be posted in central locations (lunchroom, official bulletin boards) throughout the firm.

Case Studies

Example 1

Angie is suffering from clinical depression, which requires her to work only half days for a limited period of time. Her shift only has five people, so the burden of extra work is placed on others in the group. Dick, a co-worker, begins making comments to others, not to Angie. He says: "I am sure glad someone is pulling their weight around here," "Don't say those things; they make me depressed," and "Having all this work makes me depressed. I think I'll start working half-days too." Angie complains to her supervisor, who (1) tells her to try to understand the resentment that the other workers feel about the increased workload or (2) asks her how soon she can get back to full-time work so this problem will be resolved. Analyze options (1) and (2) as though they were two separate scenarios.

Example 2

A male supervisor (John) has asked a young female employee (Maria) to "go out" with him. She refuses. The supervisor later starts making nasty remarks and innuendoes about her when they are alone. He asks her where she was on Saturday night. When she asks him how he knows she was not home, he replies that he drove to her house with a friend to "see if she wanted to party." She becomes frightened and tells a co-worker, a union representative, who decides to tell the manager. The manager knows that this same woman has had amorous relationships with other male employees, including a supervisor, and decides it was probably invited unless she complains herself. He does not speak to John or Maria. The Human Resources Department finds out about the situation when the employee quits and is encouraged by her doctor to tell the corporation. John denies all charges and Maria is visibly upset and shaking when she talks to the investigator.

Example 3

As part of a time-honored hazing activity, a male supervisor (Ronnie) transposes a picture of the head of one of his male employees (Steve) onto a sexually charged cartoon from *Playboy*. He also writes suggestive captions on the photo and shares it with the rest of the staff (a mostly male, but mixed, group). The group has a good laugh; Steve tries to ignore it. Six months later, Ronnie meets with Steve to give him feedback about "not being a good team member." Shortly after, Steve complains about the previous behavior and claims that fear of retaliation kept him from complaining earlier.

Example 4

Joe, a sergeant at a correctional facility, frequently comments about a female officer's graveyard schedule. He comments that women should not be exposed to correctional facilities and what goes on in them and asks how her husband feels about her being locked up at night with a bunch of men. The last two promotions have gone to men. The women working for Joe finally complain about Joe's favoritism toward younger men.

(continued)

Example 5

Stan is a police sergeant at a jail who supervises Emilio and Carlos, both of whom speak fluent Spanish. Many of the jail inmates also speak Spanish. Stan often overhears Emilio and Carlos speaking Spanish to each other and speaking to the inmates in Spanish. This makes Stan uncomfortable, so he tells each of them that they are no longer allowed to speak Spanish on the job. He tells them that he needs to know what they are saying to inmates and what they are saying to each other. When he hears Emilio utter a curse in Spanish, he disciplines him, and Emilio complains.

Example 6

Manuel is offended by the suggestive sexual cartoons that come over e-mail, make their way around the workgroup, and end up on the bulletin board or taped to someone's computer. When he tells Laura, his supervisor, she (1) laughs and tells him he is overly sensitive or (2) tells him she'll send out a memo about what's appropriate to put on the bulletin board, but she won't tell people what they can send on their e-mails. Consider each option separately.

Example 7

Kevin's supervisor, Barbara, sits very close to him during meetings and frequently brushes up against him when they pass in the hall. Barbara also flirts with Kevin, but only during closed-door meetings in her office. Recently, Barbara asked Kevin to stay late to discuss a project. Kevin knows this project could make or break his career. At the same time, Barbara has made it clear that people need to show they know how to get along and "go the extra mile" to get ahead. In response, Kevin (1) tells Barbara he wants to "go the extra mile" professionally, but he is not interested in a personal relationship or (b) became friendlier to Barbara and eventually consented to an affair with her, which he ended after a month because he felt so bad about it. Consider each option separately.

Example 8

Larry likes Christina, a co-worker. They have gone to lunch a few times, but she's always said she's busy when he's asked her for a date. This morning, Larry left Christina a voice mail at (a) work or (b) home, saying he woke up very early dreaming about her and how good it would feel to be holding her in his arms, stroking her beautiful hair. Consider each option separately.

Example 9

Bob is new in the all-female accounting department. He makes a mistake that costs some down time for everyone. Joyce, the supervisor for his section, yells at Bob in front of the rest of the group. When he complains to Karen, a co-worker, she tells him, "Look, if you can't take it, you shouldn't be working here."

(continued)

HANDOUT C *(continued)*

Case Study Analysis

For your assigned example, please respond to the following questions. Come to a consensus as a group, choose a spokesperson to present your group's perspective, and be ready to explain it in detail.

1. Is the behavior as described a violation of Microcosm's policy? Is it a violation of your organization's policy as currently written?

2. Assuming the person is a reasonable person, rate the severity of the behaviors/situation on a scale of 1 to 10. What variables did you use to make your decision? What role, if any, does diversity play in this situation?

3. What, if anything, could the organization have done to prevent the behaviors/situation?

4. What discipline should be imposed in this case, and on whom?

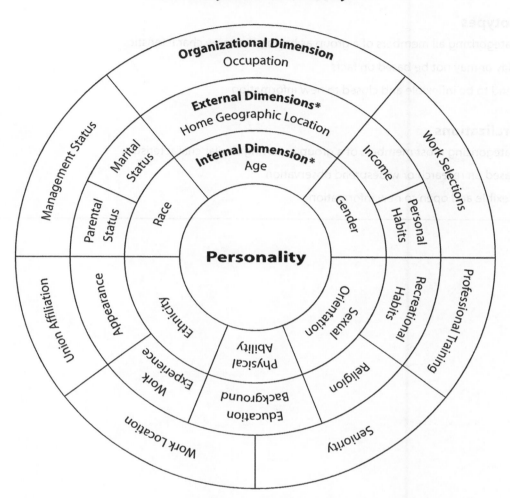

Reproduced with permission from Diverse Teams at Work: Capitalizing on the Power of Diversity *by Lee Gardenswartz and Anita Rowe, copyright 2003, Society for Human Resource Management.*

*Internal and external dimensions are adapted from Marilyn Loden and Judy Rosener, Workforce America! *(Irwin, 1991).*

HANDOUT E

Stereotypes and Generalizations

Stereotypes

- Categorizing all members of a group as having the same characteristics
- May or may not be based on facts
- Tend to be inflexible and closed to new information

Generalizations

- Categorizing most members of a group as having similar characteristics
- Based on research or widespread observation
- Flexible and open to new information

HANDOUT F

You as a Diverse Entity

Visualize a pie that makes up the cultural you. Divide this pie into cultural characteristics that are important to you (gender, religion, occupation, and so forth).

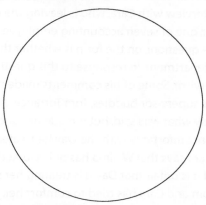

1. Identify one value that is represented from your top three cultural characteristics.

2. How do your cultural experiences/filters affect how you work with others?

3. What parts might enhance your ability to investigate? Why?

4. What parts might make investigating difficult for you? Why?

HANDOUT G

Triad Role Play

Scenario

Michael Smith, the Human Resources director of Microcosm, a high-tech company, is interviewing Cara Rodriguez. This is part of an exit interview with Cara, who is leaving the company. She has been employed as an accounting worker, one of seven accounting employees reporting to David Lee. She completed an exit form. One of the questions on the form is whether the person experienced problems with any particular people in the department. In response to this question, Cara indicated that she had problems with David Lee, her supervisor. Some of his comments made her uncomfortable. She had over-heard David talking with one of his supervisor buddies, Tom Torrance, about sex and telling raunchy jokes. She doesn't remember exactly what was said, but it made her uncomfortable. This happened more than one time. She was also very uncomfortable with the way he treated another employee, Willima (Will EE Ma) Michaels. Willima is black. Cara says that Willima has only worked for the company a couple of years, but she is a hard worker, and it is unfair that David is treating her so harshly. Willima has ended up crying several times in the bathroom and Cara has tried to comfort her. She feels that lately he was harsher on Willima and her work than on the other workers. David would yell and scream at Willima in front of the other workers. This treatment of Willima only started in the last few months; before then, she seemed to be a favorite of David's. David did not seem to yell and scream at some of the other employees. When he would yell, his face would turn red and his eyes would seem to explode out of his head. He would use profanity liberally. He only yelled at Cara a couple of times, but she got tired of it and yelled back, and he never did it again.

Cara indicates that she is leaving because she found another job because she could not stand working for David Lee one more day. She found this job very quickly; however, it has lower pay and fewer benefits.

(continued)

HANDOUT G *(continued)*

Instructions

Each of you in the triad will play the witness, the investigator (Michael Smith), or the observer. Please rotate the roles so that at the end of the exercise each person will have played each role. You will be allowed approximately 10 minutes for each role play and 5 minutes for feedback. When you are the observer, use the form below to check off points and give constructive feedback.

1. Introduction and preliminary issues

<u>Content</u>

(Role, confidentiality, purpose)

<u>Technique</u>

(Putting at ease, listening)

2. Gaining of background information (job, physical scene, as needed)

<u>Content</u>

<u>Technique</u>

3. Explore issues related to complaint

<u>Content</u>

<u>Technique</u>

4. Which of the following skills were used?

- ❑ Paraphrasing
- ❑ Summarizing
- ❑ Perception checking
- ❑ Open-ended questions
- ❑ Information giving
- ❑ Specific questions

HANDOUT H

Forming an Investigative Plan

Please use the questions and categories below to create a preliminary investigative plan for the scenario described in the Role Play Triad.

- Assess the allegations (include additional background you may need, additional complainants, and so forth).

- Identify potential violations of the Microcosm policy, Handout B. Identify what information you need to establish violations of policy.

- Identify potential witnesses. (Who in the situation or what kinds of witnesses do you want to interview and in what order and where?)

- Identify potential documents/physical evidence.

(continued)

HANDOUT H *(continued)*

- Identify possible issues of retaliation, safety, and workgroup issues that may need interim attention from management (include options for addressing these).

- Who in management will need to be informed and included?

- List potential problem areas.

Witness Summary:
Willima Michaels

Willima has worked at Microcosm for two years as a clerical worker. She was a teen mother and raised two children before she went back to school to get a degree in business administration to try to get a job as a business manager. She is good at her job and does not want to lose it. She wants to be promoted someday and is afraid that her involvement in this complaint process will have repercussions for her. She is thus very afraid of telling her story. She is still not sure if anything she has done was a violation of the policy.

Willima (Will EE Ma) has worked for David Lee for the two years she has been here. She has not really had a problem with how he supervised her work, but there have been some things that he has done that have made her uncomfortable at work.

Shortly after she started at Microcosm, David acted like he really enjoyed Willima's company. He seemed very friendly. He stopped by her desk every morning with a cup of coffee and they chatted about her life story and her ambitions. She enjoyed his company too, so they spent some time having coffee, sitting together in the cafeteria at lunch time, and occasionally going out for a beer with other co-workers. At first, it almost seemed like he was flirting with her.

David seems like a very powerful person, and he is very good friends with the big boss, Tom Torrance, so she didn't mind the attention, because she thought it could probably help her. She may even have flirted back a little.

David would tell jokes that had a sexual meaning to them, and sometimes she would laugh, and other times she would tell her own funny joke. She tried to tell mostly jokes that did not have a sexual meaning, but that were funny. But David started making comments that she did not find funny. For instance, he started joking about her "pimp." Willima thinks he meant it as a joke. She didn't understand the joke. So sometimes she just laughed. She didn't want to make him mad. And the other people in the workgroup would also laugh, so she didn't want to be the only one not laughing. Some other jokes that he told were: "Why don't Mexicans have barbeques? The beans fall through the grate" and "What did the Mexican-American wife say to her husband when he suggested that they take swimming lessons? Why? We're already here." He also told a joke that she doesn't really remember, but it was something about being able to see blacks in the dark because of their smiles.

She wanted to be a team player, and since most of the managers in Microcosm are male, she knew she had to try harder to make them like her. She was only really embarrassed a couple of times when David made comments about her body (if pressed she will say he said something about her breasts popping out of her shirt and her pants fitting snug against her legs). He complimented her on her beautiful brown skin. He also said things that were confusing, like when he told her one pair of her earrings were attractive, then when he got angry he said the same pair of earrings was not professional enough.

Most of the time at first, David seemed to treat her very politely, maybe even better than the rest of the staff. However, this changed about three months ago. She had accepted a couple of his proposals to head for beers after work, and it ended up being just the two of them. His comments became more personal when they were alone, and he asked if she had a boyfriend and told her she must have lots of men "hot for her body." He would sometimes talk about girlfriends he had when he was younger. If she told him to stop talking about sexual issues, he would tell her that she had to be tough to work at Microcosm, so she better learn to take it.

(continued)

HANDOUT I-1 *(continued)*

Finally, about three months ago she started turning down his invitations. He then started criticizing her work and yelling at her very loudly, complaining about things she had done. She didn't understand most times what she had done wrong. He also criticized her for being too direct in her communication style. She has the uncomfortable feeling that David is watching her.

Willima does not like using foul language and has never used the word "nigger" to refer to herself or anyone else.

Willima told her friend Michelle Cline about the encounters with David, and Michelle seemed to become very upset about it. Michelle did tell her to keep to herself about her problems with David, because people who "crossed" David ended up not working for Microcosm, because he and Tom were such good friends.

Confidential

The following information should be disclosed only if the investigator asks questions that directly elicits the information, that is, the witness is reluctant to disclose this information.

Willima had an affair with a male co-worker at Microcosm right after she started.

After one beer-drinking session, David touched Willima's breast. It was almost as though it was accidental as they were standing to go, but it felt intentional. Willima got very embarrassed and told him never to touch her again. He "pretended" that he did not know what she was talking about. It was shortly after this that Willima began refusing other invitations. While David never said anything to make her believe this, she believed that her job depended on continuing to endure his advances.

Willima never directly told David that she was no longer interested in his friendship; she just offered excuses on why she could not go with him. Tom saw Willima out with David for beers, but he just turned and walked away.

Witness Statement:
Tom Torrance

Tom Torrrance is shocked that anyone would accuse David Lee of not being a good supervisor. Tom has been David's supervisor for several years now. He absolutely denies ever seeing any improper behavior from David. David is the best supervisor the accounting department has ever had. Tom tries to be a mentor to the staff, always asking how they are doing, giving them encouragement. None of them has ever complained about David making sexual or ethnic jokes, including Cara Rodriguez (who is Hispanic and has just resigned) and Willima (Will-EE-ma) Michaels (who is black and is still employed). Tom remembers after-work activities with a group of people from the office, and he does not remember ever seeing anything happen that was odd or unusual or that someone would complain about. He does recall seeing Cara and Willima join in those after-work groups. He is proud of the fact that Microcosm has made great progress in diversifying its workers. Many of them have gained excellent skills and are slated for promotion. He names Michelle Cline as one who has been very successful. Michelle is also in the accounting department, reporting to David Lee, and is Caucasian. People who can get along with the team and show their strength are made of the "right stuff" and can make it.

Tom sees Willima as very bright, but with a lot of family troubles. She has had a hard life. He thinks David has taken a personal interest in helping her succeed. David does this with a lot of newer employees, because he wants to "be there" for them.

Tom has noticed that Willima seems edgy lately, not really acting like a team player, and he knows David has cautioned her about that. Tom feels that, while he wants to be supportive, they cannot tolerate the attitude problems that Willima is exhibiting.

Tom does not remember much about Cara, the employee whose exit interview started this process. He vaguely recalls some discussions with David about her, but his impression was that she was not happy here, that she was not cut out for the job. She was simply not pulling her weight.

Someone may have mentioned to him once or twice that David had a hot temper and that he was "yelling" at one of the employees. Tom did not take this complaint seriously, because he believes that a little "yelling" may be necessary to get employees to comply at times. David is a great producer, and if you get used to his direct style he is easy to get along with. Maybe Willima's problem is that she is also a very direct person, and she is just not comfortable with someone being direct back. Tom also has a hard time believing that Willima would not have said something if she had a complaint, because she is always complaining about everything.

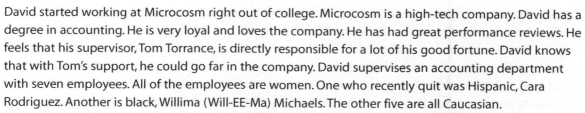

HANDOUT I-3

Witness Summary:
David Lee

David started working at Microcosm right out of college. Microcosm is a high-tech company. David has a degree in accounting. He is very loyal and loves the company. He has had great performance reviews. He feels that his supervisor, Tom Torrance, is directly responsible for a lot of his good fortune. David knows that with Tom's support, he could go far in the company. David supervises an accounting department with seven employees. All of the employees are women. One who recently quit was Hispanic, Cara Rodriguez. Another is black, Willima (Will-EE-Ma) Michaels. The other five are all Caucasian.

David admits that, at times, maybe a couple, he has made an ethnic comment. He does not really recall what he might have said, but everybody makes comments like that once in a while. He has been to the sexual harassment training sessions, but nothing was said about making comments about ethnic background, so he was not aware that this might be against company policy. No one appeared to be bothered by anything he said or did, because when he would tell jokes, he would get a big laugh. Willima, Michelle Cline, and Cara were among those laughing the loudest.

David thinks of himself as an All-American and he's proud of it. David thinks it is sad the country is falling down because illegal immigrants and legal refugees have moved in. This feeling intensified greatly after 9/11. David was raised in a large city. However, he does not think that he has a problem with different races that he knows of. He kind of feels sorry for them and wants to help them. David knows he can be rude and very direct at times, but he does that with all the employees, both male and female. He doesn't treat the women any differently, just gives them equal treatment. Nothing he has ever done or said to a woman appeared to bother her. Sometimes there are jokes told, but he has seen all the women join in the joking, including Willima and Michelle. He has heard Willima tell jokes that were very suggestive. He has had to counsel her about that. He has also heard her call the other women bitches, and she seems to act jealous of the others when they get attention. He has seen Willima act very suggestively towards one of their co-workers, rubbing up against him, and whispering in his ear. At the time he told her that was inappropriate.

David thinks Willima must have misinterpreted his attention toward her. David has a very good, mentoring relationship toward many of the employees, men and women. Some of his language is rough, but this is a team environment, and you'd better be able to take it or you should not be working here. Some women are just not cut out to be in this environment, because they can't take the pressure. Cara Rodriguez was that type of person, and that is why she did not last.

David has never touched Willima and is offended that anyone would even suggest it. He did ask her to go for coffee or beers with him, but there was nothing suggestive about it at all. David has never called Willima names or called Cara a "wetback."

Witness Summary:
B.J. Raymond

B.J. is the data processing manager at Microcosm. His office is located in a corner near the accounting area. Thus, he passes by their desks all the time. He knows David Lee, the supervisor of the clerical staff, but is not friends with him. He also knows Willima Michaels, an accounting clerk in the department, and Tom Torrance, David Lee's boss. He has talked to Cara Rodriguez, who just resigned from the company, but did not know her well and does not know why she recently left the company. He does know she had performance problems, though, because he heard David yelling at her frequently about her performance.

When B.J. heard David yelling at Cara, he heard David using swear words sometimes. David was very loud when he was yelling. The swear words he might have heard were things like "dammit" and "shit," and he may have heard "fuck" once or twice. He also heard David say things like "stupid" and "idiot" and once heard him ask Cara if her parents were retarded.

He has seen David get angry and yell at other employees. The only one he can really remember is Willima Michaels. He remembers one time when David was yelling at Willima and he said she must have been raised on a plantation because she sure didn't know how to work in an office. B.J. doesn't know what the problems were.

B.J. has had both Cara (who is Hispanic) and Willima (who is black) do work for him on his budget issues, and they both did an excellent job, so he has not seen any performance problems. Some of the other accounting clerks, who are Caucasian, do not do a good job. He has had at least two of them make major mistakes on projects he has asked them to do. When he told David about the mistakes, David just said B.J. must have given the wrong instructions. B.J. has never heard David yelling at the other employees.

When David did not seem to do anything about B.J.'s complaints about the accounting department work products, he took them to Tom Torrance, David's supervisor. Tom said that he was sure that David would handle it. Tom did not appear to take the complaint seriously, even though the mistakes cost the company a lot of money.

Confidential

The following information should be disclosed only if the investigator asks questions that directly elicits the information, that is, the witness is reluctant to disclose this information.

B.J. is uncomfortable with some of the words he heard David use to refer to Willima. He did hear him use the word "nigger" once. In reference to Cara, he also heard David use the word "wetback." He has also heard a couple of jokes told, one about Mexicans and one about blacks, but he really does not remember the details. But B.J. really does not want to get David in trouble, because he only heard these words once, and he really needs David's cooperation to get his work done. B.J. thinks that David and Tom are very good friends. They go camping, hunting, and fishing together. Because of that, B.J. has the impression that Tom overlooks a lot of the behavior that David engages in because they are friends. One time when David was yelling at Willima, and using lots of swear words, Tom was standing right there, but did nothing. B.J. also does not want to alienate Tom, so he wants this information kept very confidential.

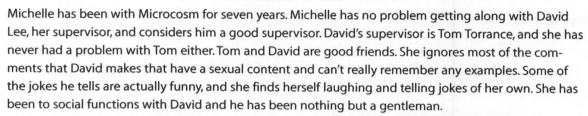

Witness Summary:
Michelle Cline

Michelle has been with Microcosm for seven years. Michelle has no problem getting along with David Lee, her supervisor, and considers him a good supervisor. David's supervisor is Tom Torrance, and she has never had a problem with Tom either. Tom and David are good friends. She ignores most of the comments that David makes that have a sexual content and can't really remember any examples. Some of the jokes he tells are actually funny, and she finds herself laughing and telling jokes of her own. She has been to social functions with David and he has been nothing but a gentleman.

Michelle believes that there have been a couple of women who have left the department, but she firmly believes that they were women who did not understand the work or how difficult and tedious it is. It is a very close-knit group of employees, and you have to get along or you will be miserable. The women who have not been able to do that have left. There has never been a man on the accounting staff, so it is hard to say if they would have had the same problems. Cara Rodriguez is one of those who just resigned because she could not take it.

Michelle remembers that there has been some mention of harassment in some of the training they have had, but she has never had a problem in the accounting department. She doesn't seem to remember exactly what they said at the training, but she does recall some of the managers saying that harassment will be "graded."

Michelle does remember both Cara Rodriguez and Willima Michaels complaining about David, but Willima was also always kind of joking around and "hanging around" David, and Michelle did not appreciate that. She thinks Willima is now mad at David because he did not return her affection. The complaints were not very specific, just that David was mean to them, yelled at them, or was "bothering" them. Michelle simply assumed they could not take the atmosphere.

Michelle has heard David yelling at both Cara and Willima. David does have a tendency to get very mad, and his face turns red and he raises his voice. He may have used a few swear words when that happened. David has never gotten mad at Michelle, and she is very glad about that, because it would probably be kind of frightening. She has not seen David get mad at the other clerical staff. She assumes that David was mad at Cara and Willima because of their work performance. She has never personally had any trouble with their work. Any projects that she has asked them to help her with they have done very well, and both women have always acted very professionally toward their work. There have been employees who were lackadaisical about their work and did not have good work product, but she never saw David yell at them.

HANDOUT J-1

Role Play Preparation and Feedback Forms

Person to be interviewed: _____

Purpose of interview

Introduction/preliminary issues (role, policy, retaliation, confidentiality, and so forth)

(continued)

HANDOUT J-1 *(continued)*

Background information

   • Historical (personnel record, etc.)

   • Physical scene

Issues to be surfaced

Follow-up issues

Role Play Feedback Guidelines

Witness Interviewed: _____

What techniques were effective?

What else would you have done?

What information discovered was pertinent?

What don't we know? What's next?

HANDOUT K

Remedies, Healing, and Aftermath

Case Study Application

Instructions: As this handout will be used for several activities, wait for the instructor's directions before filling out each section.

Potential Discipline

Potential Remedies

Debriefing Issues

Healing and Follow-Up Strategies
  • Complainant

  • Accused

  • Witnesses

Long-Term Possibilities/Problems

Who is responsible for what?

Debriefing the Workgroup Exercise

Time Issues

Initial Complaint Description

Specific Outcomes (discipline, remedies, and so on)

General Outcomes

Invitation for Feedback and Interaction

HANDOUT M

Your Organization's Follow-Up Issues

Use this form to record your group's feedback to management on any issues that need follow-up.

Policy and Procedures

Record Keeping

Training

Report Writing

Additional Issues

Appendix

Sample Policy

Respectful Workplace Anti-Harassment Policy

Microcosm is an equal employment opportunity employer. We value our diverse employees and clients and we strive to create a professional and respectful workplace. Bias, prejudice, harassment, and disrespectful behaviors are not tolerated at Microcosm, Inc.

Harassment based on race, color, sex or sexual orientation, religion, national origin, age, disability, veteran or marital status, or retaliation, including opposition to prohibited discrimination, will not be tolerated. Appropriate preventative measures shall be used to promote respect for the rights of co-workers. Remedial measures and/or corrective actions, up to and including dismissal, shall be utilized when acts of harassment occur. Each employee has an affirmative duty to maintain a workplace free of harassment and intimidation.

This policy applies to anyone who does business with Microcosm (contractors, vendors, clients, and all others). All harassment complaints, regardless of where reported or from whom, shall be taken seriously and resolved.

Roles and Responsibilities of Management

All of our leaders (supervisors and managers), through their actions, shall model respectful behavior by:

- Encouraging reports of harassment and/or discrimination incidents;

- Taking remedial measures to stop harassing behavior whenever reported or observed;

- Notifying management or Human Resources of all allegations or incidences of harassment in the workplace; and

- Ensuring that retaliatory behavior is not allowed.

Harassing Behavior

Harassment is any conduct that:

- Degrades or shows hostility toward an individual because of race, color, sex, or sexual orientation, religion, national origin, age, disability, veteran or marital status, or because of retaliation for opposition to prohibited discrimination; and/or

- Creates an intimidating, hostile, or offensive working environment through written (e-mail, computer), graphic, or verbal communications (voice mail, oral, or otherwise), including comments, jokes, slurs, or negative stereotyping or interferes with an individual's ability to do his or her work.

Additionally, sexual harassment is specifically prohibited and defined as unwelcome sexual advances, requests for sexual favors, or other verbal or physical conduct of a sexual nature when the sexual conduct has the purpose or effect of unreasonably interfering with an individual's work performance or creating an intimidating, hostile, or offensive work environment.

Examples of sexual harassment include, but are not limited to:

- Demeaning and/or derogatory harassment toward one's gender;

- Demeaning behavior, staring, pinching, touching and other physical contact, or blocking the movements of another person;

- Unwelcome sexual comments, innuendoes, jokes, or abusive personal remarks;

- Sexually explicit displays or distribution of pictures, materials, or objects in the work area;

- Offering or implying a reward or threat concerning work assignments, performance review, discipline, promotions, or other terms or conditions of employment in exchange for sexual favors;

- Unwelcome amorous advances or propositions, physical conduct, obscene gestures;

- Obscene letters, phone calls, e-mails, or unwelcome words or comments with sexual or other discriminatory meanings;

- Unwelcome requests for sexual favors or repeated social contact; and

- Sexual assault or other unwelcome sexual contact.

General Harassment

General workplace harassment is a form of offensive treatment or behavior that, to a reasonable person, creates an intimidating, hostile, or abusive work environment. Examples can include but are not limited to verbal or physical behavior that is derogatory, abusive, bullying, threatening, or disrespectful or ridiculing or under-mining an individual with vindictive or humiliating words or acts.

Retaliation Prohibited

Employees who complain of harassment or discrimination, who provide informa-tion related to such complaints, or who oppose harassing and/or discriminating behavior shall be protected against retaliation. Retaliation is considered as serious as prohibited harassment, and immediate and appropriate disciplinary action, up to and including dismissal, shall be instituted. During the complaint investigation, all parties shall be reminded that retaliation is prohibited.

Examples of retaliation can include negative actions such as, but not limited to, unwarranted poor performance evaluations; change in job duties as a consequence of reporting harassing behavior; other negative employment decisions; laughing at, ignoring, or failing to take seriously reports/complaints of harassment; or con-tinuing/escalating harassing behavior after the employee objects.

Addressing Harassment

If you feel you are being harassed or retaliated against, you are encouraged to notify any supervisor, manager, member of the Human Resources staff, or Paul Johnson, the president of Microcosm.

Harassment Complaint Investigation

Whenever we become aware of harassment, immediate remedial measures shall be taken to stop the behavior.

All allegations, regardless of where reported, shall be forwarded to the any supervisor, manager, plant manager, Human Resources, or directly to the corpo-rate offices. The complaint shall be reviewed to determine whether a detailed fact-finding investigation is appropriate.

If a fact-finding investigation is necessary, the investigation shall begin imme-diately. An investigator shall be appointed to gather and consider the relevant facts. Employees are expected to be ethical and honest throughout all proceedings. The confidentiality of all parties who are interviewed or present information about the harassment allegation shall be maintained as much as possible, with the informa-tion being disseminated only on a need-to-know basis.

The alleged harasser shall not have supervisory authority over the individual who conducts the investigation and shall not have any direct or indirect control over the investigation.

Corrective Actions

If the findings of the investigation indicate that a violation of the harassment policy has occurred, immediate and appropriate corrective and/or disciplinary action, up to and including dismissal, shall be administered. Corrective actions shall be proportional to the seriousness or repetitiveness of the offense. (An oral or written warning, training or counseling, monitoring the harasser, transfer or reassignment, demotion, reduction of wages, suspension, or dismissal may all be appropriate.)

Policy Distribution

Every employee shall be supplied with a copy of this policy each time it is updated. Additionally, the complaint reporting procedures and other information about harassment shall be posted in central locations (lunchroom, official bulletin boards) throughout the firm.

Sample Investigative Forms

Investigation Activity Log

Date	Time	Activity of Investigator

Investigator's Checklist

- ❑ Review written complaint, if any
- ❑ Check applicable policies
- ❑ Develop investigative plan
- ❑ Develop contact list for all potential witnesses
- ❑ Review personnel file of accused and complainant(s)
- ❑ Review training records
- ❑ Determine appropriate location for interviews
- ❑ Contact witnesses and arrange for interviews
- ❑ Tour work location, if appropriate
- ❑ Interview complainant first, if possible
- ❑ Interview all witnesses
- ❑ Interview accused
- ❑ Gather any additional documents, witnesses necessary
- ❑ Conduct rebuttal interviews with complainant and accused
- ❑ Prepare report
- ❑ Communicate with appropriate management regarding outcome
- ❑ Contact complainant regarding outcome
- ❑ Contact accused regarding outcome
- ❑ Aftermath debriefing with workgroup, if appropriate

Checklist for Interview with Complainant

❑ Introduction (confidentiality, fairness, complaint process, your role, policy)

❑ Complainant's role, job, working relationship with others

❑ Any rights (such as union rights, consult with counsel)

❑ Physical location where events took place

❑ Events

    ❑ How many times

    ❑ Who was present

    ❑ Where

    ❑ What was said

    ❑ What happened

    ❑ Reactions of others present

    ❑ Reactions of complainant

    ❑ Who complainant told

❑ Documents

    ❑ Memos

    ❑ E-mails

    ❑ Notes

    ❑ Diaries

    ❑ Logs

    ❑ Calendars

    ❑ Time sheets

❑ Current feelings about situation

❑ Medical attention sought

❑ Comfort in returning to workplace

❑ Anything else

Checklist for Interview with Accused

- ❏ Introduction (confidentiality, fairness, complaint process, your role, policy)
- ❏ Accused's role, job, working relationship with others, particularly complainant
- ❏ Any rights (such as union or Garrity rights, consult with counsel)
- ❏ Physical location where events took place
- ❏ Events
    - ❏ How many times
    - ❏ Who was present
    - ❏ Where
    - ❏ What was said
    - ❏ What happened
    - ❏ Reactions of others present
    - ❏ Reactions of complainant
    - ❏ Did complainant object verbally
- ❏ Documents
    - ❏ Memos
    - ❏ E-mails
    - ❏ Notes
    - ❏ Diaries
    - ❏ Logs
    - ❏ Calendars
    - ❏ Time sheets
- ❏ Anything else

Checklist for Interviews with Witnesses

- ❑ Introduction (confidentiality, fairness, complaint process, your role, policy)
- ❑ Complainant's role, job, working relationship with others
- ❑ Physical location where events took place
- ❑ Events
    - ❑ How many times
    - ❑ Who present
    - ❑ Where
    - ❑ What said
    - ❑ What happened
    - ❑ Reactions of others present
    - ❑ Reactions of complainant
    - ❑ Who witness told
- ❑ Documents
    - ❑ Memos
    - ❑ E-mails
    - ❑ Notes
    - ❑ Diaries
    - ❑ Logs
    - ❑ Calendars
    - ❑ Time sheets
- ❑ Anything else

Investigation Report

Date of Report: October 7, 2003
Date Investigation Began: October 3, 2003

Scope of Investigation

This investigation began after an exit interview with resigning employee Cara Rodriguez on October 3, 2003. That interview revealed possible conduct in violation of company policy by supervisor David Lee. The investigation initially focused on alleged sexually suggestive comments and general harassment through abusive conduct. The investigation later expanded to include alleged harassment on the basis of race or national origin, and supervisory misconduct of Mr. Lee's supervisor, Tom Torrance. This investigator interviewed six witnesses.

Initial Complaint

Supervisor David Lee "yelled" at employees; used profanity; made sexually suggestive comments about female employees' clothing or body; and may have treated some employees differently than other workers based on race/color, national origin, or gender.

Policies at Issue

Respectful Workplace Anti-Harassment Policy—Roles and Responsibilities of Management; Harassing Behavior; General Harassment; Retaliation Prohibited.

Summary of Facts Found

Allegation: David Lee would commonly use a management style that involved raising his voice to "yell" at subordinates about work performance issues.

Facts Found: Several witnesses verified that Lee used verbally abusive methods of supervision with at least two employees. One witness verified hearing him use the words "stupid" and "idiot" on one occasion when yelling at one employee. The witness also heard Lee ask a female employee if her parents were "retarded."

Allegation: David Lee told jokes and made comments in the workplace that had a sexual connotation.

Facts Found: Lee admits that he may have told suggestive jokes, but indicated that others, including the women, also told such jokes. Witnesses verified that suggestive jokes were told by Lee.

Allegation: David Lee made comments to female subordinates about their clothing or bodies that were sexually suggestive. Lee also touched one woman inappropriately on her breast.

Facts Found: Witnesses verified that the verbal comments were made to two women, indicating that Lee had called women "hot" and made comments about their breasts popping out of their clothes. Only the woman who alleged the touching and Lee witnessed that behavior; Lee denied the behavior, and no witnesses could verify that the behavior occurred. Lee also allegedly approached another woman romantically, but she declined, and no further advances were made, thus no violation of policy is apparent from that behavior.

Allegation: David Lee told jokes in the workplace derogatory to Mexican Americans. (At least one of the affected employees is of Mexican descent.)

Facts Found: Lee denied this allegation. Two witnesses verified that, on at least two occasions, Lee told jokes that were derogatory toward Mexican Americans. Another witness verified that Lee used the term "wetback."

Allegation: David Lee allegedly told jokes, made comments, and used words in the workplace derogatory to blacks. (At least one of Lee's female subordinates is black.)

Facts Found: Lee denied this allegation. Two witnesses verified that this behavior occurred. One witness verified that Lee used the word "nigger" in the workplace. Lee also made reference to a black woman's "pimp" and complimented her on her "beautiful brown skin."

Allegation: David Lee singled out the non-Caucasian employees in his workgroup for abusive behavior.

Facts Found: Lee denied this allegation. However, witnesses support the fact that the only two employees subjected to verbally abusive behavior were one Hispanic and one black worker. Witnesses did not support the idea that their behavior or performance led to their being singled out. In addition, witnesses noted performance problems with other Caucasian workers who were not subjected to similar abusive behavior.

Allegation: Tom Torrance, David Lee's supervisor, was told about, and personally observed on one occasion, Lee's verbally abusive behavior but took no action.

Facts Found: Torrance admitted this allegation.

Allegation: David Lee used profanity in the workplace.

Facts Found: Lee denied using profanity. Witnesses verified Lee's use of foul language in the workplace, including hearing him use the word "fuck" and "dammit" and "shit."*

Conclusion

Based on the facts gathered and this investigator's assessment of reliability and credibility, the complaint of a violation of the Respectful Workplace Anti-Harassment Policy is substantiated. Those who have violated that policy include supervisor David Lee and supervisor Tom Torrance.

---

*While some might find the use of these words offensive, they have a particular purpose in the report to management. Investigators should avoid the impulse to "sanitize" the nature of the behavior and conduct found. To sanitize the words of behavior diminishes the impact of the behavior. In turn, management may make the wrong decision on corrective action because the managers receiving the report did not understand the full gravity of the behavior and its impact on the workforce. While not every sordid detail needs to be shared, make sure that sanitization does not impact the result.

Federal Cases of Importance for Sexual Harassment Issues

Faragher v. City of Boca Raton (Supreme Court, 1998)

A female employee (Faragher) worked for the City of Boca Raton, Florida, from 1985 until 1990 as a lifeguard part-time and during the summer. Throughout her employment, she and other female lifeguards were sexually harassed by two of Faragher's immediate supervisors. Although the City had a policy prohibiting sexual harassment, it did not effectively communicate the policy to beach employees, and neither of the supervisors was aware of the policy. Faragher and other female lifeguards spoke informally with a third supervisor about the harassment, not as a formal complaint, but because they respected him and thought he was someone in whom they could confide. However, neither the third supervisor nor any of the victims of the harassment reported it to any of the City's management officials. Eventually, a former lifeguard reported the harassment to the City's director of personnel. After conducting an investigation, the City reprimanded and disciplined the two supervisors. Faragher resigned from her job shortly thereafter and filed suit against the City alleging that the City had subjected her to a hostile work environment in violation of Title VII.

In deciding *Faragher* and *Ellerth* (see next page), the Supreme Court distinguished between supervisor harassment that results in tangible employment action, such as a discharge, demotion, or failure to promote, and supervisor harassment that does not. The Court held that when the harassment resulted in tangible employment action, the employer is always liable for the harassment. However, when no tangible employment action is taken against the employee, an employer may establish an affirmative defense to liability or damages if it can prove by a preponderance of the evidence that it (a) "exercised reasonable care to prevent and correct promptly any sexually harassing behavior" and (b) "that the plaintiff employee unreasonably failed to take advantage of any preventive or corrective opportunities provided by the employer or to avoid harm otherwise." The Court held that proof that an employer had developed an anti-harassment policy with a complaint procedure is one method of establishing that the employer exercised reasonable care to prevent and promptly correct any sexual harassment. Similarly, proof that an employee failed to use the employer's complaint procedure will normally establish that the employee unreasonably failed to take advantage of any preventive or corrective opportunities provided by the employer or to otherwise avoid harm.

Burlington Industries, Inc. v. Ellerth (Supreme Court, 1998)

A female employee was sexually harassed by a mid-level manager at Burlington Northern. Although the manager threatened to take adverse employment action against Ellerth if she did not submit to his sexual advances, he never followed through on his threats to retaliate against her. In fact, Ellerth was promoted during her fourteen months of employment at Burlington. Ellerth never complained to anyone at Burlington Northern about the harassment, even though she knew that the company had a policy prohibiting sexual harassment. Ultimately, she resigned because of the harassment and filed suit against Burlington alleging that she had been subjected to unlawful sexual harassment and constructively discharged.

As noted previously, the Supreme Court applied the principles of first determining if a tangible employment action was taken. Here, the Court decided that there was no tangible action, and this was not a quid pro quo case. The court then applied the affirmative defense principles noted previously.

Harris v. Forklift Systems, Inc. (Supreme Court, 1993)

To prove a hostile environment under Title VII, a complainant need not show that she or he suffered severe psychological harm as a result of sexual and/or gender demeaning behavior. It is sufficient for the complainant to prove that the work environment was permeated with discriminatory behavior sufficiently severe or pervasive to create a hostile or abusive working environment for a reasonable person, and that she subjectively viewed the environment as abusive or hostile.

The decision on whether an environment is hostile or abusive is determined based on the totality of the circumstances, which may include the frequency of the discriminatory conduct, its severity, whether it is physically threatening or humiliating or a mere offensive utterance, and whether it unreasonably interferes with an employee's work performance. No single factor is required to support this proof, and it can consist of a combination of factors.

Robinson v. Shell Oil (Supreme Court, 1997)

Even a former employee is protected against discrimination under Title VII. When the employee received a poor employment reference from his former employer, Shell Oil, allegedly because he had filed a discrimination claim against Shell, the court found that he could sue for employment discrimination/retaliation under Title VII.

Meritor Savings Bank v. Vinson (Supreme Court, 1986)

A female assistant branch manager sued her male branch manager and the bank for hostile work environment sexual harassment arising out of the branch manager's alleged ongoing sexual advances toward her. Important rulings include the following:

- Hostile work environment (HWE) claims are actionable as gender discrimination under Title VII.

- Such claims can be proven by a showing that there were unwelcome, uninvited sexual advances directed at a complainant and those advances unreasonably interfered with the complainant's work environment, whether or not he or she lost economic benefits.

- Eventual acceptance of sexual advances by the victim does not defeat a hostile environment claim; however, in deciding whether the advances were unwelcome or uninvited, the court may consider the complainant's conduct, dress, and language at the time of the alleged advances.

- An employer will be liable for conduct that creates a hostile work environment if it knew or should have known about the conduct and failed to take immediate, appropriate corrective action.

- In deciding whether an employer knew or should have known about the HWE, a court will consider whether the employer had in place a clear policy against sexual harassment and an effective set of procedures that employees could use to bring claims forward for resolution.

Federal Cases Addressing the Affirmative Defense, 1998–2002

Adequacy of the Employer's Policy

Marrero v. Goya of Puerto Rico (1st Circuit, 2002)

In this case, the employer had a policy drafted by an outside law firm, but there was a credibility dispute as to whether that happened before or after plaintiff began her employment. Plaintiff was able to testify that she never saw any such policy, nor was she provided training on it. She also testified that she asked her supervisor for a copy of the policy, but it was never provided. The policy, as drafted, had an acknowledgment form, but the company could never produce a signed copy of it. In addition, the company claimed that it posted the policy on posters throughout the worksite, but a video shown at trial did not show the posters in place. This case illustrates that a good policy does you no good unless it is effectively distributed.

Bennett v. Progressive Corporation (N.D. New York, 2002)

In this case, the organization could not prove that complainant received a copy of their policy. While supervisors offered proof that "every" new employee receives a copy, they could not prove that the complainant did, and when she denied it, that was enough to raise a question of fact on that point. In addition, the court was very critical of the policy itself. With respect to a complaint procedure, the policy allegedly contained "no specific procedure for sexual harassment complaints, aside from the unhelpful advice to contact someone." While the organization contended that it had an "open door" policy and a "hotline" for reporting harassment, the court noted that such avenues were "geared to any run-of-the-mill behavior an employee deems inappropriate" and held that such measures were insufficient to meet the affirmative defense.

Cardenas v. Massey (3rd Circuit, October 2001)

In a case involving harassment based on national origin (Mexican American), the court stated that having a policy is in itself insufficient to establish an affirmative defense. The court indicated that, in addition to a policy, the employer would also have to show that it was effectively carried out.

Dowdy v. North Carolina (4th Circuit, Unpublished, November 2001)

The employer had a policy that clearly listed to whom to report complaints. The plaintiff chose to report her complaint to someone other than those listed. While she expressed a generalized fear of retaliation as an excuse for not following the policy, the court held that was not enough and that the employer could rely on distribution of the policy as proof of reasonable care to prevent harassment.

Stricker v. Cesford Construction Co. (N.D. Iowa, 2001)

The court held that the policy was inadequate because there was only one channel for reporting harassment (the EEO officer) and the policy provided no information on how to contact that person. In addition, the policy did not define "sexual harassment." Finally, the policy did not include an express statement that harassment would not be tolerated, did not indicate that those who engage in harassment would be disciplined, and did not prohibit retaliation.

Matira v. Bald Head Island Management Incorporated (4th Circuit, July 2001)

In this case the court indicated that a policy was not ambiguous in prohibiting harassment and providing avenues of reporting complaints. The plaintiff pointed to supervisors' testimony indicating that they were "fuzzy" on details of an orientation on the policy, but the court said that was not enough to show that the policy was ineffective. The court stated that the policy clearly defined to whom sexual harassment should be reported. The plaintiff argued that she did not report because she needed time to gather enough evidence so that her story would be believed. The court ruled that her duty was to report the behavior, then it was up to the company to investigate the complaint, so that was not a sufficient excuse for failing to follow the policy.

Reese v. Meritor Automotive Inc. (4th Circuit, March 2001)

In this case, the employer had a handbook that (1) defined harassment and (2) encouraged reporting. The employer provided classes for all employees on harassment issues. The court noted that the employee was aware of the policy, as evidenced by the fact that she had previously complained on behalf of a co-worker and the harassment stopped, and she had been the subject of a complaint when she told an off-color joke, and she was reprimanded. When she reported this complaint, the offender was suspended and then asked to resign at the completion of the investigation. The policy contained a hotline number to report violations and provided multiple lines of reporting. The court noted that the employee had a duty, under these circumstances, to report harassment. The plaintiff argued that, because she and the offender were seen together on premises a lot, there was a duty to inquire as to their relationship. The court refused to place such a duty on the company, as that would require prying into the private relationships of employees. Here, the plaintiff should have complained, and she did not for a period of time, so any damage arising from her failure to complain she could not recover for.

Smith v. First Union National Bank (4th Circuit, 2000)
In this case, in addition to the investigation defects noted under this same case in the "Adequacy of the Investigation" on page 225, the court found that a policy was defective when it implied that only sexual advances constituted sexual harassment.

Wyatt v. Hunt Plywood Company (5th Circuit, 2002)
Here, the organization preserved the affirmative defense by including multiple avenues for a complaint to reach upper management. Complainant had been subjected to harassment by a co-worker and had complained to a first-level supervisor. That supervisor did nothing about the harassment, and in fact also began harassing the complainant. The court upheld the affirmative defense, however, because the organization's policy indicated that the complainant could go to others higher in the supervisory chain to complain. The court issued this ruling despite the complainant's testimony that she was admonished many times not to "go over [the supervisor's head]." The court held that did not excuse the failure to take advantage of the policy's invitation to report to higher management.

Miller v. Woodharbor Molding & Millworks (N.D. Iowa, 2000)
Here, the court noted that in order to constitute an effective policy, which is required under *Faragher* and *Ellerth*, the employer must have in place (1) training for supervisors on what constitutes sexual harassment; (2) an express anti-retaliation provision in the policy; and (3) multiple complaint channels for reporting the harassment conduct. Here, the company had a policy, but when supervisors were asked under oath whether they were aware of the policy they had no knowledge of it. There was no anti-retaliation policy and no formal complaint procedure. The court concluded that the employer did not exercise reasonable care.

Walker v. Thompson (5th Circuit, 2000)

The danger of an inadequate policy is underlined in this case, where the court noted that, while the employer had a policy, it did not address racial harassment, which is the conduct that was alleged here. That defect, along with defects under this same case in the "Adequacy of the Investigation" on page 225, stripped the employer of the ability to assert the affirmative defense.

Hertzberg v. SRAM Corporation (7th Circuit, August 2001)

The court was critical of the company policy when the evidence revealed that employees were not provided with ready access to the policy and that no information was given on the avenues of complaining about harassment. This was a case involving co-worker harassment, so the affirmative defense did not apply, but the court used the same standard to determine whether punitive damages should be available.

Haugerud v. Amery School District (7th Circuit, August 2001)

This case demonstrates a situation where the employer did everything right up to a critical point, but their own policy tripped them up. The employer had a policy against harassment in place, it included a complaint process, and they conducted "in services" (training) regularly to let everyone know of the policy. However, in the policy, the school district indicated that the employee could complain to an outside agency of discrimination (the state human rights agency or the EEOC). This plaintiff did not complain internally and instead complained to the outside agency. When the employer tried to argue that the plaintiff had not fulfilled the duty to complain, the court pointed to the employer's own policy, which indicated that was a way for the employee to bring the complaint to the employer's attention. The mistake that the employer made was in then treating the case as a "litigation" case and defending the external complaint, without performing an investigation or taking remedial action. This case illustrates two points: (1) employers should be careful about including external complaint options in their policies if they want to handle complaints internally and (2) employers should investigate all complaints appropriately, regardless of whether they are received through internal or external sources.

Dockery v. Dayton-Hudson Corp. (7th Circuit, Unpublished, 2001)

This case involved both age and race (African American) harassment. The employer had a policy in place, and the plaintiff admitted that he had it but was too busy to read it and never used the complaint procedures in it to complain. The employer was entitled to the affirmative defense.

Molnar v. Booth (7th Circuit, 2000)

The court refused to allow the affirmative defense because the employer's policy only contained a general anti-discrimination policy and did not address sexual harassment. The trial testimony also revealed that employees were "extremely confused" about the definition of sexual harassment.

Madison v. IBP, Inc. (8th Circuit, June 2001)

In this male-on-male gender and race harassment case, the court was not really critical of the employer's policy, stating that the policy was in place, and the employer also had an affirmative action plan and provided training for all supervisors annually on the "Legal Aspects of Supervision," which included harassment issues. However, as seen on page 231 in "Adequacy of the Remedial Action," the remedial action of the employer fell far short of the mark.

Zelaya v. Eastern & Western Hotel Corp. (9th Circuit, Unpublished, March 2001)

This case demonstrates what an employer did correctly in promulgating and distributing a policy. The company had what the court noted was a reasonable anti-harassment policy, posted in multiple locations in both English and Spanish. The HR department had bilingual employees prepared to take complaints. In fact, the plaintiff had previously made complaints about other things to a Spanish-speaking employee in HR. She failed to complain about harassment, and the employer was entitled to the affirmative defense.

Wright v. Anixter, Inc. (9th Circuit, August 1999)

In this gender discrimination and sexual harassment case, the court noted that the employer had a policy prohibiting harassment in place, and it provided notice of the right to report complaints and alternatives on how to report. Plaintiff knew the policy was posted in her work location and knew where to report her complaint. However, she claimed she did not like confrontation, and so was reluctant to report her complaint. The court said that was not enough for her to be able to avoid her duty to report, and the employer won. (Of course, it helped that the employer conducted an immediate investigation when she did complain and fired the offending employee five days after the complaint was received and acknowledged.)

Montero v. AGCO (9th Circuit, September 1999)

In this sexual harassment case, the plaintiff did not complain until four months after the harassment had stopped. The employer had a policy in place that (a) defined harassment; (b) identified a complaint procedure; (c) provided for discipline for violation of the policy; and (d) ensured no retaliation for reporting. The court noted that the plaintiff had received the policy and a separate memo outlining the policy, as well as two other updated pamphlets during her employment. Plaintiff also knew who to contact, yet she waited two years to complain. Her claim was rejected, particularly based on the response from the employer when she did complain. (See discussion in "Adequacy of the Remedial Action" on page 233.)

Nichols v. Azteca Restaurant Enterprises (9th Circuit, 2001)

In a case involving male on male harassment, the court was not as critical of the policy as of the response following harassment. (See "Adequacy of the Remedial Action" on page 232.) As to the policy, the court noted that (1) the employer had a policy that defined harassment; (2) the policy provided the reporting procedures; (3) the policy indicated that violations of the policy would be disciplined; and (4) the policy prohibited retaliation for reporting. The court also noted that the plaintiff was aware of the company policy and the reporting procedure and had attended mandatory training on the issue provided to all company employees. Thus, the court ruled that the employer had done all it could to prevent harassment from occurring. However, the company was denied the affirmative defense because of their failure to correct the problem once aware of it.

Harrison v. Eddy Potash, Inc. (10th Circuit, April 2001)

The employer here had a policy prohibiting harassment, but no copies were provided to employees and copies were not posted in the work areas. The policy was also basically ignored. There was no training on the policy and no mention of it in the workplace. Plaintiff was not told of the policy when hired. The court said that the employer must not only show reasonable care in promulgating the policy, but must also show reasonable care in distributing the policy.

Frederick v. Sprint/United Management Co. (11th Circuit, April 2001)

In this sexual harassment case, the employer had a policy in place, it was distributed to all employees and posted in all offices, or so they thought. They also had a code of conduct that allowed reporting of harassment to an "Ethics Hotline." A later policy also had an anti-harassment statement, with a different method of reporting complaints. Plaintiff complained to another supervisor and allegedly was advised not to file a complaint with Human Resources. This then created confusion over whether the earlier policy allowed reporting outside the supervisory chain, and there was confusion over what could be reported on the hotline. Plaintiff also testified that she never received the policy, and it was not posted in her work location. She also indicated that she did finally receive the later policy, but only after she requested a copy directly from HR. The court held that a jury must decide whether the affirmative defense was available under these circumstances, even though the employer clearly took immediate action (a two-week investigation after which the harasser was fired) once they became "aware" of the complaint.

Church v. Maryland (D. Maryland, January 2002)

The court approved of a policy that: (1) identified the prohibited conduct, (2) protected against retaliation, (3) described the complaint procedure, (4) provided alternatives to reporting, (5) described a prompt investigation, and (6) promised prompt remedial action. Once the employer has demonstrated a reasonably designed and reasonably effective policy, the plaintiff must show how it is deficient. Here, the plaintiff merely pointed to a belief that the policy would not be enforced, despite training for all new employees and periodic training for supervisors on the harassment policy. The court said that the affirmative defense applied.

May v. AutoZone Stores, Inc. (N.D. Mississippi, December 2001)

The employer had a policy in place, but plaintiff did not receive it until eight months after she was employed. This, along with defects in the complaint procedure and the training, created a question of fact for a jury to decide on whether the employer was reasonable in preventing and correcting harassment. The fact that the employer had established an 800 number for reporting and provided five different alternatives to reporting complaints did little good in the face of evidence that the policy was not effectively communicated.

Knutson v. Brownstein (S.D. New York, December 2001)

In a case involving a claim of an age-hostile work environment, the court noted that a policy and complaint procedure existed, but there was a dispute about whether the plaintiff received the complaint. The adequacy of supervisory understanding of the policy was also at issue when plaintiff testified that he complained but was told that the employer could do nothing. The affirmative defense was denied.

Queener v. Windy Hill, Ltd. (Ohio, Unpublished, December 2001)

In a third-party harassment case, the court indicated it will apply similar analysis to the affirmative defense even in a non-supervisory negligence case. The plaintiff was allegedly harassed by an independent contractor janitor. The employer had a policy in place, plaintiff admitted she was aware of it, and the policy had a complaint procedure. Nevertheless, the plaintiff waited until a few days prior to quitting to complain, after she had already been offered an alternative position. The court held the employer was not negligent.

Adequacy of Training

Hertzberg v. SRAM Corporation (7th Circuit, August 2001)

This was a case involving co-worker harassment, so the affirmative defense did not apply, but the court used the same standard to determine whether punitive damages should be available. In a case that highlights the importance of supervisory training, plaintiff complained to a supervisor, to which he responded: "You are being too emotional, just like a woman." Another time she complained, the supervisor put his hand on her knee and told her he would "take care of it." However, the evidence showed that management just "shrugged off" these complaints. The employer was not entitled to take advantage of the affirmative defense.

Wilburn v. Fleet Financial Group, Inc. (D. Connecticut, 2001)

In this case, the court noted the deficiency of training on the sexual harassment policy as a reason to deny the affirmative defense. While the policy indicated that there would be yearly training, the unit where the harassment occurred had none. In addition, the supervisor in charge testified that he never distributed the policy, never held a meeting to review the policy, and did not even know that the policy existed.

Miller v. Woodharbor Molding & Millworks (N.D. Iowa, 2000)

The court used lack of supervisory training as one factor for holding that the employer did not take reasonable care to prevent harassment.

Passantino v. Johnson & Johnson Consumer Products (9th Circuit, April 2000)

While the court did not specifically focus on training, this case highlights a mistake made in responding to a complaint that proper training may have avoided. When the plaintiff had complained about co-workers, supervisors told her that it was her problem if she could not get along with co-workers. Her performance evaluation was then marked down in the area of relationships with peers, while the offending employees were not marked down. She then complained to an EEO officer and was allegedly told that "she would have to live with the burden if she chose to pursue a formal complaint" and coming forward "could have many ramifications."

May v. AutoZone Stores, Inc. (N.D. Mississippi, December 2001)

The employer contended that it had adequate training on its policy because it provided an orientation for all new employees and kept records of attendance at a video training it provided periodically. However, the employer was unable to produce attendance records for the alleged harasser to show that he attended the training and was unable to refute plaintiff's assertion that she never had an orientation nor attended the video training session.

Dowdy v. North Carolina (4th Circuit, Unpublished, November 2001)

The employer had a six-hour training session, which the plaintiff attended. This was a factor in allowing the affirmative defense.

Adequacy of the Complaint Procedure

Jones v. Rent-a-Center, Inc. (D. Kansas, 2002)

The organization could not obtain a summary judgment on the affirmative defense where there was evidence that the complainant had told her "supervisor" of the allegations, but he had done nothing. While the organization did not consider that individual to be a supervisor, the complainant did, and the individual himself testified that he was the complainant's supervisor. Even though the organization responded promptly when a higher level supervisor learned of the allegations, this was enough to keep the organization in court.

EEOC v. R&R Ventures (4th Circuit, March 2001)

In a case that also underscores the inadequacy of supervisory training, the affirmative defense was denied in a case where the plaintiff complained to several managers, but one said that the plaintiff was "overreacting" and the others did nothing. See discussion on page 225 regarding the "Adequacy of the Investigation."

Gawley v. Indiana University (7th Circuit, December 2001)

In assessing the affirmative defense in a sexual harassment complaint, the court noted that the University had a complaint procedure in place and as soon as the plaintiff complained, the University's response stopped the harassment. (Plaintiff had waited seven months to complain.) The court specifically noted that the complaint procedure had alternatives for plaintiff to use in reporting the harassment. The affirmative defense was allowed.

Miller v. Woodharbor Molding & Millworks (N.D. Iowa, 2000)

The court used the lack of a complaint procedure in the policy as one factor in holding that the employer failed to exercise reasonable care.

Casiano v. AT&T Corporation (5th Circuit, June 2000)

In a case involving a female supervisor harassing a male employee, the affirmative defense was allowed because the plaintiff failed to take advantage of the policy in place. There were three policy documents prohibiting harassment, and plaintiff was told of the policy at hire and provided with updated copies of the policy later. Plaintiff never complained with a description of the offending conduct until he had his attorney write a letter to the employer. Also see discussion in "Adequacy of the Investigation" on page 225.

Jackson v. Arkansas Department of Education (8th Circuit, December 2001)

The employer was able to use the affirmative defense in part because it had an adequate complaint procedure in place, but the plaintiff did not complain for nine months, refused to use the internal complaint procedure and instead reported her complaints to EEOC, and refused to use the internal investigation and remedial process. See further discussion in "Adequacy of the Investigation" on page 226.

Lagunovich v. Findlay City School System (N.D. Ohio, November 2001)

In a national origin harassment case, the court held that there was a question of fact for a jury to decide on whether there was a reasonable response by the employer. The employer had a policy and the employee was aware of it, but an investigation was not conducted until the employee complained to the assistant superintendent, and nothing had been done to act on prior complaints to a supervisor. However, once the assistant superintendent became aware of the complaint, it was immediately acted on and the employee failed to complain further.

Adequacy of the Investigation

Dowling v. The Home Depot (E.D. Pennsylvania, 2003)

In this co-employee harassment case, the court was critical of the organization's investigation, saying that the investigator concluded that the complainant's allegations were unsubstantiated "after interviewing only [the complainant] by telephone." The court implied that a jury might find this investigation to be inadequate. The court also pointed to the inadequacy of the response in determining that the organization may be found liable.

Hatley v. Hilton Hotels Corp. (5th Circuit, 2002)

In this case the jury denied the organization an affirmative defense, even though the investigator testified that she had done everything she could to investigate the complaints. However, there was other evidence from five employees that many prior complaints had been submitted to the same investigator and nothing had ever been done. The court held that this evidence was sufficient to support the jury's finding that the investigation was inadequate.

Lumhoo v. The Home Depot USA (E.D. New York, September 2002)

The court denied the affirmative defense where a manager did not conduct an investigation into complaints of racial harassment because he decided that the allegations were not credible. This case illustrates that you should never draw that conclusion *before* conducting the investigation!

Bennett v. Progressive Corporation (N.D. New York, 2002)

Here the court was critical of the organization's investigation because they had assigned a person who had no experience in investigating sexual harassment complaints, and who had only been working at the organization for four or five months. In addition, both of the central figures in the harassment incidents were intimately involved in making decisions about the investigation. Neither of those individuals had any experience in investigating harassment either. There were also no specific procedures to follow in conducting an investigation. While the investigation was completed in four days, the court used that as a strike against the organization, because of the complexity of the factual issues.

McGrath v. Nassau County Health Care Corporation (E.D. New York, 2001)

In this case, the court held that when the organization wanted to assert the affirmative defense, based on the adequacy of the investigation, the organization waived the attorney-client privilege. The organization was thus required to produce their attorney's report of the investigation, her handwritten investigative notes, and any parts of the report that had been deleted or redacted.

Cardenas v. Massey (3rd Circuit, October 2001)

The court was critical of the investigation into a national origin harassment claim because the employer (1) required a "formal" complaint before launching an investigation; (2) took ten months to complete the investigation; and (3) failed to address one important aspect of the complaint, that of discrimination in pay based on national origin. The court noted that the complainant had submitted previous complaints, which were never acted on, and had requested to deal with it on his own because of fear of reprisals. The court was critical of the employer's actions in not acting on the prior complaints.

EEOC v. R&R Ventures (4th Circuit, March 2001)

When the employer did finally investigate the plaintiff's complaints, there were no interviews conducted of the complainant or harasser. Needless to say, this was not viewed as an adequate investigation.

Matira v. Bald Head Island Management Incorporated (4th Circuit, July 2001)

The court noted the adequacy of the investigation where the employer immediately suspended the alleged harasser for four days without pay, took only eleven days to investigate, and, at the conclusion of the investigation, terminated the harasser.

Smith v. First Union National Bank (4th Circuit, 2000)

The employer's investigation was deemed defective because the investigator had never conducted an investigation before, never asked the alleged harasser whether he made the comments alleged, and simply counseled him to improve his management style and "smile more."

Walker v. Thompson (5th Circuit, 2000)

In this investigation, the employer was criticized because the investigator failed to interview obvious witnesses and failed to find harassment even after uncovering evidence of obviously racist incidents.

Casiano v. AT&T (5th Circuit, June 2000)

The court noted that once a complaint was received from the employee's attorney, there was a swift investigation, which included interviewing eleven employees. This contributed to the availability of the affirmative defense.

Gawley v. Indiana University (7th Circuit, December 2001)

While a plaintiff in a sexual harassment case contended that the investigation was inadequate, the court noted that the harassment stopped, thus providing evidence that the investigation and remedial action were effective. Plaintiff did not provide any further evidence to show that the investigation was inadequate despite the fact that the harassment stopped. Thus, the affirmative defense was allowed.

Tutman v. WBBM-TV, Inc. (7th Circuit, 2000)

In this racial harassment case, the employer escaped liability where the investigation began the same day as the alleged incident and took only two weeks from beginning to discipline.

Beard v. Flying J, Inc. (8th Circuit, September 2001)

The court was not impressed with the employer's investigation. Management learned of the complaint through co-workers and conducted an investigation. However, they interviewed only the complainant and the harasser and decided the evidence was inconclusive. When someone else then complained, the employer began another investigation, interviewed six co-workers, including the plaintiff, and concluded that harassment had occurred. They suspended the co-worker, but then allowed him to come back to work. The court denied the employer's request to apply the affirmative defense as a matter of law.

Jackson v. Arkansas Department of Education (8th Circuit, December 2001)

The employer was able to use the affirmative defense because once they became aware of the complaint they launched a thorough investigation immediately, which resulted in remedial action. See "Adequacy of the Remedial Action" on page 231.

Henderson v. Simmons Food (8th Circuit, 2000)

In this case the court was critical of the investigation because the investigator interviewed the alleged harassers and witnesses without an interpreter, although they spoke only broken English. This resulted in the witnesses misunderstanding some of the employer's questions and the harasser continuing much of his offensive behavior.

Fielder v. United Airlines Corp. (9th Circuit, July 2000)

This case, involving co-worker harassment, illustrates the importance of training and an adequate investigation and response. The court looked at the affirmative defense factors in determining whether punitive damages were appropriate. In this case, after the complainant reported the harassment, the supervisor confronted the harasser, but he denied the conduct. The supervisor did nothing except tell the complainant not to talk about it. He did not tell the harasser not to talk about it, and the harasser did talk about it. The workplace became divided, the co-workers sided with the harasser and made the plaintiff's workplace unbearable. The issue for the court, after that botched investigation, was whether the actions of co-workers in making plaintiff's life miserable could be actionable retaliation. The court found liability. Thus, a retaliation case was born of a botched investigation.

Passantino v. Johnson & Johnson Consumer Products (9th Circuit, April 2000)

In this case, the court noted that the investigation found that there was no discrimination because of a salary analysis that compared plaintiff to other male employees. However, the salary analysis used in the investigation contained false information, revealed by a comparison between the salary analysis and the actual performance evaluations of the male employees. This underlines the importance of checking source documents if they are important to the analysis. Not every document created by management will be entirely trustworthy.

Pacheco v. New Life Bakery (9th Circuit, July 1999)

The court was very critical of the investigation in this case, as it should have been. The "investigation" was conducted by the harasser's sister, assisted by the harasser's father and brother! (It was a family-owned business, and the harasser was a member of the family!) During the investigation, other female employees were not interviewed. Finally, there was no finding of harassment, even though the harasser admitted some of the conduct occurred. Along with the other significant errors made by the employer in this case, the investigation errors were particularly harmful. See "Adequacy of the Remedial Action" on page 233.

Wright v. Anixter, Inc. (9th Circuit, August 1999)

As part of the remedial action in this case, the company fired the offending supervisor within five days of the complaint. The vice president then met with employees to assure them that there would be no further harassment and no retaliation. Nonetheless, the plaintiff left the job six days later, citing a general feeling of discomfort. The court held that this could not be attributed to the employer, and the employer escaped liability.

Meadows v. County of Tulare (9th Circuit, September 1999)

This case illustrates what will happen when the employer follows through with a complete investigation, but the complainant fails to cooperate. Once plaintiff finally complained nine years after the harassment began (even though a policy was in place and she knew of the policy), the employer began an immediate independent investigation but plaintiff refused to cooperate in the investigation and offered only general descriptions of her complaint, citing a generalized fear of retaliation. The court said that the employer had no liability.

Cadena v. Pacesetter Corp. (10th Circuit, 2000)

The court found the investigation in this case to be "inadequate, if not a complete sham" where the official in charge of investigation conceded that she (1) did not speak with the complainant; (2) did not interview the alleged harasser; (3) did not interview any other potential witnesses; (4) admitted she did not know the identities of the complainant or the alleged harasser; and (5) was unsure if she had been told the nature of the complaint or its specifics.

Adequacy of the Remedial Action

Munroe v. Compaq Computer Corporation (D. New Hampshire, 2002)

In this case, the organization was unable to prevail on summary judgment on the affirmative defense because, while they acted promptly when the plaintiff complained of harassment, the organization had failed to act when previous complaints had been taken, and they failed to monitor the continuing conduct of the supervisor.

Hussain v. Long Island Railroad Company (S.D. New York, September 2002)

The court in this case found that there was a question of fact requiring a jury trial on whether the employer's response was prompt. The employer took five months to take corrective action.

Lumhoo v. The Home Depot USA (E.D. New York, September 2002)

The court held that there was a question for the jury where the employer did not respond to allegations of racial harassment prior to a physical assault, and then in response to that incident, merely put a memo in the employee's file.

Van Alstyne v. Ackerly Group, Inc. (2nd Circuit, May 2001)

The employer did a good job of remedying the harassment here once it knew about it. Plaintiff did not report it, even though she knew the policy and knew that the company had fired other employees for harassment. When she did report it, she refused to meet with the investigator, then met with the investigator only with her attorney present. The investigator went ahead and promptly met with her and her attorney within ten days, then did further investigation. During the interim, the investigator continued to check in with the complainant. The employer told the complainant that her supervisor could not terminate her. A higher level supervisor began checking in with her on a regular basis. She was told she did not have to attend meetings with her supervisor without a third party present. She was told that her supervisor had been warned that he was to have no personal contact with her. The company also offered to pay for counseling. The company also asked her if there was any further problem or anything else they could do for her, and she indicated no. Four months later, the supervisor was asked to resign. The court held that the company had established the affirmative defense as a matter of law.

Cooke v. County of Suffolk (2nd Circuit, June 2001)

This case demonstrates that, even when the harassing conduct is extremely egregious, the employer's response can insulate it from liability. Here, plaintiff was harassed for a year and claimed she was eventually raped by a supervisor. Other supervisors noticed that she appeared distressed during this time and encouraged her to disclose the problems. She revealed very little, requested confidentiality of the vague complaints she made, and refused to file a complaint despite urging from various supervisors. Finally, another supervisor filed a complaint on her behalf, and it was immediately investigated and the harasser fired. The employer was entitled to the affirmative defense because once they were made aware of the extent and nature of the complaint, they took immediate action.

Howley v. Town of Stratford (2nd Circuit, 2000)

The employer took five weeks to discipline the harasser and then only imposed a two-day weekend suspension and recommended that he apologize. He never did and the employer did not force him to. That employer was not allowed the affirmative defense.

Miller v. Woodharbor Molding & Millworks (N.D. Iowa, 2000)

Where the complainant reported the harassment to a supervisor, but no investigation was ever conducted and nothing was done, the employer lost on its bid to assert the affirmative defense.

Cardenas v. Massey (3rd Circuit, October 2001)

The court was critical of the employer's efforts at remedial action in a national origin harassment case, noting that the employer made temporary transfers of the complaining party that would have left him reporting to the same supervisors that he had complained about.

EEOC v. R&R Ventures (4th Circuit, March 2001)

In a final death knell to the employer's reliance on the affirmative defense, the employer took no remedial action at all in response to the plaintiff's complaints.

Smith v. First Union National Bank (4th Circuit, 2000)

The employer's remedy fell short when it merely instructed the harasser to improve his management style and "smile more" and refused to remove plaintiff from the alleged harasser's proximity, despite a recommendation of an EAP counselor that she should not work for the alleged harasser.

Casiano v. AT&T (5th Circuit, June 2000)

The court noted that there was an immediate suspension of the alleged harasser, and this constituted swift and appropriate remedial action.

Pollard v. E.I. DuPont de Nemours Co. (Supreme Court, 2001)

The employer's reaction in this case was to tell the male co-workers not to behave inappropriately. The court found that fell short because of substantial evidence that several members of management knew of the harassing situation, both through complaints and first-hand observation, but allowed the situation to fester without definitive action on the part of management.

Gawley v. Indiana University (7th Circuit, December 2001)

While plaintiff in a sexual harassment case contended that the act of giving a warning to the offender was inadequate, the court noted that the harassment stopped, thus providing evidence that the investigation and remedial action was effective. Plaintiff did not provide any further evidence to show that the remedial action was inadequate despite the fact that the harassment stopped. Thus, the affirmative defense was allowed.

Johnson v. West (7th Circuit, 2000)

The employer's response was adequate here, where the company separated the plaintiff and the alleged harasser and continued to investigate even after the plaintiff requested that the employer stop.

Tutman v. WBBM-TV, Inc. (7th Circuit, 2000)

The employer's response was deemed sufficient where the company promised no more contact with the harasser, reprimanded the harasser, sent him to sensitivity training, forced him to apologize, and re-circulated non-discrimination policies to employees.

Jackson v. Arkansas Department of Education (8th Circuit, December 2001)

The employer was able to use the affirmative defense because they immediately changed the hours of plaintiff and defendant so they would have no contact and checked back with the plaintiff for two weeks, every day, to see if she was comfortable with the arrangement. Ten months later, the employer discovered that the offending employee had lied during the investigation, and he was immediately terminated. The court held that the remedial action was appropriate, and the affirmative defense was allowed.

Madison v. IBP, Inc. (8th Circuit, June 2001)

In this case the employer's efforts, while starting out well, fizzled at a critical time and the employee was awarded a judgment of $1.7M. The court used the affirmative defense standards to determine the entitlement to punitive damages in a gender and race harassment case. The employee complained to the plant manager and the personnel director, but they ignored the complaints, failed to investigate, and although they claimed they counseled four people about their behavior, no documentation was included in those personnel files. The court thus found that no real discipline was administered. The court also disapproved of several practices to "discourage" the reporting of complaints, including: (1) telling the harassers the name of the person complaining and (2) placing a note in the victim's personnel file indicating "counseling for sexual harassment."

Little v. Windemere Relocation, Inc. (9th Circuit, 2002)

This case involved harassment by an "important" client, which included rape of the complainant. However, when the complainant reported to company officials that she had been raped, the officials first told her that she would be reassigned and that she should seek therapy. However, the organization's president continued to ask her how the account was developing, thus indicating that she had not been reassigned. When she disclosed the rape to the president, he told her he did not want to hear about it, then cut her pay. When she complained about the pay cut, she was told to go home and think about it for two days, because the president "did not want any clouds in the office." When she continued to complain, the president terminated her and told her to clean out her desk. The Ninth Circuit ruled that this behavior in response to the client's conduct was a continuation of the harassment, and since the company did not deal effectively with the situation, they were liable.

Taylor v. Nickels and Dimes, Inc. (N.D. Texas, 2002)

In this case, the court praised the organization for reacting swiftly and correctly when harassment was reported. The organization had a policy and instructed all its employees on the policy. They also posted a notice in the workplace. When complainant had raised allegations, she had been terminated for insubordination. She was immediately reinstated and placed on administrative leave. The investigation began immediately. The harasser was instructed not to retaliate, and work shifts were rescheduled to avoid contact between complainant and the harasser. Complainant was assigned to a different supervisor. The court indicated that the organization had satisfied the affirmative defense by its prompt and thorough response.

Nichols v. Azteca Restaurant Enterprises (9th Circuit, 2001)

In this case of male on male harassment, the Court held that the employer's efforts fell short when the complaint was received, because the employer (1) did not conduct an investigation, (2) did not speak with the offenders to correct or discipline, and (3) placed the remedial burden on the victim, by telling him that they would take action if the harassment continued, and only after he returned with another complaint. Further, the harassment did not end.

Petet v. Equity Residential Properties Trust (9th Circuit, Unpublished, August 2000)

In this case the employer never completed an investigation and rehired the harasser, but their biggest problem was that they offered to transfer the complainant. The court said the offer to transfer was itself insufficient because remedies cannot target the victim.

Passantino v. Johnson & Johnson Consumer Products (9th Circuit, April 2000)

The delicacy with which post-complaint training must be handled is illustrated by this case, where the employer chose to have an employee meeting after the complaint was investigated. At that meeting, which included all employees, management indicated that everyone should "shape up and act professionally" or they would be "off the team." While seemingly well-intentioned, the plaintiffs, because of prior communications from management discouraging complaints, interpreted this as a public rebuke directed at them.

Pacheco v. New Life Bakery (9th Circuit, July 1999)

The employer's principal defense in this case was that the harassment had stopped and that there should be no liability. The court struggled with that issue because the employer had no policy prohibiting harassment, there was no reprimand or discipline to the harasser, but the harassment for this victim stopped. The court ruled that it is not enough to escape liability to show that the harassment stopped, because the employer has done nothing to remedy the harassment. The court noted that there are two purposes to correction: (1) end the current harassment and (2) deter future harassment. While the harassment ended, either through luck or through the employer's efforts, the danger of future harassment continued unabated because of a lack of action by the employer. If harassment occurred, the result must be more than a mere request to refrain from the conduct in the future, but instead some consequences must occur to the harasser to deter future harassment.

Montero v. AGCO (9th Circuit, September 1999)

When plaintiff finally complained two years after the harassment began, the employer immediately offered her paid administrative leave during the investigation (even though the harassment had stopped four months earlier), took only eleven days from complaint to the completion of the investigation and corrective action, fired one employee, and disciplined two others. Complainant was then assured that the offenders had been disciplined and that there would be no retaliation. A new manager was hired, and the employer met with all employees and reminded them of the no retaliation rule. Plaintiff refused to return to work, and her claim was rejected.

Jones v. Illinois Department of Transportation (N.D. Illinois, November 2001)

In a case involving co-worker racial harassment, the court used the same analysis as the affirmative defense to determine whether the employer was negligent. Here the remedial action was swift, and the employer (1) suspended the offending employee for three days without pay and (2) provided updated diversity training for all. Further, the civil rights office visited the outlying offices to reinforce the "zero tolerance" policy. No further harassment occurred. The court held the employer was not negligent.

Enforcement Guidelines Issued by EEOC

EEOC Enforcement Guidance: Vicarious Employer Liability for Unlawful Harassment by Supervisors

I.   Introduction

In *Burlington Industries, Inc. v. Ellerth,* 118 S. Ct. 2257 (1998), and *Faragher v. City of Boca Raton,* 118 S. Ct. 2275 (1998), the Supreme Court made clear that employers are subject to vicarious liability for unlawful harassment by supervisors. The standard of liability set forth in these decisions is premised on two principles: (1) an employer is responsible for the acts of its supervisors and (2) employers should be encouraged to prevent harassment and employees should be encouraged to avoid or limit the harm from harassment. In order to accommodate these principles, the Court held that an employer is always liable for a supervisor's harassment if it culminates in a tangible employment action. However, if it does not, the employer may be able to avoid liability or limit damages by establishing an affirmative defense that includes two necessary elements:

(a) the employer exercised reasonable care to prevent and correct promptly any harassing behavior, and

(b) the employee unreasonably failed to take advantage of any preventive or corrective opportunities provided by the employer or to avoid harm otherwise.

While the *Faragher* and *Ellerth* decisions addressed sexual harassment, the Court's analysis drew on standards set forth in cases involving harassment on other protected bases. Moreover, the Commission has always taken the position that the same basic standards apply to all types of prohibited harassment.[1] Thus, the standard of liability set forth in the decisions applies to all forms of unlawful harassment. (See Section II, next page.)

Harassment remains a pervasive problem in American workplaces. The number of harassment charges filed with the EEOC and state fair employment practices agencies has risen significantly in recent years. For example, the number of sexual harassment charges has increased from 6,883 in fiscal year 1991 to 15,618 in fiscal year 1998. The number of racial harassment charges rose from 4,910 to 9,908 charges in the same time period.

While the anti-discrimination statutes seek to remedy discrimination, their primary purpose is to prevent violations. The Supreme Court, in *Faragher* and *Ellerth*, relied on Commission guidance that has long advised employers to take all necessary steps to prevent harassment.[2] The new affirmative defense gives credit for such preventive efforts by an employer, thereby "implement[ing] clear statutory policy and complement[ing] the Government's Title VII enforcement efforts."[3]

The question of liability arises only after there is a determination that unlawful harassment occurred. Harassment does not violate federal law unless it involves discriminatory treatment on the basis of race, color, sex, religion, national origin, age of 40 or older, disability, or protected activity under the anti-discrimination statutes. Furthermore, the anti-discrimination statutes are not a "general civility code."[4] Thus federal law does not prohibit simple teasing, offhand comments, or isolated incidents that are not "extremely serious."[5] Rather, the conduct must be "so objectively offensive as to alter the 'conditions' of the victim's employment."[6] The conditions of employment are altered only if the harassment culminated in a tangible employment action or was sufficiently severe or pervasive to create a hostile work environment.[7] Existing Commission guidance on the standards for determining whether challenged conduct rises to the level of unlawful harassment remains in effect.

This document supersedes previous Commission guidance on the issue of vicarious liability for harassment by supervisors.[8] The Commission's long-standing guidance on employer liability for harassment by co-workers remains in effect—an employer is liable if it knew or should have known of the misconduct, unless it can show that it took immediate and appropriate corrective action.[9] The standard is the same in the case of non-employees, but the employer's control over such individuals' misconduct is considered.[10]

II. The Vicarious Liability Rule Applies to Unlawful Harassment on All Covered Bases

The rule in *Ellerth* and *Faragher* regarding vicarious liability applies to harassment by supervisors based on race, color, sex (whether or not of a sexual nature[11]), religion, national origin, protected activity,[12] age, or disability.[13] Thus, employers should establish anti-harassment policies and complaint procedures covering all forms of unlawful harassment.[14]

III. Who Qualifies as a Supervisor?

A. Harasser in Supervisory Chain of Command

An employer is subject to vicarious liability for unlawful harassment if the harassment was committed by "a supervisor with immediate (or successively higher) authority over the employee."[15] Thus, it is critical to determine whether the person who engaged in unlawful harassment had supervisory authority over the complainant.

The federal employment discrimination statutes do not contain or define the term "supervisor."[16] The statutes make employers liable for the discriminatory acts of their "agents,"[17] and supervisors are agents of their employers. However, agency principles "may not be transferable in all their particulars" to the federal employment discrimination statutes.[18] The determination of whether an individual has sufficient authority to qualify as a "supervisor" for purposes of vicarious liability cannot be resolved by a purely mechanical application of agency law.[19] Rather, the purposes of the anti-discrimination statutes and the reasoning of the Supreme Court decisions on harassment must be considered.

The Supreme Court, in *Faragher* and *Ellerth*, reasoned that vicarious liability for supervisor harassment is appropriate because supervisors are aided in such misconduct by the authority that the employers delegated to them.[20] Therefore, that authority must be of a sufficient magnitude so as to assist the harasser explicitly or implicitly in carrying out the harassment. The determination as to whether a harasser had such authority is based on his or her job function rather than job title (e.g., "team leader") and must be based on the specific facts.

An individual qualifies as an employee's "supervisor" if:

a. the individual has authority to undertake or recommend tangible employment decisions affecting the employee; or

b. the individual has authority to direct the employee's daily work activities.

1. Authority to Undertake or Recommend Tangible Employment Actions

An individual qualifies as an employee's "supervisor" if he or she is authorized to undertake tangible employment decisions affecting the employee. "Tangible employment decisions" are decisions that significantly change another employee's employment status. (For a detailed explanation of what constitutes a tangible employment action, see subsection IV(B), on page 238.) Such actions include, but are not limited to, hiring, firing, promoting, demoting, and reassigning the employee. As the Supreme Court stated, "[t]angible employment actions fall within the special province of the supervisor."[21]

An individual whose job responsibilities include the authority to recommend tangible job decisions affecting an employee qualifies as his or her supervisor even if the individual does not have the final say. As the Supreme Court recognized in *Ellerth*, a tangible employment decision "may be subject to review by higher level supervisors."[22] As long as the individual's recommendation is given substantial weight by the final decision maker(s), that individual meets the definition of supervisor.

2. Authority to Direct Employee's Daily Work Activities

An individual who is authorized to direct another employee's day-to-day work activities qualifies as his or her supervisor even if that individual does not have the authority to undertake or recommend tangible job decisions. Such an individual's ability to commit harassment is enhanced by his or her authority to increase the employee's workload or assign undesirable tasks, and hence it is appropriate to consider such a person a "supervisor" when determining whether the employer is vicariously liable.

In *Faragher*, one of the harassers was authorized to hire, supervise, counsel, and discipline lifeguards, while the other harasser was responsible for making the lifeguards' daily work assignments and supervising their work and fitness training.[23] There was no question that the Court viewed them both as "supervisors," even though one of them apparently lacked authority regarding tangible job decisions.[24]

An individual who is temporarily authorized to direct another employee's daily work activities qualifies as his or her "supervisor" during that time period. Accordingly, the employer would be subject to vicarious liability if that individual commits unlawful harassment of a subordinate while serving as his or her supervisor.

On the other hand, someone who merely relays other officials' instructions regarding work assignments and reports back to those officials does not have true supervisory authority. Furthermore, someone who directs only a limited number of tasks or assignments would not qualify as a "supervisor." For example, an individual whose delegated authority is confined to coordinating a work project of limited scope is not a "supervisor."

B. Harasser Outside Supervisory Chain of Command

In some circumstances, an employer may be subject to vicarious liability for harassment by a supervisor who does not have actual authority over the employee. Such a result is appropriate if the employee reasonably believed that the harasser had such power.[25] The employee might have such a belief because, for example, the chains of command are unclear. Alternatively, the employee might reasonably believe that a harasser with broad delegated powers has the ability to significantly influence employment decisions affecting him or her even if the harasser is outside the employee's chain of command.

If the harasser had no actual supervisory power over the employee, and the employee did not reasonably believe that the harasser had such authority, then the standard of liability for co-worker harassment applies.

IV. Harassment by Supervisor That Results in a Tangible Employment Action

A. Standard of Liability

An employer is always liable for harassment by a supervisor on a prohibited basis that culminates in a tangible employment action. No affirmative defense is available in such cases.[26] The Supreme Court recognized that this result is appropriate because an employer acts through its supervisors, and a supervisor's undertaking of a tangible employment action constitutes an act of the employer.[27]

B. Definition of "Tangible Employment Action"

A tangible employment action is "a significant change in employment status."[28] Unfulfilled threats are insufficient. Characteristics of a tangible employment action are:[29]

1. A tangible employment action is the means by which the supervisor brings the official power of the enterprise to bear on subordinates, as demonstrated by the following:

    * It requires an official act of the enterprise;

    * It usually is documented in official company records;

    * It may be subject to review by higher level supervisors; and

    * It often requires the formal approval of the enterprise and use of its internal processes.

2. A tangible employment action usually inflicts direct economic harm.

3. A tangible employment action, in most instances, can only be caused by a supervisor or other person acting with the authority of the company.

    Examples of tangible employment actions include:[30]

    * Hiring and firing;

    * Promotion and failure to promote;

    * Demotion;[31]

- Undesirable reassignment;
- A decision causing a significant change in benefits;
- Compensation decisions; and
- Work assignment.

Any employment action qualifies as "tangible" if it results in a significant change in employment status. For example, significantly changing an individual's duties in his or her existing job constitutes a tangible employment action regardless of whether the individual retains the same salary and benefits.[32] Similarly, altering an individual's duties in a way that blocks his or her opportunity for promotion or salary increases also constitutes a tangible employment action.[33]

On the other hand, an employment action does not reach the threshold of "tangible" if it results in only an insignificant change in the complainant's employment status. For example, altering an individual's job title does not qualify as a tangible employment action if there is no change in salary, benefits, duties, or prestige, and the only effect is a bruised ego.[34] However, if there is a significant change in the status of the position because the new title is less prestigious and thereby effectively constitutes a demotion, a tangible employment action would be found.[35]

If a supervisor undertakes or recommends a tangible job action based on a subordinate's response to unwelcome sexual demands, the employer is liable and cannot raise the affirmative defense. The result is the same whether the employee rejects the demands and is subjected to an adverse tangible employment action or submits to the demands and consequently obtains a tangible job benefit.[36] Such harassment previously would have been characterized as "quid pro quo." It would be a perverse result if the employer is foreclosed from raising the affirmative defense if its supervisor denies a tangible job benefit based on an employee's rejection of unwelcome sexual demands, but can raise the defense if its supervisor grants a tangible job benefit based on submission to such demands. The Commission rejects such an analysis. In both those situations the supervisor undertakes a tangible employment action on a discriminatory basis. The Supreme Court stated that there must be a significant change in employment status; it did not require that the change be adverse in order to qualify as tangible.[37]

If a challenged employment action is not "tangible," it may still be considered, along with other evidence, as part of a hostile environment claim that is subject to the affirmative defense. In *Ellerth*, the Court concluded that there was no tangible employment action because the supervisor never carried out his threats of job harm. *Ellerth* could still proceed with her claim of harassment, but the claim was properly "categorized as a hostile work environment claim which requires a showing of severe or pervasive conduct." 118 S. Ct. at 2265.

C. Link Between Harassment and Tangible Employment Action

When harassment culminates in a tangible employment action, the employer cannot raise the affirmative defense. This sort of claim is analyzed like any other case in which a challenged employment action is alleged to be discriminatory. If the employer produces evidence of a non-discriminatory explanation for the tangible employment action, a determination must be made whether that explanation is a pretext designed to hide a discriminatory motive.

For example, if an employee alleged that she was demoted because she refused her supervisor's sexual advances, a determination would have to be made whether the demotion was because of her response to the advances, and hence because of her sex. Similarly, if an employee alleges that he was discharged after being subjected to severe or pervasive harassment by his supervisor based on his national origin, a determination would have to be made whether the discharge was because of the employee's national origin.

A strong inference of discrimination will arise whenever a harassing supervisor undertakes or has significant input into a tangible employment action affecting the victim,[38] because it can be "assume[d] that the harasser . . . could not act as an objective, non-discriminatory decision maker with respect to the plaintiff."[39] However, if the employer produces evidence of a non-discriminatory reason for the action, the employee will have to prove that the asserted reason was a pretext designed to hide the true discriminatory motive.

If it is determined that the tangible action was based on a discriminatory reason linked to the preceding harassment, relief could be sought for the entire pattern of misconduct culminating in the tangible employment action, and no affirmative defense is available.[40] However, the harassment preceding the tangible employment action must be severe or pervasive in order to be actionable.[41] If the tangible employment action was based on a non-discriminatory motive, then the employer would have an opportunity to raise the affirmative defense to a claim based on the preceding harassment.[42]

V. Harassment by Supervisor That Does Not Result in a Tangible Employment Action

A. Standard of Liability

When harassment by a supervisor creates an unlawful hostile environment but does not result in a tangible employment action, the employer can raise an affirmative defense to liability or damages, which it must prove by a preponderance of the evidence. The defense consists of two necessary elements:

(a) the employer exercised reasonable care to prevent and correct promptly any harassment; and

(b) the employee unreasonably failed to take advantage of any preventive or corrective opportunities provided by the employer or to avoid harm otherwise.

B. Effect of Standard

If an employer can prove that it discharged its duty of reasonable care and that the employee could have avoided all of the harm but unreasonably failed to do so, the employer will avoid all liability for unlawful harassment.[43] For example, if an employee was subjected to a pattern of disability-based harassment that created an unlawful hostile environment, but the employee unreasonably failed to complain to management before she suffered emotional harm and the employer exercised reasonable care to prevent and promptly correct the harassment, then the employer will avoid all liability.

If an employer cannot prove that it discharged its duty of reasonable care and that the employee unreasonably failed to avoid the harm, the employer will be liable. For example, if unlawful harassment by a supervisor occurred and the employer failed to exercise reasonable care to prevent it, the employer will be liable even if the employee unreasonably failed to complain to management or even if the employer took prompt and appropriate corrective action when it gained notice.[44]

In most circumstances, if employers and employees discharge their respective duties of reasonable care, unlawful harassment will be prevented and there will be no reason to consider questions of liability. An effective complaint procedure "encourages employees to report harassing conduct before it becomes severe or pervasive,"[45] and if an employee promptly utilizes that procedure, the employer can usually stop the harassment before actionable harm occurs.[46]

In some circumstances, however, unlawful harassment will occur and harm will result despite the exercise of requisite legal care by the employer and employee. For example, if an employee's supervisor directed frequent, egregious racial epithets at him that caused emotional harm virtually from the outset, and the employee promptly complained, corrective action by the employer could prevent further harm but might not correct the actionable harm that the employee already had suffered.[47] Alternatively, if an employee complained about harassment before it became severe or pervasive, remedial measures undertaken by the employer might fail to stop the harassment before it reaches an actionable level, even if those measures are reasonably calculated to halt it. In these circumstances, the employer will be liable because the defense requires proof that it exercised reasonable legal care and that the employee unreasonably failed to avoid the harm. While a notice-based negligence standard would absolve the employer of liability, the standard set forth in *Ellerth* and *Faragher* does not. As the Court explained, vicarious liability sets a "more stringent standard" for the employer than the "minimum standard" of negligence theory.[48]

While this result may seem harsh to a law-abiding employer, it is consistent with liability standards under the anti-discrimination statutes which generally make employers responsible for the discriminatory acts of their supervisors.[49] If, for example, a supervisor rejects a candidate for promotion because of national origin–based bias, the employer will be liable regardless of whether the employee complained to higher management and regardless of whether higher management had any knowledge about the supervisor's motivation.[50] Harassment is the only type of discrimination carried out by a supervisor for which an employer can avoid liability, and that limitation must be construed narrowly. The employer will be shielded from liability for harassment by a supervisor only if it proves that it exercised reasonable care in preventing and correcting the harassment and that the employee unreasonably failed to avoid all of the harm. If both parties exercise reasonable care, the defense will fail.

In some cases, an employer will be unable to avoid liability completely, but may be able to establish the affirmative defense as a means to limit damages.[51] The defense only limits damages where the employee reasonably could have avoided some but not all of the harm from the harassment. In the example above, in which the supervisor used frequent, egregious racial epithets, an unreasonable delay by the employee in complaining could limit damages but not eliminate liability entirely. This is because a reasonably prompt complaint would have reduced, but not eliminated, the actionable harm.[52]

C. First Prong of Affirmative Defense: Employer's Duty to Exercise Reasonable Care

The first prong of the affirmative defense requires a showing by the employer that it undertook reasonable care to prevent and promptly correct harassment. Such reasonable care generally requires an employer to establish, disseminate, and enforce an anti-harassment policy and complaint procedure and to take other reasonable steps to prevent and correct harassment. The steps described below are not mandatory requirements—whether or not an employer can prove that it exercised reasonable care depends on the particular factual circumstances and, in some cases, the nature of the employer's workforce. Small employers may be able to effectively prevent and correct harassment through informal means, while larger employers may have to institute more formal mechanisms.[53]

There are no "safe harbors" for employers based on the written content of policies and procedures. Even the best policy and complaint procedure will not alone satisfy the burden of proving reasonable care if, in the particular circumstances of a claim, the employer failed to implement its process effectively.[54] If, for example, the employer has an adequate policy and complaint procedure and properly responded to an employee's complaint of harassment, but management ignored previous complaints by other employees about the same harasser, then the employer has not exercised reasonable care in preventing the harassment.[55] Similarly, if the employer has an adequate policy and complaint procedure but an official failed to carry out his or her responsibility to conduct an effective investigation of a harassment complaint, the employer has not discharged its duty to exercise reasonable care. Alternatively, lack of a formal policy and complaint procedure will not defeat the defense if the employer exercised sufficient care through other means.

1. Policy and Complaint Procedure

It generally is necessary for employers to establish, publicize, and enforce anti-harassment policies and complaint procedures. As the Supreme Court stated, "Title VII is designed to encourage the creation of anti-harassment policies and effective grievance mechanisms." *Ellerth*, 118 S. Ct. at 2270. While the Court noted that this "is not necessary in every instance as a matter of law,"[56] failure to do so will make it difficult for an employer to prove that it exercised reasonable care to prevent and correct harassment.[57] (See Section V(C)(3), on page 251, for discussion of preventive and corrective measures by small businesses.)

An employer should provide every employee with a copy of the policy and complaint procedure, and redistribute it periodically. The policy and complaint procedure should be written in a way that will be understood by all employees in the employer's workforce. Other measures to ensure effective dissemination of the policy and complaint procedure include posting them in central locations and incorporating them into employee handbooks. If feasible, the employer should provide training to all employees to ensure that they understand their rights and responsibilities.

An anti-harassment policy and complaint procedure should contain, at a minimum, the following elements:

- A clear explanation of prohibited conduct;
- Assurance that employees who make complaints of harassment or provide information related to such complaints will be protected against retaliation;
- A clearly described complaint process that provides accessible avenues of complaint;
- Assurance that the employer will protect the confidentiality of harassment complaints to the extent possible;

- A complaint process that provides a prompt, thorough, and impartial investigation; and

- Assurance that the employer will take immediate and appropriate corrective action when it determines that harassment has occurred.

The above elements are explained in the following subsections.

a. Prohibition Against Harassment An employer's policy should make clear that it will not tolerate harassment based on sex (with or without sexual conduct), race, color, religion, national origin, age, disability, and protected activity (i.e., opposition to prohibited discrimination or participation in the statutory complaint process). This prohibition should cover harassment by anyone in the workplace—supervisors, co-workers, or non-employees.[58] Management should convey the seriousness of the prohibition. One way to do that is for the mandate to "come from the top," i.e., from upper management.

The policy should encourage employees to report harassment before it becomes severe or pervasive. While isolated incidents of harassment generally do not violate federal law, a pattern of such incidents may be unlawful. Therefore, to discharge its duty of preventive care, the employer must make clear to employees that it will stop harassment before it rises to the level of a violation of federal law.

b. Protection Against Retaliation An employer should make clear that it will not tolerate adverse treatment of employees because they report harassment or provide information related to such complaints. An anti-harassment policy and complaint procedure will not be effective without such an assurance.[59]

Management should undertake whatever measures are necessary to ensure that retaliation does not occur. For example, when management investigates a complaint of harassment, the official who interviews the parties and witnesses should remind these individuals about the prohibition against retaliation. Management also should scrutinize employment decisions affecting the complainant and witnesses during and after the investigation to ensure that such decisions are not based on retaliatory motives.

c. Effective Complaint Process An employer's harassment complaint procedure should be designed to encourage victims to come forward. To that end, it should clearly explain the process and ensure that there are no unreasonable obstacles to complaints. A complaint procedure should not be rigid, since that could defeat the goal of preventing and correcting harassment. When an employee complains to management about alleged harassment, the employer is obligated to investigate the allegation regardless of whether it conforms to a particular format or is made in writing.

The complaint procedure should provide accessible points of contact for the initial complaint.[60] A complaint process is not effective if employees are always required to complain first to their supervisors about alleged harassment, since the supervisor may be a harasser.[61] Moreover, reasonable care in preventing and correcting harassment requires an employer to instruct all supervisors to report complaints of harassment to appropriate officials.[62]

It is advisable for an employer to designate at least one official outside an employee's chain of command to take complaints of harassment. For example, if the employer has an office of human resources, one or more officials in that office could be authorized to take complaints. Allowing an employee to bypass his or her chain of command provides additional assurance that the complaint will be handled in an impartial manner, since an employee who reports harassment by his or her supervisor may feel that officials within the chain of command will more readily believe the supervisor's version of events.

It also is important for an employer's anti-harassment policy and complaint procedure to contain information about the time frames for filing charges of unlawful harassment with the EEOC or state fair employment practice agencies and to explain that the deadline runs from the last date of unlawful harassment, not from the date that the complaint to the employer is resolved.[63] While a prompt complaint process should make it feasible for an employee to delay deciding whether to file a charge until the complaint to the employer is resolved, he or she is not required to do so.[64]

d. Confidentiality   An employer should make clear to employees that it will protect the confidentiality of harassment allegations to the extent possible. An employer cannot guarantee complete confidentiality, since it cannot conduct an effective investigation without revealing certain information to the alleged harasser and potential witnesses. However, information about the allegation of harassment should be shared only with those who need to know about it. Records relating to harassment complaints should be kept confidential on the same basis.[65]

A conflict between an employee's desire for confidentiality and the employer's duty to investigate may arise if an employee informs a supervisor about alleged harassment, but asks him or her to keep the matter confidential and take no action. Inaction by the supervisor in such circumstances could lead to employer liability. While it may seem reasonable to let the employee determine whether to pursue a complaint, the employer must discharge its duty to prevent and correct harassment.[66] One mechanism to help avoid such conflicts would be for the employer to set up an informational phone line which employees can use to discuss questions or concerns about harassment on an anonymous basis.[67]

e. Effective Investigative Process An employer should set up a mechanism for a prompt, thorough, and impartial investigation into alleged harassment. As soon as management learns about alleged harassment, it should determine whether a detailed fact-finding investigation is necessary. For example, if the alleged harasser does not deny the accusation, there would be no need to interview witnesses, and the employer could immediately determine appropriate corrective action.

If a fact-finding investigation is necessary, it should be launched immediately. The amount of time that it will take to complete the investigation will depend on the particular circumstances.[68] If, for example, multiple individuals were allegedly harassed, then it will take longer to interview the parties and witnesses.

It may be necessary to undertake intermediate measures before completing the investigation to ensure that further harassment does not occur. Examples of such measures are making scheduling changes so as to avoid contact between the parties; transferring the alleged harasser; or placing the alleged harasser on non-disciplinary leave with pay pending the conclusion of the investigation. The complainant should not be involuntarily transferred or otherwise burdened, since such measures could constitute unlawful retaliation.

The employer should ensure that the individual who conducts the investigation will objectively gather and consider the relevant facts. The alleged harasser should not have supervisory authority over the individual who conducts the investigation and should not have any direct or indirect control over the investigation. Whoever conducts the investigation should be well-trained in the skills that are required for interviewing witnesses and evaluating credibility.

i. Questions to Ask Parties and Witnesses When detailed fact-finding is necessary, the investigator should interview the complainant, the alleged harasser, and third parties who could reasonably be expected to have relevant information. Information relating to the personal lives of the parties outside the workplace would be relevant only in unusual circumstances. When interviewing the parties and witnesses, the investigator should refrain from offering his or her opinion.

The following are examples of questions that may be appropriate to ask the parties and potential witnesses. Any actual investigation must be tailored to the particular facts.

Questions to Ask the Complainant

- Who, what, when, where, and how: Who committed the alleged harassment? What exactly occurred or was said? When did it occur and is it still ongoing? Where did it occur? How often did it occur? How did it affect you?

- How did you react? What response did you make when the incident(s) occurred or afterwards?

- How did the harassment affect you? Has your job been affected in any way?
- Are there any persons who have relevant information? Was anyone present when the alleged harassment occurred? Did you tell anyone about it? Did anyone see you immediately after episodes of alleged harassment?
- Did the person who harassed you harass anyone else? Do you know whether anyone complained about harassment by that person?
- Are there any notes, physical evidence, or other documentation regarding the incident(s)?
- How would you like to see the situation resolved?
- Do you know of any other relevant information?

Questions to Ask the Alleged Harasser

- What is your response to the allegations?
- If the harasser claims that the allegations are false, ask why the complainant might lie.
- Are there any persons who have relevant information?
- Are there any notes, physical evidence, or other documentation regarding the incident(s)?
- Do you know of any other relevant information?

Questions to Ask Third Parties

- What did you see or hear? When did this occur? Describe the alleged harasser's behavior toward the complainant and toward others in the workplace.
- What did the complainant tell you? When did s/he tell you this?
- Do you know of any other relevant information?
- Are there other persons who have relevant information?

ii. Credibility Determinations If there are conflicting versions of relevant events, the employer will have to weigh each party's credibility. Credibility assessments can be critical in determining whether the alleged harassment in fact occurred. Factors to consider include:

- Inherent plausibility: Is the testimony believable on its face? Does it make sense?
- Demeanor: Did the person seem to be telling the truth or lying?
- Motive to falsify: Did the person have a reason to lie?

- Corroboration: Is there witness testimony (such as testimony by eye-witnesses, people who saw the person soon after the alleged incidents, or people who discussed the incidents with him or her at around the time that they occurred) or physical evidence (such as written documentation) that corroborates the party's testimony?

- Past record: Did the alleged harasser have a history of similar behavior in the past?

None of the above factors are determinative as to credibility. For example, the fact that there are no eye-witnesses to the alleged harassment by no means necessarily defeats the complainant's credibility, since harassment often occurs behind closed doors. Furthermore, the fact that the alleged harasser engaged in similar behavior in the past does not necessarily mean that he or she did so again.

iii. Reaching a Determination Once all of the evidence is in, interviews are finalized, and credibility issues are resolved, management should make a determination as to whether harassment occurred. That determination could be made by the investigator, or by a management official who reviews the investigator's report. The parties should be informed of the determination.

In some circumstances, it may be difficult for management to reach a determination because of direct contradictions between the parties and a lack of documentary or eye-witness corroboration. In such cases, a credibility assessment may form the basis for a determination, based on factors such as those set forth above.

If no determination can be made because the evidence is inconclusive, the employer should still undertake further preventive measures, such as training and monitoring.

f. Assurance of Immediate and Appropriate Corrective Action An employer should make clear that it will undertake immediate and appropriate corrective action, including discipline, whenever it determines that harassment has occurred in violation of the employer's policy. Management should inform both parties about these measures.[69]

Remedial measures should be designed to stop the harassment, correct its effects on the employee, and ensure that the harassment does not recur. These remedial measures need not be those that the employee requests or prefers, as long as they are effective.

In determining disciplinary measures, management should keep in mind that the employer could be found liable if the harassment does not stop. At the same time, management may have concerns that overly punitive measures may subject the employer to claims such as wrongful discharge, and may simply be inappropriate.

To balance the competing concerns, disciplinary measures should be proportional to the seriousness of the offense.[70] If the harassment was minor, such as a small number of "off-color" remarks by an individual with no prior history of similar misconduct, then counseling and an oral warning might be all that is necessary. On the other hand, if the harassment was severe or persistent, then suspension or discharge may be appropriate.[71]

Remedial measures should not adversely affect the complainant. Thus, for example, if it is necessary to separate the parties, then the harasser should be transferred (unless the complainant prefers otherwise).[72] Remedial responses that penalize the complainant could constitute unlawful retaliation and are not effective in correcting the harassment.[73]

Remedial measures also should correct the effects of the harassment. Such measures should be designed to put the employee in the position s/he would have been in had the misconduct not occurred.

Examples of Measures to Stop the Harassment and Ensure That It Does Not Recur

- Oral[74] or written warning or reprimand;
- Transfer or reassignment;
- Demotion;
- Reduction of wages;
- Suspension;
- Discharge;
- Training or counseling of harasser to ensure that s/he understands why his or her conduct violated the employer's anti-harassment policy; and
- Monitoring of harasser to ensure that harassment stops.

Examples of Measures to Correct the Effects of the Harassment

- Restoration of leave taken because of the harassment;
- Expungement of negative evaluation(s) in employee's personnel file that arose from the harassment;
- Reinstatement;
- Apology by the harasser;
- Monitoring treatment of employee to ensure that s/he is not subjected to retaliation by the harasser or others in the workplace because of the complaint; and
- Correction of any other harm caused by the harassment (e.g., compensation for losses).

2. Other Preventive and Corrective Measures

An employer's responsibility to exercise reasonable care to prevent and correct harassment is not limited to implementing an anti-harassment policy and complaint procedure. As the Supreme Court stated, "the employer has a greater opportunity to guard against misconduct by supervisors than by common workers; employers have greater opportunity and incentive to screen them, train them, and monitor their performance." *Faragher*, 118 S. Ct. at 2291.

An employer's duty to exercise due care includes instructing all of its supervisors and managers to address or report to appropriate officials complaints of harassment regardless of whether they are officially designated to take complaints[75] and regardless of whether a complaint was framed in a way that conforms to the organization's particular complaint procedures.[76] For example, if an employee files an EEOC charge alleging unlawful harassment, the employer should launch an internal investigation even if the employee did not complain to management through its internal complaint process.

Furthermore, due care requires management to correct harassment regardless of whether an employee files an internal complaint, if the conduct is clearly unwelcome. For example, if there are areas in the workplace with graffiti containing racial or sexual epithets, management should eliminate the graffiti and not wait for an internal complaint.[77]

An employer should ensure that its supervisors and managers understand their responsibilities under the organization's anti-harassment policy and complaint procedure. Periodic training of those individuals can help achieve that result. Such training should explain the types of conduct that violate the employer's anti-harassment policy; the seriousness of the policy; the responsibilities of supervisors and managers when they learn of alleged harassment; and the prohibition against retaliation.

An employer should keep track of its supervisors' and managers' conduct to make sure that they carry out their responsibilities under the organization's anti-harassment program.[78] For example, an employer could include such compliance in formal evaluations.

Reasonable preventive measures include screening applicants for supervisory jobs to see if any have a record of engaging in harassment. If so, it may be necessary for the employer to reject a candidate on that basis or to take additional steps to prevent harassment by that individual.

Finally, it is advisable for an employer to keep records of all complaints of harassment. Without such records, the employer could be unaware of a pattern of harassment by the same individual. Such a pattern would be relevant to credibility assessments and disciplinary measures.[79]

3. Small Businesses

It may not be necessary for an employer of a small workforce to implement the type of formal complaint process described previously. If it puts into place an effective, informal mechanism to prevent and correct harassment, a small employer could still satisfy the first prong of the affirmative defense to a claim of harassment.[80] As the Court recognized in *Faragher*, an employer of a small workforce might informally exercise sufficient care to prevent harassment.[81]

For example, such an employer's failure to disseminate a written policy against harassment on protected bases would not undermine the affirmative defense if it effectively communicated the prohibition and an effective complaint procedure to all employees at staff meetings. An owner of a small business who regularly meets with all of his or her employees might tell them at monthly staff meetings that he or she will not tolerate harassment and that anyone who experiences harassment should bring it "straight to the top."

If a complaint is made, the business, like any other employer, must conduct a prompt, thorough, and impartial investigation and undertake swift and appropriate corrective action where appropriate. The questions set forth in Section V(C)(1)(e)(i), on page 246, can help guide the inquiry and the factors set forth in Section V(C)(1)(e)(ii) should be considered in evaluating the credibility of each of the parties.

D. Second Prong of Affirmative Defense: Employee's Duty to Exercise Reasonable Care

The second prong of the affirmative defense requires a showing by the employer that the aggrieved employee "unreasonably failed to take advantage of any preventive or corrective opportunities provided by the employer or to avoid harm otherwise." *Faragher*, 118 S. Ct. at 2293; *Ellerth*, 118 S. Ct. at 2270.

This element of the defense arises from the general theory "that a victim has a duty 'to use such means as are reasonable under the circumstances to avoid or minimize the damages' that result from violations of the statute." *Faragher*, 18 S. Ct. at 2292, quoting *Ford Motor Co. v. EEOC*, 458 U.S. 219, 231 n.15 (1982). Thus an employer who exercised reasonable care as described in subsection V(C), on page 242, is not liable for unlawful harassment if the aggrieved employee could have avoided all of the actionable harm. If some but not all of the harm could have been avoided, then an award of damages will be mitigated accordingly.[82]

A complaint by an employee does not automatically defeat the employer's affirmative defense. If, for example, the employee provided no information to support his or her allegation, gave untruthful information, or otherwise failed to cooperate in the investigation, the complaint would not qualify as an effort to avoid harm. Furthermore, if the employee unreasonably delayed complaining, and an earlier complaint could have reduced the harm, then the affirmative defense could operate to reduce damages.

Proof that the employee unreasonably failed to use any complaint procedure provided by the employer will normally satisfy the employer's burden.[83] However, it is important to emphasize that an employee who failed to complain does not carry a burden of proving the reasonableness of that decision. Rather, the burden lies with the employer to prove that the employee's failure to complain was unreasonable.

1. Failure to Complain

A determination as to whether an employee unreasonably failed to complain or otherwise avoid harm depends on the particular circumstances and information available to the employee at that time.[84] An employee should not necessarily be expected to complain to management immediately after the first or second incident of relatively minor harassment. Workplaces need not become battlegrounds where every minor, unwelcome remark based on race, sex, or another protected category triggers a complaint and investigation. An employee might reasonably ignore a small number of incidents, hoping that the harassment will stop without resort to the complaint process.[85] The employee may directly say to the harasser that s/he wants the misconduct to stop, and then wait to see if that is effective in ending the harassment before complaining to management. If the harassment persists, however, then further delay in complaining might be found unreasonable.

There might be other reasonable explanations for an employee's delay in complaining or entire failure to utilize the employer's complaint process. For example, the employee might have had reason to believe that:[86]

- Using the complaint mechanism entailed a risk of retaliation;
- There were obstacles to complaints; and
- The complaint mechanism was not effective.

To establish the second prong of the affirmative defense, the employer must prove that the belief or perception underlying the employee's failure to complain was unreasonable.

a. Risk of Retaliation   An employer cannot establish that an employee unreasonably failed to use its complaint procedure if that employee reasonably feared retaliation. Surveys have shown that employees who are subjected to harassment frequently do not complain to management due to fear of retaliation.[87] To assure employees that such a fear is unwarranted, the employer must clearly communicate and enforce a policy that no employee will be retaliated against for complaining of harassment.

b. Obstacles to Complaints An employee's failure to use the employer's complaint procedure would be reasonable if that failure was based on unnecessary obstacles to complaints. For example, if the process entailed undue expense by the employee,[88] inaccessible points of contact for making complaints,[89] or unnecessarily intimidating or burdensome requirements, failure to invoke it on such a basis would be reasonable.

An employee's failure to participate in a mandatory mediation or other alternative dispute resolution process also does not constitute unreasonable failure to avoid harm. While an employee can be expected to cooperate in the employer's investigation by providing relevant information, an employee can never be required to waive rights, either substantive or procedural, as an element of his or her exercise of reasonable care.[90] Nor must an employee have to try to resolve the matter with the harasser as an element of exercising due care.

c. Perception That Complaint Process Was Ineffective An employer cannot establish the second prong of the defense based on the employee's failure to complain if that failure was based on a reasonable belief that the process was ineffective. For example, an employee would have a reasonable basis to believe that the complaint process is ineffective if the procedure required the employee to complain initially to the harassing supervisor. Such a reasonable basis also would be found if he or she was aware of instances in which co-workers' complaints failed to stop harassment. One way to increase employees' confidence in the efficacy of the complaint process would be for the employer to release general information to employees about corrective and disciplinary measures undertaken to stop harassment.[91]

2. Other Efforts to Avoid Harm

Generally, an employer can prove the second prong of the affirmative defense if the employee unreasonably failed to utilize its complaint process. However, such proof will not establish the defense if the employee made other efforts to avoid harm.

For example, a prompt complaint by the employee to the EEOC or a state fair employment practices agency while the harassment is ongoing could qualify as such an effort. A union grievance could also qualify as an effort to avoid harm.[92] Similarly, a staffing firm worker who is harassed at the client's workplace might report the harassment either to the staffing firm or to the client, reasonably expecting that either would act to correct the problem.[93] Thus the worker's failure to complain to one of those entities would not bar him or her from subsequently bringing a claim against it.

With these and any other efforts to avoid harm, the timing of the complaint could affect liability or damages. If the employee could have avoided some of the harm by complaining earlier, then damages would be mitigated accordingly.

VI. Harassment by "Alter Ego" of Employer

A. Standard of Liability

An employer is liable for unlawful harassment whenever the harasser is of a sufficiently high rank to fall "within that class . . . who may be treated as the organization's proxy." *Faragher*, 118 S. Ct. at 2284.[94] In such circumstances, the official's unlawful harassment is imputed automatically to the employer.[95] Thus the employer cannot raise the affirmative defense, even if the harassment did not result in a tangible employment action.

B. Officials Who Qualify as "Alter Egos" or "Proxies"

The Court, in *Faragher*, cited the following examples of officials whose harassment could be imputed automatically to the employer:

- President[96]
- Owner[97]
- Partner[98]
- Corporate officer

Faragher, 118 S. Ct. at 2284

VII. Conclusion

The Supreme Court's rulings in *Ellerth* and *Faragher* create an incentive for employers to implement and enforce strong policies prohibiting harassment and effective complaint procedures. The rulings also create an incentive for employees to alert management about harassment before it becomes severe and pervasive. If employers and employees undertake these steps, unlawful harassment can often be prevented, thereby effectuating an important goal of the anti-discrimination statutes.

Notes

[1]See, e.g., 29 C.F.R. § 1604.11 n. 1 ("The principles involved here continue to apply to race, color, religion or national origin"); EEOC Compliance Manual Section 615.11(a) (BNA) 615:0025 ("Title VII law and agency principles will guide the determination of whether an employer is liable for age harassment by its supervisors, employees, or non-employees").

[2]See 1980 Guidelines at 29 C.F.R. § 1604.11(f) and Policy Guidance on Current Issues of Sexual Harassment, Section E, 8 FEP Manual 405:6699 (Mar. 19, 1990), quoted in *Faragher*, 118 S. Ct. at 2292.

[3]*Faragher*, 118 S. Ct. at 2292.

[4]*Oncale v. Sundowner Offshore Services, Inc.*, 118 S. Ct. 998, 1002 (1998).

[5]*Faragher,* 118 S. Ct. at 2283. However, when isolated incidents that are not "extremely serious" come to the attention of management, appropriate corrective action should still be taken so that they do not escalate. See Section V(C)(1)(a), on page 244.

[6]*Oncale,* 118 S. Ct. at 1003.

[7]Some previous Commission documents classified harassment as either "quid pro quo" or hostile environment. However, it is now more useful to distinguish between harassment that results in a tangible employment action and harassment that creates a hostile work environment, since that dichotomy determines whether the employer can raise the affirmative defense to vicarious liability. Guidance on the definition of "tangible employment action" appears in Section IV(B), on page 238.

[8]The guidance in this document applies to federal sector employers, as well as all other employers covered by the statutes enforced by the Commission.

[9]29 C.F.R. § 1604.11(d).

[10]The Commission will rescind Subsection 1604.11(c) of the 1980 Guidelines on Sexual Harassment, 29 CFR § 1604.11(c). In addition, the following Commission guidance is no longer in effect: Subsection D of the 1990 Policy Statement on Current Issues in Sexual Harassment ("Employer Liability for Harassment by Supervisors"), EEOC Compliance Manual (BNA) N:4050–58 (3/19/90); and EEOC Compliance Manual Section 615.3(c) (BNA) 6:15–0007–0008.

    The remaining portions of the 1980 Guidelines, the 1990 Policy Statement, and Section 615 of the Compliance Manual remain in effect. Other Commission guidance on harassment also remains in effect, including the Enforcement Guidance on *Harris v. Forklift Sys., Inc.*, EEOC Compliance Manual (BNA) N:4071 (3/8/94) and the Policy Guidance on Employer Liability for Sexual Favoritism, EEOC Compliance Manual (BNA) N:5051 (3/19/90).

[11]Harassment that is targeted at an individual because of his or her sex violates Title VII even if it does not involve sexual comments or conduct. Thus, for example, frequent, derogatory remarks about women could constitute unlawful harassment even if the remarks are not sexual in nature. See 1990 Policy Guidance on Current Issues of Sexual Harassment, subsection C(4) ("sex-based harassment—that is, harassment not involving sexual activity or language—may also give rise to Title VII liability . . . if it is 'sufficiently patterned or pervasive' and directed at employees because of their sex").

[12]"Protected activity" means opposition to discrimination or participation in proceedings covered by the anti-discrimination statutes. Harassment based on protected activity can constitute unlawful retaliation. See EEOC Compliance Manual Section 8 ("Retaliation") (BNA) 614:001 (May 20, 1998).

[13]For cases applying *Ellerth* and *Faragher* to harassment on different bases, see *Hafford v. Seidner*, 167 F. 3d 1074, 1080 (6th Cir. 1999) (religion and race); *Breeding v. Arthur J. Gallagher and Co.*, 164 F. 3d 1151, 1158 (8th Cir. 1999) (age); *Allen v. Michigan Department of Corrections*, 165 F. 3d 405, 411 (6th Cir. 1999) (race); *Richmond-Hopes v. City of Cleveland*, No. 97–3595, 1998 WL 808222 at *9 (6th Cir. Nov. 16, 1998) (unpublished) (retaliation); *Wright-Simmons v. City of Oklahoma City*, 155 F. 3d 1264, 1270 (10th Cir. 1998) (race); *Gotfryd v. Book Covers, Inc.*, No. 97 C 7696, 1999 WL 20925 at *5 (N.D. Ill. Jan. 7, 1999) (national origin). See also *Wallin v. Minnesota Department of Corrections*, 153 F. 3d 681, 687 (8th Cir. 1998) (assuming without deciding that ADA hostile environment claims are modeled after Title VII claims), cert. denied, 119 S. Ct. 1141 (1999).

[14]The majority's analysis in both *Faragher* and *Ellerth* drew on the liability standards for harassment on other protected bases. It is therefore clear that the same standards apply. See *Faragher*, 118 S. Ct. at 2283 (in determining appropriate standard of liability for sexual harassment by supervisors, Court "drew upon cases recognizing liability for discriminatory harassment based on race and national origin"); *Ellerth*, 118 S. Ct. at 2268 (Court imported concept of "tangible employment action" in race, age, and national origin discrimination cases for resolution of vicarious liability in sexual harassment cases). See also cases cited in n.13, above.

[15]*Ellerth*, 118 S. Ct. at 2270; *Faragher*, 118 S. Ct. at 2293.

[16]Numerous statutes contain the word "supervisor," and some contain definitions of the term. See, e.g., 12 U.S.C. § 1813(r) (definition of "State bank supervisor" in legislation regarding Federal Deposit Insurance Corporation); 29 U.S.C. § 152(11) (definition of "supervisor" in National Labor Relations Act); 42 U.S.C. § 8262(2) (definition of "facility energy supervisor" in Federal Energy Initiative legislation). The definitions vary depending on the purpose and structure of each statute. The definition of the word "supervisor" under other statutes does not control, and is not affected by, the meaning of that term under the employment discrimination statutes.

[17]See 42 U.S.C. 2000e(a) (Title VII); 29 U.S.C. 630(b) (ADEA); and 42 U.S.C. §12111(5)(A) (ADA) (all defining "employer" as including any agent of the employer).

[18]*Meritor Savings Bank, FSB v. Vinson*, 477 U.S. 57, 72 (1986); *Faragher*, 118 S. Ct. at 2290 n.3; *Ellerth*, 118 S. Ct. at 2266.

[19]See *Faragher*, 118 S. Ct. at 2288 (analysis of vicarious liability "calls not for a mechanical application of indefinite and malleable factors set forth in the restatement . . . but rather an inquiry into the reasons that would support a conclusion that harassing behavior ought to be held within the scope of a supervisor's employment . . . ") and at 2290 n.3 (agency concepts must be adapted to the practical objectives of the antidiscrimination statutes).

[20]*Faragher*, 118 S. Ct. at 2290; *Ellerth*, 118 S. Ct. at 2269.

[21]*Ellerth*, 118 S. Ct. at 2269.

[22]*Ellerth*, 118 S. Ct. at 2269.

[23]*Faragher*, 118 S. Ct. at 2280. For a more detailed discussion of the harassers' job responsibilities, see *Faragher*, 864 F. Supp. 1552, 1563 (S.D. Fla. 1994).

[24]See *Grozdanich v. Leisure Hills Health Center*, 25 F. Supp. 2d 953, 973 (D. Minn., 1998) ("it is evident that the Supreme Court views the term 'supervisor' as more expansive than as merely including those employees whose opinions are dispositive on hiring, firing, and promotion"; thus, "charge nurse" who had authority to control plaintiff's daily activities and recommend discipline qualified as "supervisor" and therefore rendered employer vicariously liable under Title VII for his harassment of plaintiff, subject to affirmative defense).

[25]See *Ellerth*, 118 S. Ct. at 2268 ("If, in the unusual case, it is alleged there is a false impression that the actor was a supervisor, when he in fact was not, the victim's mistaken conclusion must be a reasonable one"); *Llampallas v. Mini-Circuit Lab, Inc.*, 163 F. 3d 1236, 1247 (11th Cir. 1998) ("Although the employer may argue that the employee had no actual authority to take the employment action against the plaintiff, apparent authority serves just as well to impute liability to the employer for the employee's action").

[26]Of course, traditional principles of mitigation of damages apply in these cases, as well as all other employment discrimination cases. See generally *Ford Motor Co. v. EEOC*, 458 U.S. 219 (1982).

[27]*Ellerth*, 118 S. Ct. at 2269; *Faragher*, 118 S. Ct. 2284–85. See also *Durham Life Insurance Co., v. Evans*, 166 F. 3d 139, 152 (3rd Cir. 1999) ("A supervisor can only take a tangible adverse employment action because of the authority delegated by the employer . . . and thus the employer is properly charged with the consequences of that delegation").

[28]*Ellerth*, 118 S. Ct. at 2268.

[29]All listed criteria are set forth in *Ellerth*, 118 S. Ct. at 2269.

[30]All listed examples are set forth in *Ellerth* and/or *Faragher*. See *Ellerth*, 118 S. Ct. at 2268 and 2270; *Faragher*, 118 S. Ct. at 2284, 2291, and 2293.

[31]Other forms of formal discipline would qualify as well, such as suspension. Any disciplinary action undertaken as part of a program of progressive discipline is "tangible" because it brings the employee one step closer to discharge.

[32]The Commission disagrees with the Fourth Circuit's conclusion in *Reinhold v. Commonwealth of Virginia*, 151 F. 3d 172 (4th Cir. 1998), that the plaintiff was not subjected to a tangible employment action where the harassing supervisor "dramatically increased her workload," *Reinhold*, 947 F. Supp. 919, 923 (E.D. Va. 1996), denied her the opportunity to attend a professional conference, required her to monitor and discipline a co-worker, and generally gave her undesirable assignments. The Fourth Circuit ruled that the plaintiff had not been subjected to a tangible employment action because she had not "experienced a change in her employment status akin to a demotion or a reassignment entailing significantly different job responsibilities." 151 F. 3d at 175. It is the Commission's view that the Fourth Circuit misconstrued

Faragher and *Ellerth.* While minor changes in work assignments would not rise to the level of tangible job harm, the actions of the supervisor in *Reinhold* were substantial enough to significantly alter the plaintiff's employment status.

[33]See *Durham,* 166 F. 3d at 152–53 (assigning insurance salesperson heavy load of inactive policies, which had a severe negative impact on her earnings, and depriving her of her private office and secretary, were tangible employment actions); *Bryson v. Chicago State University,* 96 F. 3d 912, 917 (7th Cir. 1996) ("Depriving someone of the building blocks for . . . a promotion . . . is just as serious as depriving her of the job itself").

[34]See *Flaherty v. Gas Research Institute,* 31 F. 3d 451, 457 (7th Cir. 1994) (change in reporting relationship requiring plaintiff to report to former subordinate, while may be bruising plaintiff's ego, did not affect his salary, benefits, and level of responsibility and therefore could not be challenged in ADEA claim), cited in *Ellerth,* 118 S. Ct. at 2269.

[35]See *Crady v. Liberty Nat. Bank & Trust Co. of Ind.,* 993 F. 2d 132, 136 (7th Cir. 1993) ("A materially adverse change might be indicated by a termination of employment, a demotion evidenced by a decrease in wage or salary, a less distinguished title, a material loss of benefits, significantly diminished material responsibilities, or other indices that might be unique to the particular situation"), quoted in *Ellerth,* 118 S. Ct. at 2268–69.

[36]See *Nichols v. Frank,* 42 F. 3d 503, 512–13 (9th Cir. 1994) (employer vicariously liable where its supervisor granted plaintiff's leave requests based on her submission to sexual conduct), cited in *Faragher,* 118 S. Ct. at 2285.

[37]See *Ellerth,* 118 S. Ct. at 2268 and *Faragher,* 118 S. Ct. at 2284 (listed examples of tangible employment actions that included both positive and negative job decisions: hiring and firing; promotion and failure to promote).

[38]The link could be established even if the harasser was not the ultimate decision maker. See, e.g., *Shager v Upjohn Co.,* 913 F. 2d 398, 405 (7th Cir. 1990) (noting that committee rather than the supervisor fired plaintiff, but employer was still liable because committee functioned as supervisor's "cat's paw"), cited in *Ellerth,* 118 S. Ct. at 2269.

[39]*Llampallas,* 163 F. 3d at 1247.

[40]*Ellerth,* 118 S. Ct. at 2270 ("[n]o affirmative defense is available . . . when the supervisor's harassment culminates in a tangible employment action . . ."); *Faragher,* 118 S. Ct. at 2293 (same). See also *Durham,* 166 F. 3d at 154 ("When harassment becomes adverse employment action, the employer loses the affirmative defense, even if it might have been available before"); *Lissau v. Southern Food Services, Inc.,* 159 F. 3d 177, 184 (4th Cir. 1998) (the affirmative defense "is not available in a hostile work environment case when the supervisor takes a tangible employment action against the employee as part of the harassment") (Michael, J., concurring).

[41]*Ellerth,* 118 S. Ct. at 2265. Even if the preceding acts were not severe or pervasive, they still may be relevant evidence in determining whether the tangible employment action was discriminatory.

[42]See *Lissau v. Southern Food Service, Inc.,* 159 F. 3d at 182 (if plaintiff could not prove that her discharge resulted from her refusal to submit to her supervisor's sexual harassment, then the defendant could advance the affirmative defense); *Newton v. Caldwell Laboratories,* 156 F. 3d 880, 883 (8th Cir. 1998) (plaintiff failed to prove that her rejection of her supervisor's sexual advances was the reason that her request for a transfer was denied and that she was discharged; her claim was therefore categorized as one of hostile environment harassment); *Fierro v. Saks Fifth Avenue,* 13 F. Supp. 2d 481, 491 (S.D. N.Y. 1998) (plaintiff claimed that his discharge resulted from national origin harassment but court found that he was discharged because of embezzlement; thus, employer could raise affirmative defense as to the harassment preceding the discharge).

[43]See *Faragher,* 118 S. Ct. at 2292 ("If the victim could have avoided harm, no liability should be found against the employer who had taken reasonable care").

[44]See, e.g., *EEOC v. SBS Transit, Inc.,* No. 97–4164, 1998 WL 903833 at *1 (6th Cir. Dec. 18, 1998) (unpublished) (lower court erred when it reasoned that employer liability for sexual harassment is negated if the employer responds adequately and effectively once it has notice of the supervisor's harassment; that standard conflicts with affirmative defense which requires proof that employer "took reasonable care to prevent and correct promptly any sexually harassing behavior and that the plaintiff employee unreasonably failed to take advantage of preventative or corrective opportunities provided by the employer").

[45]*Ellerth,* 118 S. Ct. at 2270.

[46]See *Indest v. Freeman Decorating, Inc.,* 168 F. 3d 795, 803 (5th Cir. 1999) ("when an employer satisfies the first element of the Supreme Court's affirmative defense, it will likely forestall its own vicarious liability for a supervisor's discriminatory conduct by nipping such behavior in the bud") (Wiener, J., concurring in *Indest,* 164 F. 3d 258 (5th Cir. 1999)). The Commission agrees with Judge Wiener's concurrence in *Indest* that the court in that case dismissed the plaintiff's claims on an erroneous basis. The plaintiff alleged that her supervisor made five crude sexual comments or gestures to her during a week-long convention. She reported the incidents to appropriate management officials who investigated the matter and meted out appropriate discipline. No further incidents of harassment occurred. The court noted that it was "difficult to conclude" that the conduct to which the plaintiff was briefly subjected created an unlawful hostile environment. Nevertheless, the court went on to consider liability. It stated that *Ellerth* and *Faragher* do not apply where the plaintiff quickly resorted to the employer's grievance procedure and the employer took prompt remedial action. In such a case, according to the court, the employer's quick response exempts it from liability. The Commission agrees with Judge Wiener that *Ellerth* and *Faragher* do control the analysis in such cases, and that an employee's

prompt complaint to management forecloses the employer from proving the affirmative defense. However, as Judge Wiener pointed out, an employer's quick remedial action will often thwart the creation of an unlawful hostile environment, rendering any consideration of employer liability unnecessary.

[47]See *Greene v. Dalton*, 164 F. 3d 671, 674 (D.C. Cir. 1999) (in order for defendant to avoid all liability for sexual harassment leading to rape of plaintiff "it must show not merely that [the plaintiff] inexcusably delayed reporting the alleged rape . . . but that, as a matter of law, a reasonable person in [her] place would have come forward early enough to prevent [the] harassment from becoming 'severe or pervasive'").

[48]*Ellerth*, 118 S. Ct. at 2267.

[49]Under this same principle, it is the Commission's position that an employer is liable for punitive damages if its supervisor commits unlawful harassment or other discriminatory conduct with malice or with reckless indifference to the employee's federally protected rights. (The Supreme Court will determine the standard for awarding punitive damages in *Kolstad v. American Dental Association*, 119 S. Ct. 401 (1998) (granting certiorari).) The test for imposition of punitive damages is the mental state of the harasser, not of higher level officials. This approach furthers the remedial and deterrent objectives of the anti-discrimination statutes, and is consistent with the vicarious liability standard set forth in *Faragher* and *Ellerth*.

[50]Even if higher management proves that evidence it discovered after-the-fact would have justified the supervisor's action, such evidence can only limit remedies, not eliminate liability. *McKennon v. Nashville Banner Publishing Co.*, 513 U.S. 352, 360–62 (1995).

[51]See *Faragher*, 118 S. Ct. at 2293, and *Ellerth*, 118 S. Ct. at 2270 (affirmative defense operates either to eliminate liability or limit damages).

[52]See *Faragher*, 118 S. Ct. at 2292 ("if damages could reasonably have been mitigated no award against a liable employer should reward a plaintiff for what her own efforts could have avoided").

[53]See Section V(C)(3) for a discussion of preventive and corrective care by small employers.

[54]See *Hurley v. Atlantic City Police Dept.*, No. 96–5634, 96–5633, 96–5661, 96–5738, 1999 WL 150301 (3d Cir. March 18, 1999) ("*Ellerth* and *Faragher* do not, as the defendants seem to assume, focus mechanically on the formal existence of a sexual harassment policy, allowing an absolute defense to a hostile work environment claim whenever the employer can point to an anti-harassment policy of some sort"; defendant failed to prove affirmative defense where it issued written policies without enforcing them, painted over offensive graffiti every few months only to see it go up again in minutes, and failed to investigate sexual harassment as it investigated and punished other forms of misconduct).

[55]See *Dees v. Johnson Controls World Services, Inc.*, 168 F. 3d 417, 422 (11th Cir. 1999) (employer can be held liable despite its immediate and appropriate corrective action in response to harassment complaint if it had knowledge of the harassment prior to the complaint and took no corrective action).

[56]*Ellerth,* 118 S. Ct. at 2270.

[57]A union grievance and arbitration system does not fulfill this obligation. Decision making under such a system addresses the collective interests of bargaining unit members, while decision making under an internal harassment complaint process should focus on the individual complainant's rights under the employer's anti-harassment policy.

An arbitration, mediation, or other alternative dispute resolution process also does not fulfill the employer's duty of due care. The employer cannot discharge its responsibility to investigate complaints of harassment and undertake corrective measures by providing employees with a dispute resolution process. For further discussion of the impact of such procedures on the affirmative defense, see Section V(D)(1)(b), on page 253.

Finally, a federal agency's formal, internal EEO complaint process does not, by itself, fulfill its obligation to exercise reasonable care. That process only addresses complaints of violations of the federal EEO laws, while the Court, in *Ellerth*, made clear that an employer should encourage employees "to report harassing conduct before it becomes severe or pervasive." *Ellerth,* 118 S. Ct. at 2270. Furthermore, the EEO process is designed to assess whether the agency is liable for unlawful discrimination and does not necessarily fulfill the agency's obligation to undertake immediate and appropriate corrective action.

[58]Although the affirmative defense does not apply in cases of harassment by co-workers or non-employees, an employer cannot claim lack of knowledge as a defense to such harassment if it did not make clear to employees that they can bring such misconduct to the attention of management and that such complaints will be addressed. See *Perry v. Ethan Allen,* 115 F. 3d 143, 149 (2d Cir. 1997) ("When harassment is perpetrated by the plaintiff's co-workers, an employer will be liable if the plaintiff demonstrates that 'the employer either provided no reasonable avenue for complaint or knew of the harassment but did nothing about it'"), cited in *Faragher,* 118 S. Ct. at 2289. Furthermore, an employer is liable for harassment by a co-worker or non-employer if management knew or should have known of the misconduct, unless the employer can show that it took immediate and appropriate corrective action. 29 C.F.R. § 1604.11(d). Therefore, the employer should have a mechanism for investigating such allegations and undertaking corrective action, where appropriate.

[59]Surveys have shown that a common reason for failure to report harassment to management is fear of retaliation. See, e.g., Louise F. Fitzgerald & Suzanne Swan, "Why Didn't She Just Report Him? The Psychological and Legal Implications of Women's

Responses to Sexual Harassment," 51 *Journal of Social Issues* 117, 121–22 (1995) (citing studies). Surveys also have shown that a significant proportion of harassment victims are worse off after complaining. *Id.* at 123–24; see also Patricia A. Frazier, "Overview of Sexual Harassment from the Behavioral Science Perspective," paper presented at the American Bar Association National Institute on Sexual Harassment at B-17 (1998) (reviewing studies that show frequency of retaliation after victims confront their harasser or filed formal complaints).

[60]See *Wilson v. Tulsa Junior College,* 164 F. 3d 534, 541 (10th Cir. 1998) (complaint process deficient where it permitted employees to bypass the harassing supervisor by complaining to director of personnel services, but the director was inaccessible due to hours of duty and location in separate facility).

[61]*Faragher,* 118 S. Ct. at 2293 (in holding as matter of law that City did not exercise reasonable care to prevent the supervisors' harassment, Court took note of fact that City's policy "did not include any assurance that the harassing supervisors could be bypassed in registering complaints"); *Meritor Savings Bank, FSB v. Vinson,* 471 U.S. 57, 72 (1986).

[62]See *Wilson,* 164 F. 3d at 541 (complaint procedure deficient because it only required supervisors to report "formal" as opposed to "informal" complaints of harassment); *Varner v. National Super Markets Inc.,* 94 F. 3d 1209, 1213 (8th Cir. 1996), cert. denied, 519 U.S. 1110 (1997) (complaint procedure is not effective if it does not require supervisor with knowledge of harassment to report the information to those in position to take appropriate action).

[63]It is particularly important for federal agencies to explain the statute of limitations for filing formal EEO complaints, because the regulatory deadline is only 45 days and employees may otherwise assume they can wait whatever length of time it takes for management to complete its internal investigation.

[64]If an employer actively misleads an employee into missing the deadline for filing a charge by dragging out its investigation and assuring the employee that the harassment will be rectified, then the employer would be "equitably estopped" from challenging the delay. See *Currier v. Radio Free Europe/Radio Liberty, Inc.,* 159 F. 3d 1363, 1368 (D.C. Cir. 1998) ("an employer's affirmatively misleading statements that a grievance will be resolved in the employee's favor can establish an equitable estoppel"); *Miranda v. B & B Cash Grocery Store, Inc.,* 975 F. 2d 1518, 1531 (11th Cir. 1992) (tolling is appropriate where plaintiff was led by defendant to believe that the discriminatory treatment would be rectified); *Miller v. Beneficial Management Corp.,* 977 F. 2d 834, 845 (3d Cir. 1992) (equitable tolling applies where employer's own acts or omission has lulled the plaintiff into foregoing prompt attempt to vindicate his rights).

[65]The sharing of records about a harassment complaint with prospective employers of the complainant could constitute unlawful retaliation. See Compliance Manual Section 8 ("Retaliation), subsection II D (2), (BNA) 614:0005 (5/20/98).

[66]One court has suggested that it may be permissible to honor such a request, but that when the harassment is severe, an employer cannot just stand by, even if requested to do so. *Torres v. Pisano,* 116 F. 3d 625 (2d Cir.), cert. denied, 118 S. Ct. 563(1997).

[67]Employers may hesitate to set up such a phone line due to concern that it may create a duty to investigate anonymous complaints, even if based on mere rumor. To avoid any confusion as to whether an anonymous complaint through such a phone line triggers an investigation, the employer should make clear that the person who takes the calls is not a management official and can only answer questions and provide information. An investigation will proceed only if a complaint is made through the internal complaint process or if management otherwise learns about alleged harassment.

[68]See, e.g., *Van Zant v. KLM Royal Dutch Airlines,* 80 F. 3d 708, 715 (2d Cir. 1996) (employer's response prompt where it began investigation on the day that complaint was made, conducted interviews within two days, and fired the harasser within ten days); *Steiner v. Showboat Operating Co.,* 25 F. 3d 1459, 1464 (9th Cir. 1994) (employer's response to complaints inadequate despite eventual discharge of harasser where it did not seriously investigate or strongly reprimand supervisor until after plaintiff filed charge with state FEP agency), cert. denied, 513 U.S. 1082 (1995); *Saxton v. AT&T,* 10 F. 3d 526, 535 (7th Cir 1993) (investigation prompt where it was begun one day after complaint and a detailed report was completed two weeks later); *Nash v. Electrospace Systems, Inc.,* 9 F. 3d 401, 404 (5th Cir. 1993) (prompt investigation completed within one week); *Juarez v. Ameritech Mobile Communications, Inc.,* 957 F. 2d 317, 319 (7th Cir. 1992) (adequate investigation completed within four days).

[69]Management may be reluctant to release information about specific disciplinary measures that it undertakes against the harasser, due to concerns about potential defamation claims by the harasser. However, many courts have recognized that limited disclosures of such information are privileged. For cases addressing defenses to defamation claims arising out of alleged harassment, see *Duffy v. Leading Edge Products,* 44 F. 3d 308, 311 (5th Cir. 1995) (qualified privilege applied to statements accusing plaintiff of harassment); *Garziano v. E.I. DuPont de Nemours & Co.,* 818 F. 2d 380 (5th Cir. 1987) (qualified privilege protects employer's statements in bulletin to employees concerning dismissal of alleged harasser); *Stockley v. AT&T,* 687 F. Supp. 764 (E.D. N.Y. 1988) (statements made in course of investigation into sexual harassment charges protected by qualified privilege).

[70]*Mockler v. Multnomah County,* 140 F. 3d 808, 813 (9th Cir. 1998).

[71]In some cases, accused harassers who were subjected to discipline and subsequently exonerated have claimed that the disciplinary action was discriminatory. No discrimination will be found if the employer had a good faith belief that such action was warranted and there is no evidence that it undertook less punitive measures against similarly situated employees outside his or her protected class who were

accused of harassment. In such circumstances, the Commission will not find pretext based solely on an after-the-fact conclusion that the disciplinary action was inappropriate. See *Waggoner v. City of Garland Tex.*, 987 F. 2d 1160, 1165 (5th Cir. 1993) (where accused harasser claims that disciplinary action was discriminatory, "[t]he real issue is whether the employer reasonably believed the employee's allegation [of harassment] and acted on it in good faith, or to the contrary, the employer did not actually believe the co-employee's allegation but instead used it as a pretext for an otherwise discriminatory dismissal").

[72]See *Steiner v. Showboat Operating Co.*, 25 F. 3d 1459, 1464 (9th Cir. 1994) (employer remedial action for sexual harassment by supervisor inadequate where it twice changed plaintiff's shift to get her away from supervisor rather than change his shift or work area), cert. denied, 513 U.S. 1082 (1995).

[73]See *Guess v. Bethlehem Steel Corp.*, 913 F. 2d 463, 465 (7th Cir. 1990) ("a remedial measure that makes the victim of sexual harassment worse off is ineffective per se").

[74]An oral warning or reprimand would be appropriate only if the misconduct was isolated and minor. If an employer relies on oral warnings or reprimands to correct harassment, it will have difficulty proving that it exercised reasonable care to prevent and correct such misconduct.

[75]See *Varner*, 94 F. 3d at 1213 (complaint procedure is not effective if it does not require supervisor with knowledge of harassment to report the information to those in position to take appropriate action), cert. denied, 117 S. Ct. 946 (1997); accord *Wilson v. Tulsa Junior College*, 164 F. 3d at 541.

[76]See *Wilson*, 164 F. 3d at 541 (complaint procedure deficient because it only required supervisors to report "formal" as opposed to "informal" complaints of harassment).

[77]See, e.g., *Splunge v. Shoney's, Inc.*, 97 F. 3d 488, 490 (11th Cir. 1996) (where harassment of plaintiffs was so pervasive that higher management could be deemed to have constructive knowledge of it, employer was obligated to undertake corrective action even though plaintiffs did not register complaints); *Fall v. Indiana Univ. Bd. of Trustees*, 12 F. Supp. 2d 870, 882 (N.D. Ind. 1998) (employer has constructive knowledge of harassment by supervisors where it "was so broad in scope and so permeated the workplace that it must have come to the attention of someone authorized to do something about it").

[78]In *Faragher*, the City lost the opportunity to establish the affirmative defense in part because "its officials made no attempt to keep track of the conduct of supervisors." *Faragher*, 118 S. Ct. at 2293.

[79]See subsections V(C)(1)(e)(ii), on page 247, and V(C)(2), on page 250.

[80]If the owner of the business commits unlawful harassment, then the business will automatically be found liable under the alter ego standard and no affirmative defense can be raised. See Section VI, on page 254.

[81]*Faragher*, 118 S. Ct. at 2293.

[82]*Faragher,* 118 S. Ct. at 2292 ("If the victim could have avoided harm, no liability should be found against the employer who had taken reasonable care, and if damages could reasonably have been mitigated no award against a liable employer should reward a plaintiff for what her own efforts could have avoided").

[83]*Ellerth,* 118 S. Ct. at 2270; *Faragher,* 118 S. Ct. at 2293. See also *Scrivner v. Socorro Independent School District,* 169 F. 3d 969, 971 (5th Cir., 1999) (employer established second prong of defense where harassment began during summer, plaintiff misled investigators inquiring into anonymous complaint by denying that harassment occurred, and plaintiff did not complain about the harassment until the following March).

[84]The employee is not required to have chosen "the course that events later show to have been the best." Restatement (Second) of Torts § 918, comment c.

[85]See *Corcoran v. Shoney's Colonial, Inc.,* 24 F. Supp. 2d 601, 606 (W.D. Va. 1998) ("Though unwanted sexual remarks have no place in the work environment, it is far from uncommon for those subjected to such remarks to ignore them when they are first made").

[86]See *Faragher,* 118 S. Ct. at 2292 (defense established if plaintiff unreasonably failed to avail herself of "a proven, effective mechanism for reporting and resolving complaints of sexual harassment, available to the employee without undue risk or expense"). See also restatement (Second) of Torts § 918, comment c (tort victim "is not barred from full recovery by the fact that it would have been reasonable for him to make expenditures or subject himself to pain or risk; it is only when he is unreasonable in refusing or failing to take action to prevent further loss that his damages are curtailed").

[87]See n. 59, above.

[88]See *Faragher,* 118 S. Ct. at 2292 (employee should not recover for harm that could have been avoided by utilizing a proven, effective complaint process that was available "without undue risk or expense").

[89]See *Wilson,* 164 F. 3d at 541 (complaint process deficient where official who could take complaint was inaccessible due to hours of duty and location in separate facility).

[90]See Policy Statement on Mandatory Binding Arbitration of Employment Discrimination Disputes as a Condition of Employment, EEOC Compliance Manual (BNA) N:3101 (7/10/97).

[91]For a discussion of defamation claims and the application of a qualified privilege to an employer's statements about instances of harassment, see n. 69, above.

[92]See *Watts v. Kroger Company,* 170 F. 3d 505, 510 (5th Cir. 1999) (plaintiff made effort "to avoid harm otherwise" where she filed a union grievance and did not utilize the employer's harassment complaint process; both the employer and union procedures were corrective mechanisms designed to avoid harm).

[93]Both the staffing firm and the client may be legally responsible, under the anti-discrimination statutes, for undertaking corrective action. See Enforcement Guidance: Application of EEO Laws to Contingent Workers Placed by Temporary Employment Agencies and Other Staffing Firms, EEOC Compliance Manual (BNA) N:3317 (12/3/97).

[94]See also *Ellerth,* 118 S. Ct. at 2267 (under agency principles an employer is indirectly liable "where the agent's high rank in the company makes him or her the employer's alter ego"); *Harrison v. Eddy Potash, Inc.,* 158 F. 3d 1371, 1376 (10th Cir. 1998) ("the Supreme Court in Burlington acknowledged an employer can be held vicariously liable under Title VII if the harassing employee's 'high rank in the company makes him or her the employer's alter ego'").

[95]*Faragher,* 118 S. Ct. at 2284.

[96]The Court noted that the standards for employer liability were not at issue in the case of *Harris v. Forklift Systems,* 510 U.S. 17 (1993), because the harasser was the president of the company. *Faragher,* 118 S. Ct. at 2284.

[97]An individual who has an ownership interest in an organization, receives compensation based on its profits, and participates in managing the organization would qualify as an "owner" or "partner." *Serapion v. Martinez,* 119 F. 3d 982, 990 (1st Cir. 1997), cert. denied, 118 S. Ct. 690 (1998).

[98]*Id.*

Policy Guidance on Current Issues of Sexual Harassment (1990)

A. Determining Whether Sexual Conduct Is Unwelcome

Sexual harassment is "unwelcome . . . verbal or physical conduct of a sexual nature . . ." 29 C.F.R. § 1604.11(a). Because sexual attraction may often play a role in the day-to-day social exchange between employees, "the distinction between invited, uninvited-but-welcome, offensive-but-tolerated, and flatly rejected" sexual advances may well be difficult to discern. *Barnes v. Costle*, 561 F. 2d 983, 999, 14 EPD 7755 (D.C. Cir. 1977) (J. MacKinnon, concurring). But this distinction is essential because sexual conduct becomes unlawful only when it is unwelcome. The Eleventh Circuit provided a general definition of "unwelcome conduct" in *Henson v. City of Dundee*, 682 F. 2d at 903: the challenged conduct must be unwelcome "in the sense that the employee did not solicit or incite it, and in the sense that the employee regarded the conduct as undesirable or offensive."

When confronted with conflicting evidence as to welcomeness, the Commission looks "at the record as a whole and at the totality of circumstances . . ." 29 C.F.R. § 1604.11(b), evaluating each situation on a case-by-case basis. When there is some indication of welcomeness or when the credibility of the parties is at issue, the charging party's claim will be considerably strengthened if she made a contemporaneous complaint or protest.[7] (Footnotes start at 7 because this document is an extract from a larger document. The full document can be accessed at www.eeoc.gov.) Particularly when the alleged harasser may have some reason (e.g., prior consensual relationship) to believe that the advances will be welcomed, it is important for the victim to communicate that the conduct is unwelcome. Generally, victims are well-advised to assert their right to a workplace free from sexual harassment. This may stop the harassment before it becomes more serious. A contemporaneous complaint or protest may also provide persuasive evidence that the sexual harassment in fact occurred as alleged (see infra Section B). Thus, in investigating sexual harassment charges, it is important to develop detailed evidence of the circumstances and nature of any such complaints or protests, whether to the alleged harasser, higher management, co-workers or others.[8]

While a complaint or protest is helpful to charging party's case, it is not a necessary element of the claim. Indeed, the Commission recognizes that victims may fear repercussions from complaining about the harassment and that such fear may explain a delay in opposing the conduct. If the victim failed to complain or delayed in complaining, the investigation must ascertain why. The relevance of whether the victim has complained varies depending on "the nature of the sexual advances and the context in which the alleged incidents occurred." 29 C.F.R. § 1604.11(b).[9]

> *Example—Charging Party (CP) alleges that her supervisor subjected her to unwelcome sexual advances that created a hostile work environment. The investigation into her charge discloses that her supervisor began making intermittent sexual advances to her in June 1987, but she did not complain to management about the harassment. After the harassment continued and worsened, she filed a charge with EEOC in June 1988. There is no evidence CP welcomed the advances. CP states that she feared that complaining about the harassment would cause her to lose her job. She also states that she initially believed she could resolve the situation herself, but as the harassment became more frequent and severe, she said she realized that intervention by EEOC was necessary. The investigator determines CP is credible and concludes that the delay in complaining does not undercut CP's claim.*

When welcomeness is at issue, the investigation should determine whether the victim's conduct is consistent, or inconsistent, with her assertion that the sexual conduct is unwelcome.[10]

In *Vinson*, the Supreme Court made clear that voluntary submission to sexual conduct will not necessarily defeat a claim of sexual harassment. The correct inquiry "is whether [the employee] by her conduct indicated that the alleged sexual advances were unwelcome, not whether her actual participation in sexual intercourse was voluntary." 106 S. Ct. at 2406 (emphasis added). *See also* Commission Decision No. 84–1 ("acquiescence in sexual conduct at the workplace may not mean that the conduct is welcome to the individual").

In some cases the courts and the Commission have considered whether the complainant welcomed the sexual conduct by acting in a sexually aggressive manner, using sexually oriented language, or soliciting the sexual conduct. Thus, in *Gan v. Kepro Circuit Systems*, 27 EPD 32,379 (E.D. Mo. 1982), the plaintiff regularly used vulgar language, initiated sexually oriented conversations with her co-workers, asked male employees about their marital sex lives and whether they engaged in extramarital affairs, and discussed her own sexual encounters. In rejecting the plaintiff's claim of "hostile environment" harassment, the court found that any propositions or sexual remarks by co-workers were "prompted by her own sexual aggressiveness and her own sexually explicit conversations" *Id.* at 23,648.[11] And in *Vinson,* the Supreme Court held that testimony about the plaintiff's provocative dress and publicly expressed sexual fantasies is not *per se* inadmissible but the trial court should carefully weigh its relevance against the potential for unfair prejudice. 106 S. Ct. at 2407.

Conversely, occasional use of sexually explicit language does not necessarily negate a claim that sexual conduct was unwelcome. Although a charging party's use of sexual terms or off-color jokes may suggest that sexual comments by others in that situation were not unwelcome, more extreme and abusive or persistent comments or a physical assault will not be excused, nor would "quid pro quo" harassment be allowed.

Any past conduct of the charging party that is offered to show "welcomeness" must relate to the alleged harasser. In *Swentek v. US Air, Inc.,* 830 F. 2d 552, 557, 44 EPD 37,457 (4th Cir. 1987), the Fourth Circuit held the district court wrongly concluded that the plaintiff's own past conduct and use of foul language showed that "she was the kind of person who could not be offended by such comments and therefore welcomed them generally," even though she had told the harasser to leave her alone. Emphasizing that the proper inquiry is "whether plaintiff welcomed the particular conduct in question from the alleged harasser," the court of appeals held that "Plaintiff's use of foul language or sexual innuendo in a consensual setting does not waive 'her legal protections against unwelcome harassment.'" 830 F. 2d at 557 (quoting *Katz v. Dole,* 709 F. 2d 251, 254 n. 3, 32 EPD 33,639 (4th Cir. 1983)). Thus, evidence concerning a charging party's general character and past behavior toward others has limited, if any, probative value and does not substitute for a careful examination of her behavior toward the alleged harasser.

A more difficult situation occurs when an employee first willingly participates in conduct of a sexual nature but then ceases to participate and claims that any continued sexual conduct has created a hostile work environment. Here the employee has the burden of showing that any further sexual conduct is unwelcome, work-related harassment. The employee must clearly notify the alleged harasser that his conduct is no longer welcome.[12] If the conduct still continues, her failure to bring the matter to the attention of higher management or the EEOC is evidence, though not dispositive, that any continued conduct is, in fact, welcome or unrelated to work.[13] In any case, however, her refusal to submit to the sexual conduct cannot be the basis for denying her an employment benefit or opportunity; that would constituted a "quid pro quo" violation.

B. Evaluating Evidence of Harassment

The Commission recognizes that sexual conduct may be private and unacknowledged, with no eyewitnesses. Even sexual conduct that occurs openly in the workplace may appear to be consensual. Thus the resolution of a sexual harassment claim often depends on the credibility of the parties. The investigator should question the charging party and the alleged harasser in detail. The Commission's investigation also should search thoroughly for corroborative evidence of any nature.[14] Supervisory and managerial employees, as well as co-workers, should be asked about their knowledge of the alleged harassment.

In appropriate cases, the Commission may make a finding of harassment based solely on the credibility of the victim's allegation. As with any other charge of discrimination, a victim's account must be sufficiently detailed and internally consistent so as to be plausible, and lack of corroborative evidence where such evidence logically should exist would undermine the allegation.[15] By the same token, a general denial by the alleged harasser will carry little weight when it is contradicted by other evidence.[16]

Of course, the Commission recognizes that a charging party may not be able to identify witnesses to the alleged conduct itself. But testimony may be obtained from persons who observed the charging party's demeanor immediately after an alleged incident of harassment. Persons with whom she discussed the incident—such as co-workers, a doctor or a counselor—should be interviewed. Other employees should be asked if they noticed changes in charging party's behavior at work or in the alleged harasser's treatment of charging party. As stated earlier, a contemporaneous complaint by the victim would be persuasive evidence both that the conduct occurred and that it was unwelcome (*see supra* Section A). So too is evidence that other employees were sexually harassed by the same person.

The investigator should determine whether the employer was aware of any other instances of harassment and if so what the response was. Where appropriate the Commission will expand the case to include class claims.[17]

Example—Charging Party (CP) alleges that her supervisor made unwelcome sexual advances toward her on frequent occasions while they were alone in his office. The supervisor denies this allegation. No one witnessed the alleged advances. CP's inability to produce eyewitnesses to the harassment does not defeat her claim. The resolution will depend on the credibility of her allegations versus that of her supervisor's. Corroborating, credible evidence will establish her claim. For example, three co-workers state that CP looked distraught on several occasions after leaving the supervisor's office, and that she informed them on those occasions that he had sexually propositioned and touched her. In addition, the evidence shows that CP had complained to the general manager of the office about the incidents soon after they occurred. The corroborating witness testi-

mony and her complaint to higher management would be sufficient to establish her claim. Her allegations would be further buttressed if other employees testified that the supervisor propositioned them as well.

If the investigation exhausts all possibilities for obtaining corroborative evidence, but finds none, the Commission may make a cause finding based solely on a reasoned decision to credit the charging party's testimony.[18]

In a "quid pro quo" case, a finding that the employer's asserted reasons for its adverse action against the charging party are pretextual will usually establish a violation.[19] The investigation should determine the validity of the employer's reasons for the charging party's termination. If they are pretextual and if the sexual harassment occurred, then it should be inferred that the charging party was terminated for rejecting the employer's sexual advances, as she claims. Moreover, if the termination occurred because the victim complained, it would be appropriate to find, in addition, a violation of section 704(a).

C. Determining Whether a Work Environment Is "Hostile"

The Supreme Court said in *Vinson* that for sexual harassment to violate Title VII, it must be "sufficiently severe or pervasive 'to alter the conditions of [the victim's] employment and create an abusive working environment.'" 106 S. Ct. at 2406 (quoting *Henson v. City of Dundee*, 682 F. 2d at 904. Since "hostile environment" harassment takes a variety of forms, many factors may affect this determination, including: (1) whether the conduct was verbal or physical, or both; (2) how frequently it was repeated; (3) whether the conduct was hostile and patently offensive; (4) whether the alleged harasser was a co-worker or a supervisor; (5) whether the others joined in perpetrating the harassment; and (6) whether the harassment was directed at more than one individual.

In determining whether unwelcome sexual conduct rises to the level of a "hostile environment" in violation of Title VII, the central inquiry is whether the conduct "unreasonably interfer[es] with an individual's work performance" or creates "an intimidating, hostile, or offensive working environment." 29 C.F.R. § 1604.11(a)(3). Thus, sexual flirtation or innuendo, even vulgar language that is trivial or merely annoying, would probably not establish a hostile environment.

1. Standard for Evaluating Harassment

In determining whether harassment is sufficiently severe or pervasive to create a hostile environment, the harasser's conduct should be evaluated from the objective standpoint of a "reasonable person." Title VII does not serve "as a vehicle for vindicating the petty slights suffered by the hypersensitive." *Zabkowicz v. West Bend*

Co., 589 F. Supp. 780, 784, 35 EPD 34, 766 (E.D. Wis. 1984). See also *Ross v. Comsat*, 34 FEP cases 260, 265 (D. Md. 1984), rev'd on other grounds, 759 F. 2d 355 (4th Cir. 1985). Thus, if the challenged conduct would not substantially affect the work environment of a reasonable person, no violation should be found.

> *Example—Charging Party alleges that her co-worker made repeated unwelcome sexual advances toward her. An investigation discloses that the alleged "advances" consisted of invitations to join a group of employees who regularly socialized at dinner after work. The co-worker's invitations, viewed in that context and from the perspective of a reasonable person, would not have created a hostile environment and therefore did not constitute sexual harassment.*

A "reasonable person" standard also should be applied to be a more basic determination of whether challenged conduct is of a sexual nature. Thus, in the above example, a reasonable person would not consider the co-worker's invitations sexual in nature, and on that basis as well no violation would be found.

This objective standard should not be applied in a vacuum, however. Consideration should be given to the context in which the alleged harassment took place. As the Sixth Circuit has stated, the trier of fact must "adopt the perspective of a reasonable person's reaction to a similar environment under similar or like circumstances." *Highlander v. K.F.C. National Management Co.*, 805 F. 2d 644, 650, 41 EPD 36,675 (6th Cir. 1986).[20]

The reasonable person standard should consider the victim's perspective and not stereotyped notions of acceptable behavior. For example, the Commission believes that a workplace in which sexual slurs, displays of "girlie" pictures, and other offensive conduct abound can constitute a hostile work environment even if many people deem it to be harmless or insignificant. Cf. *Rabidue v. Osceola Refining Co.*, 805 F. 2d 611, 626, 41 EPD 36,643 (6th Cir. 1986) (Keith, C.J., dissenting), cert. denied, 107 S. Ct. 1983, 42 EPD 36,984 (1987). *Lipsett v. University of Puerto Rico*, 864 F. 2d 881, 898 48 EPD 38,393 (1st Cir. 1988).

2. Isolated Instances of Harassment

Unless the conduct is quite severe, a single incident or isolated incidents of offensive sexual conduct or remarks generally do not create an abusive environment. As the Court noted in *Vinson*, "mere utterance of an ethnic or racial epithet which engenders offensive feelings in an employee would not affect the conditions of employment to a sufficiently significant degree to violate Title VII." 106 S. Ct. at 2406 (quoting *Rogers v. EEOC*, 454 F. 2d 234, 4 EPD 7597 (5th Cir. 1971), cert. denied, 406 U.S. 957, 4 EPD 7838 (1972)). A "hostile environment" claim generally requires a showing of a pattern of offensive conduct.[21] In contrast, in "quid pro quo" cases a single sexual advance may constitute harassment if it is linked to the granting or denial of employment benefits.[22]

But a single, unusually severe incident of harassment may be sufficient to constitute a Title VII violation; the more severe the harassment, the less need to show a repetitive series of incidents. This is particularly true when the harassment is physical.[23] Thus, in *Barrett v. Omaha National Bank*, 584 F. Supp, 22, 35 FEP Cases 585 (D. Neb. 1983), aff'd, 726 F. 2d 424, 33 EPD 34,132 (8th Cir. 1984), one incident constituted actionable sexual harassment. The harasser talked to the plaintiff about sexual activities and touched her in an offensive manner while they were inside a vehicle from which she could not escape.[24]

The Commission will presume that the unwelcome, intentional touching of a charging party's intimate body areas is sufficiently offensive to alter the condition of her working environment and constitute a violation of Title VII. More so than in the case of verbal advances or remarks, a single unwelcome physical advance can seriously poison the victim's working environment. If an employee's supervisor sexually touches that employee, the Commission normally would find a violation. In such situations, it is the employer's burden to demonstrate that the unwelcome conduct was not sufficiently severe to create a hostile work environment.

When the victim is the target of both verbal and non-intimate physical conduct, the hostility of the environment is exacerbated and a violation is more likely to be found. Similarly, incidents of sexual harassment directed at other employees in addition to the charging party are relevant to a showing of hostile work environment. *Hall v. Gus Construction Co.*, 842 F. 2d 1010, 46 EPD 37,905 (8th Cir. 1988); *Hicks v. Gates Rubber Co.*, 833 F. 2d 1406, 44 EPD 37,542 (10th Cir. 1987); *Jones v. Flagship International*, 793 F. 2d 714, 721 n.7, 40 EPD 36,392 (5th Cir. 1986), cert. denied, 107 S. Ct. 952, 41 EPD 36,708 (1987).

3. Non-Physical Harassment

When the alleged harassment consists of verbal conduct, the investigation should ascertain the nature, frequency, context, and intended target of the remarks. Questions to be explored might include:

- Did the alleged harasser single out the charging party?
- Did the charging party participate?
- What was the relationship between the charging party and the alleged harasser(s)?
- Were the remarks hostile and derogatory?

No one factor alone determines whether particular conduct violates Title VII. As the Guidelines emphasize, the Commission will evaluate the totality of the circumstances. In general, a woman does not forfeit her right to be free from sexual harassment by choosing to work in an atmosphere that has traditionally included vulgar, anti-female language. However, in *Rabidue v. Osceola Refining Co.*, 805 F. 2d

611, 41 EPD 36,643 (6th Cir. 1986), cert. denied, 107 S. Ct. 1983, 42 EPD 36,984 (1987), the Sixth Circuit rejected the plaintiff's claim of harassment in such a situation.[25]

One of the factors the court found relevant was "the lexicon of obscenity that pervaded the environment of the workplace both before and after the plaintiff's introduction into its environs, coupled with the reasonable expectations of the plaintiff upon voluntarily entering that environment." 805 F. 2d at 620. Quoting the district court, the majority noted that in some work environments, "'humor and language are rough hewn and vulgar. Sexual jokes, sexual conversations, and girlie magazines may abound. Title VII was not meant to—or can—change this.'" *Id.* at 620–21. The court also considered the sexual remarks and poster at issue to have a "de minimus effect on the plaintiff's work environment when considered in the context of a society that condones and publicly features and commercially exploits open displays of written and pictorial erotica at the newsstands, on prime-time television, at the cinema, and in other public places." *Id.* at 622.

The Commission believes these factors rarely will be relevant and agrees with the dissent in *Rabidue* that a woman does not assume the risk of harassment by voluntarily entering an abusive, anti-female environment. "Title VII's precise purpose is to prevent such behavior and attitudes from poisoning the work environment of classes protected under the Act." 805 F. 2d at 626 (Keith, J., dissenting in part and concurring in part). Thus, in a decision disagreeing with *Rabidue*, a district court found that a hostile environment was established by the presence of pornographic magazines in the workplace and vulgar employee comments concerning them; offensive sexual comments made to and about plaintiff and other female employees by her supervisor; sexually oriented pictures in a company-sponsored movie and slide presentation; sexually oriented pictures and calendars in the workplace; and offensive touching of plaintiff by a co-worker. *Barbetta v. Chemlawn Services Corp.,* 669 F. Supp. 569, 45 EPD 37,568 (W.D. N.Y. 1987). The court held that the proliferation of pornography and demeaning comments, if sufficiently continuous and pervasive, "may be found to create an atmosphere in which women are viewed as men's sexual playthings rather than as their equal co-workers." *Barbetta,* 669 F. Supp. at 573. The Commission agrees that, depending on the totality of circumstances, such an atmosphere may violate Title VII. See also *Waltman v. International Paper Co.,* 875 F. 2d 468, 50 EPD 39,106 (5th Cir. 1989), in which the 5th Circuit endorsed the Commission's position in its amicus brief that evidence of ongoing sexual graffiti in the workplace, not all of which was directed at the plaintiff, was relevant to her claim of harassment. *Bennett v. Coroon & Black Corp.,* 845 F. 2d 104, 46 EPD 37,955 (5th Cir. 1988) (the posting of obscene cartoons in an office men's room bearing the plaintiff's name and depicting her engaged in crude and deviant sexual activities could create a hostile work environment).

4. Sex-Based Harassment

Although the Guidelines specifically address conduct that is sexual in nature, the Commission notes that sex-based harassment—that is, harassment not involving sexual activity or language—may also give rise to Title VII liability (just as in the case of harassment based on race, national origin, or religion) if it is "sufficiently patterned or pervasive" and directed at employees because of their sex. *Hicks v. Gates Rubber Co.,* 833 F. 2d at 1416; *McKinney v. Dole,* 765 F. 2d 1129, 1138, 37 EPD 35,339 (D.C. Cir. 1985).

Acts of physical aggression, intimidation, hostility or unequal treatment based on sex may be combined with incidents of sexual harassment to establish the existence of discriminatory terms and conditions of employment. *Hall v. Gus Construction Co.,* 842 F. 2d 1014; *Hicks v. Gates Rubber Co.,* 833 F. 2d at 1416.

5. Constructive Discharge

Claims of "hostile environment" sexual harassment often are coupled with claims of constructive discharge. If constructive discharge due to a hostile environment is proven, the claim will also become one of "quid pro quo" harassment.[26] It is the position of the Commission and a majority of courts that an employer is liable for constructive discharge when it imposes intolerable working conditions in violation of Title VII when those conditions foreseeably would compel a reasonable employee to quit, whether or not the employer specifically intended to force the victim's resignation. See *Derr v. Gulf Oil Corp.,* 796 F. 2d 340, 343–44, 41 EPD 36,468 (10th Cir. 1986); *Goss v. Exxon Office Systems Co.,* 747 F .2d 885, 888, 35 EPD 34, 768 (3d Cir. 1984); *Nolan v. Cleland,* 686 F. 2d 806, 812–15, 30 EPD 33,029 (9th Cir. 1982); *Held v. Gulf Oil Co.,* 684 F. 2d 427, 432, 29 EPD 32,968 (6th Cir. 1982); *Clark v. Marsh,* 655 F. 2d 1168, 1175 n.8, 26 EPD 32,082 (D.C. Cir. 1981); *Bourque v. Powell Electrical Manufacturing Co.,* 617 F. 2d 61, 65, 23 EPD 30,891 (5th Cir. 1980); Commission Decision 84–1, CCH EEOC Decision 6839. However, the Fourth Circuit requires proof that the employer imposed the intolerable conditions with the intent of forcing the victim to leave. See *EEOC v. Federal Reserve Bank of Richmond,* 698 F. 2d 633, 672, 30 EPD 33,269 (4th Cir. 1983). But this case is not a sexual harassment case and the Commission believes it is distinguishable because specific intent is not likely to be present in "hostile environment" cases.

An important factor to consider is whether the employer had an effective internal grievance procedure. (See Section E, Preventive and Remedial Action.) The Commission argued in its *Vinson* brief that if an employee knows that effective avenues of complaint and redress are available, then the availability of such avenues itself becomes a part of the work environment and overcomes, to the degree it is effective, the hostility of the work environment. As Justice Marshall noted in his opinion in *Vinson,* "Where a complainant without good reason bypassed an internal complaint procedure she knew to be effective, a court may be reluctant to find constructive termination . . . " 106 S. Ct. at 2411 (Marshall, J., concurring in part and dissenting in part). Similarly, the court of appeals in *Dornhecker v. Malibu Grand Prix Corp.*, 828 F. 2d 307, 44 EPD 37,557 (5th Cir. 1987), held the plaintiff was not constructively discharged after an incident of harassment by a co-worker because she quit immediately, even though the employer told her she would not have to work with him again, and she did not give the employer a fair opportunity to demonstrate it could curb the harasser's conduct.

D. [Deleted 6/1999]

E. Preventive and Remedial Action

1. Preventive Action

The EEOC'S Guidelines encourage employers to:

take all steps necessary to prevent sexual harassment from occurring, such as affirmatively raising the subject, expressing strong disapproval, developing appropriate sanctions, informing employees of their right to raise and how to raise the issue of harassment under Title VII, and developing methods to sensitize all concerned.

29 C.F.R. § 1604.11(f). An effective preventive program should include an explicit policy against sexual harassment that is clearly and regularly communicated to employees and effectively implemented. The employer should affirmatively raise the subject with all supervisory and non-supervisory employees, express strong disapproval, and explain the sanctions for harassment. The employer should also have a procedure for resolving sexual harassment complaints. The procedure should be designed to "encourage victims of harassment to come forward" and should not require a victim to complain first to the offending supervisor. See *Vinson*, 106 S. Ct. at 2408. It should ensure confidentiality as much as possible and provide effective remedies, including protection of victims and witnesses against retaliation.

2. Remedial Action

Since Title VII

". . . affords employees the right to work in an environment free from discriminatory intimidation, ridicule, and insult" (Vinson, 106 S. Ct. at 2405), an employer is liable for failing to remedy known hostile or offensive work environ-

ments. See, e.g., Garziano v. E.I. DuPont de Nemours & Co., *818 F. 2d 380, 388, 43 EPD 37,171 (5th Cir. 1987) (*Vinson *holds employers have an "affirmative duty to eradicate 'hostile or offensive' work environments");* Bundy v. Jackson, *641 F. 2d 934, 947, 24 EPD 31,439 (D.C. Cir. 1981) (employer violated Title VII by failing to investigate and correct sexual harassment despite notice);* Tompkins v. Public Service Electric & Gas Co., *568 F. 2d 1044, 1049, 15 EPD 7954 (3d Cir. 1977) (same);* Henson v. City of Dundee, *682 F. 2d 897, 905, 15 EPD 32,993 (11th Cir. 1982) (same);* Munford v. James T. Barnes & Co., *441 F. Supp. 459, 466 16 EPD 8233 (E.D. Mich. 1977) (employer has an affirmative duty to investigate complaints of sexual harassment and to deal appropriately with the offending personnel; "failure to investigate gives tactic support to the discrimination because the absence of sanctions encourages abusive behavior").*[27]

When an employer receives a complaint or otherwise learns of alleged sexual harassment in the workplace, the employer should investigate promptly and thoroughly. The employer should take immediate and appropriate corrective action by doing whatever is necessary to end the harassment, make the victim whole by restoring lost employment benefits or opportunities, and prevent the misconduct from recurring. Disciplinary action against the offending supervisor or employee, ranging from reprimand to discharge, may be necessary. Generally, the corrective action should reflect the severity of the conduct. See Waltman v. International Paper Co., 875 F. 2d at 479 (appropriateness of remedial action will depend on the severity and persistence of the harassment and the effectiveness of any initial remedial steps). Dornhecker v. Malibu Grand Prix Corp., 828 F. 2d 307, 309–10, 44 EPD 37,557 (5th Cir. 1987) (the employer's remedy may be "assessed proportionately to the seriousness of the offense"). The employer should make follow-up inquiries to ensure the harassment has not resumed and the victim has not suffered retaliation.

Recent Court decisions illustrate appropriate and inappropriate responses by employers. In Barrett v. Omaha National Bank, 726 F. 2d 424, 33 EPD 34,132 (8th Cir. 1984), the victim informed her employer that her co-worker had talked to her about sexual activities and touched her in an offensive manner. Within four days of receiving this information, the employer investigated the charges, reprimanded the guilty employee, placed him on probation, and warned him that further misconduct would result in discharge. A second co-worker who had witnessed the harassment was also reprimanded for not intervening on the victim's behalf or reporting the conduct. The court ruled that the employer's response constituted immediate and appropriate corrective action, and on this basis found the employer not liable.

In contrast, in Yates v. Avco Corp., 819 F. 2d 630, 43 EPD 37,086 (6th Cir. 1987), the court found the employer's policy against sexual harassment failed to function effectively. The victim's first-level supervisor had responsibility for reporting and correcting harassment at the company, yet he was the harasser. The employer told the victims not to go to the EEOC. While giving the accused harasser administrative leave pending investigation, the employer made the plaintiffs take sick leave, which was never credited back to them and was recorded in their personnel files as excessive absenteeism without indicating they were absent because of sexual harassment. Similarly, in Zabkowicz v. West Bend Co., 589 F. Supp. 780, 35 EPD 34,766 (E.D. Wis. 1984), co-workers harassed the plaintiff over a period of nearly four years in a manner the court described as "malevolent" and "outrageous." Despite the plaintiff's numerous complaints, her supervisor took no remedial action other than to hold occasional meetings at which he reminded employees of the company's policy against offensive conduct. The supervisor never conducted an investigation or disciplined any employees until the plaintiff filed an EEOC charge, at which time one of the offending co-workers was discharged and three others were suspended. The court held the employer liable because it failed to take immediate and appropriate corrective action.[28]

When an employer asserts it has taken remedial action, the Commission will investigate to determine whether the action was appropriate and, more important, effective. The EEOC investigator should, of course, conduct an independent investigation of the harassment claim, and the Commission will reach its own conclusion as to whether the law has been violated. If the Commission finds that the harassment has been eliminated, all victims made whole, and preventive measures instituted, the Commission normally will administratively close the charge because of the employer's prompt remedial action.[29]

Notes

[7]For a complaint to be "contemporaneous," it should be made while the harassment is ongoing or shortly after it has ceased. For example, a victim of "hostile environment" harassment who resigns her job because working conditions have become intolerable would be considered to have made a contemporaneous complaint if she notified the employer of the harassment at the time of her departure or shortly thereafter. The employer has a duty to investigate and, if it finds the allegations true, to take remedial action including offering reinstatement (see infra Section E).

[8]Even when unwelcomeness is not at issue, the investigation should develop this evidence in order to aid in making credibility determinations (see infra p. 12).

[9]A victim of harassment need not always confront her harasser directly so long as her conduct demonstrates the harasser's behavior is unwelcome. See, e.g., *Lipsett v. University of Puerto Rico,* 864 F. 2d 881, 898, 48 EPD 38,393 (1st Cir. 1988) ("In some instances a woman may have the responsibility for telling the man directly that his comments or conduct is unwelcome. In other instances, however, a women's consistent failure to respond to suggestive comments or gestures may be sufficient to communicate that the man's conduct is unwelcome"); Commission Decision No. 84–1, CCH EEOC Decisions 6839 (although charging parties did not confront their supervisor directly about his sexual remarks and gestures for fear of losing their jobs, evidence showing that they demonstrated through comments and actions that his conduct was unwelcome was sufficient to support a finding of harassment).

[10]Investigators and triers of fact rely on objective evidence, rather than subjective, uncommunicated feelings. For example, in *Ukarish v. Magnesium Electron,* 33 EPD 34,087 (D. N.J. 1983), the court rejected the plaintiff's claim that she was sexually harassed by her co-worker's language and gestures; although she indicated in her personal diary that she did not welcome the banter, she made no objection and indeed appeared to join in "as one of the boys." *Id.* At 32,118. In *Sardigal v. St. Louis National Stockyards Co.,* 41 EPD 36,613 (S.D. Ill. 1986), the plaintiff's allegation was found not credible because she visited her alleged harasser at the hospital and at his brother's home, and allowed him to come into her home alone at night after the alleged harassment occurred. Similarly, in the *Vinson* case, the district court noted the plaintiff had twice refused transfers to other offices located away from the alleged harasser. (In a particular charge, the significance of a charging party's refusing an offer to transfer will depend upon her reasons for doing so.)

[11]See also *Ferguson v. E.I. DuPont de Nemours and Co.,* 560 F. Supp. 1172, 33 EPD 34,131 (D. Del. 1983) ("sexually aggressive conduct and explicit conversation on the part of the plaintiff may bar a cause of action for [hostile environment] sexual harassment"); *Reichman v. Bureau of Affirmative Action,* 536 F. Supp. 1149, 1172, 30 FEP Cases 1644 (M.D. Pa. 1982) (where plaintiff behaved "in a very flirtatious and provocative manner" around the alleged harasser, asked him to have dinner at her house on several occasions despite his repeated refusals, and continued to conduct herself in a similar manner after the alleged harassment, she could not claim the alleged harassment was unwelcome).

[12]In Commission Decision No. 84–1, CCH Employment Practices Guide 6839, the Commission found that active participation in sexual conduct at the workplace, e.g., by "using dirty remarks and telling dirty jokes," may indicate that the sexual advances complained of were not unwelcome. Thus, the Commission found that no harassment occurred with respect to an employee who had joined in the telling of bawdy jokes and the use of vulgar language during her first two months on the job, and failed to provide subsequent notice that the conduct was no longer welcome. By actively participating in the conduct, the charging party had created the impression among her co-workers that she welcomed the sort of sexually oriented banter that

she later asserted was objectionable. Simply ceasing to participate was insufficient to show the continuing activity was no longer welcome to her. See also *Loftin Boggs v. City of Meridian*, 633 F. Supp. 1323, 41 FEP Cases 532 (S.D. Miss. 1986) (plaintiff initially participated in and initiated some of the crude language that was prevalent on the job; if she later found such conduct offensive, she should have conveyed this by her own conduct and her reaction to her co-workers' conduct).

[13]However, if the harassing supervisor engages in conduct that is sufficiently pervasive and work-related, it may place the employer on notice that the conduct constitutes harassment.

[14]As the court said in *Henson v. City of Dundee*, 682 F. 2d at 912 n. 25, "In a case of alleged sexual harassment which involves close questions of credibility and subjective interpretation, the existence of corroborative evidence or the lack thereof is likely to be crucial."

[15]In *Sardigal v. St. Louis National Stockyards Co.*, 41 EPD 36,613 at 44,694 (S.D. Ill. 1986), the plaintiff, a waitress, alleged she was harassed over a period of nine months in a restaurant at noontime, when there was a "constant flow of waitresses or customers" around the area where the offenses allegedly took place. Her allegations were not credited by the district court because no individuals came forward with testimony to support her.

[16]See Commission Decision No. 81–17, CCH EEOC Decisions (1983) 6757 (violation of Title VII found where charging party alleged that her supervisor made repeated sexual advances toward her; although the supervisor denied the allegations, statements of other employees supported them).

[17]Class complaints in the federal sector are governed by the requirements of 29 C.F.R. § 1613 Subpart F.

[18]In Commission Decision No. 82–13, CCH EEOC Decisions (1983) 6832, the Commission stated that a "bare assertion" of sexual harassment "cannot stand without some factual support." To the extent this decision suggests a charging party can never prevail based solely on the credibility of her own testimony, that decision is overruled.

[19]See, e.g., *Bundy v. Jackson*, 641 F. 2d 934, 953, 24, EPD 31,439 (D.C. Cir. 1981).

[20]In *Highlander* and also in *Rabidue v. Osceola Refining Co.*, 805 F. 2d 611, 41 EPD 36,643 (6th Cir. 1986), cert. denied, 107 S. Ct. 1983, 42 EPD 36,984 (1987), the Sixth Circuit required an additional showing that the plaintiff suffered some degree of psychological injury. *Highlander*, 805 F. 2d at 650; *Rabidue*, 805 F. 2d at 620. However, it is the Commission's position that it is sufficient for the charging party to show that the harassment was unwelcome and that it would have substantially affected the work environment of a reasonable person.

[21]See, e.g., *Scott v. Sears, Roebuck and Co.*, 798 F. 2d 210, 214, 41 EPD 36,439 (7th Cir. 1986) (offensive comments and conduct of co-workers were "too isolated and lacking the repetitive and debilitation effect necessary to maintain a hostile environment claim"); *Moylan v. Maries County*, 792 F. 2d 746, 749 40 EPD 36,228 (8th Cir. 1986)

(single incident or isolated incidents of harassment will not be sufficient to establish a violation; the harassment must be sustained and nontrivial); *Downes v. Federal Aviation Administration*, 775 F. 2d 288, 293, 38 EPD 35,590 (D.C. Cir. 1985 (Title VII does not create a claim of sexual harassment "for each and every crude joke or sexually explicit remark made on the job.[A] *pattern* of offensive conduct must be proved"); *Sapp v. City of Warner-Robins*, 655 F. Supp. 1043, 43 FEP Cases 486 (M.D. Ga. 1987) (co-worker's single effort to get the plaintiff to go out with him did not create an abusive working environment); *Freedman v. American Standard*, 41 FEP Cases 471 (D. N.J. 1986) (plaintiff did not suffer a hostile environment from the receipt of an obscene message from her co-workers and sexual solicitation from one co-worker); *Hollis v. Fleetguard, Inc.*, 44 FEP Cases 1527 (M.D. Tenn. 1987) (plaintiff's co-worker's requests, on four occasions over a four-month period, that she have a sexual affair with him, followed by his coolness toward her and avoidance of her did not constitute a hostile environment; there was not evidence he coerced, pressured, or abused the plaintiff after she rejected his advances).

[22]See *Neville v. Taft Broadcasting Co.*, 42 FEP Cases 1314 (W.D. N.Y. 1987) (one sexual advance, rebuffed by plaintiff, may establish a prima facie case of "quid pro quo" harassment but is not severe enough to create a hostile environment).

[23]The principles for establishing employer liability, set forth in Section D, are to be applied to cases involving physical contact in the same manner that they are applied in other cases.

[24]See also *Gilardi v. Schroeder*, 672 F. Supp. 1043, 45 FEP Cases 283 (N.D. Ill. 1986) (plaintiff who was drugged by employer's owner and raped while unconscious, and then was terminated at insistence of owner's wife, was awarded $133,000 in damages for harassment and intentional infliction of emotional distress); Commission Decision No. 83–1, CCH EEOC Decisions (1983) 6834 (violation found where the harasser forcibly grabbed and kissed charging party while they were alone in a storeroom); Commission Decision No. 84–3, CCH Employment Practices Guide 6841 (violation found where the harasser slid his hand under the charging party's skirt and squeezed her buttocks).

[25]The alleged harasser, a supervisor of another department who did not supervise plaintiff but worked with her regularly, "was an extremely vulgar and crude individual who customarily made obscene comments about women generally, and, on occasion, directed such obscenities to the plaintiff." 805 F. 2d at 615. The plaintiff and other female employees were exposed daily to displays of nude or partially clad women in posters in male employees' offices. 805 F. 2d at 623-24 (Keith, J., dissenting in part and concurring in part). Although the employees told management they were disturbed and offended, the employer did not reprimand the supervisor.

[26]However, while an employee's failure to utilize effective grievance procedures will not shield an employer from liability for "quid pro quo" harassment, such failure may defeat a claim of constructive discharge. See discussion of impact of grievance procedures later in this section, and Section D(2)(c)(2).

[27]The employer's affirmative duty was first enunciated in cases of harassment based on race or national origin. See, e.g., *United States v. City of Buffalo*, 457 F. Supp. 612, 632–35, 18 EPD 8899 (W.D. N.Y. 1978), modified in part, 633 F. 2d 643, 24 EPD 31,333 (2d Cir. 1980) (employer violated Title VII by failing to issue strong policy directive against racial slurs and harassment of black police officers, to conduct full investigations, and to take appropriate disciplinary action); *EEOC v. Murphy Motor Freight Lines, Inc.*, 488 Supp. 381, 385–86, 22 EPD 30,888 (D. Minn. 1980) (defendant violated Title VII because supervisors knew or should have known of co-workers' harassment of black employees, but took inadequate steps to eliminate it).

[28]See also *Delgado v. Lehman*, 665 F. Supp. 460, 44 EPD 37,517 (E.D. Va. 1987) (employer failed to conduct follow-up inquiry to determine if hostile environment had dissipated); *Salazar v. Church's Fried Chicken, Inc.*, 44 FEP Cases 472 (S.D. Tex. 1987) (employer's policy inadequate because plaintiff, as a part-time teenage employee, could have concluded a complaint would be futile because the alleged harasser was the roommate of her store manager); *Brooms v. Regal Tube Co.*, 44 FEP Cases 1119 (N.D. Ill. 1987) (employer liable when a verbal reprimand proved ineffective and employer took no further action when informed of the harasser's persistence).

[29]For appropriate procedures, see §§ 4.4(e) and 15 of Volume I of the Compliance Manual.

The U.S. Equal Employment Opportunity Commission Enforcement Guidelines

Harris v. Forklift Systems:
Necessity of Psychological Injury 3/8/94

In *Harris v. Forklift Sys., Inc.,* No. 92–1168 slip op. (Nov. 9, 1993), the Supreme Court considered whether a plaintiff was required to prove psychological injury in order to prevail on a cause of action alleging hostile environment sexual harassment under Title VII of the Civil Rights Act of 1964, as amended, 42 U.S.C. §§ 2000e et seq. A unanimous Court held that if a workplace is permeated with behavior that is severe or pervasive enough to create a discriminatorily hostile or abusive working environment, Title VII is violated regardless of whether the plaintiff suffered psychological harm. The Court's decision reaffirms *Meritor Savings Bank v. Vinson,* 477 U.S. 57, 40 EPD 36,159 (1986), and is consistent with existing Commission policy on hostile environment harassment. Consequently, the Commission will continue to conduct investigations in hostile environment harassment cases in the same manner as it has previously.

Background

In *Harris,* the plaintiff, Teresa Harris, brought a Title VII action against her former employer, Forklift Systems, Inc. ("Forklift"), an equipment rental company, alleging that Forklift had created a sexually hostile work environment. Harris had worked for Forklift as a manager from April 1985 to October 1987. The case was heard by a magistrate who found that during the period of Harris' employment, Forklift's president, Charles Hardy, subjected Harris to numerous offensive remarks and unwanted sexual innuendoes. Specifically, the court found that Hardy had, on a number of occasions, asked plaintiff and other female employees to retrieve coins from his front pants pocket, asked plaintiff and other female employees to retrieve objects that he had thrown on the ground in front of them and commented, using sexual innuendo, about plaintiff's and other female employees' attire. On other occasions, he remarked to plaintiff in the presence of other employees: "You're a woman, what do you know," "You're a dumb ass woman," and "We need a man as the rental manager." In addition, he once remarked in the presence of other employees, as well as a client, that he and Harris should "go to the Holiday Inn to negotiate [Harris'] raise." *Harris*, slip op. at 1.

In August 1987, Harris complained to Hardy that she found his behavior offensive. Although Hardy apologized and promised to desist, in September 1987 he suggested in the presence of other employees that plaintiff had promised sexual favors to a customer in order to secure an account. Shortly thereafter, Harris tendered her resignation and filed a Title VII action against Forklift alleging hostile environment sexual harassment.

The district court dismissed the case, concluding that Harris had failed to support her claim of sexual harassment. The court found, however, that "Hardy is a vulgar man [who] demeans the female employees at his work place." *Harris v. Forklift Sys., Inc.*, 60 EPD 42,070 (M.D. Tenn. 1991). Moreover, the court stated that "[a] reasonable woman manager under like circumstances would have been offended by Hardy." *Id.* Nevertheless, the court concluded that this was not enough to support a claim of sexual harassment. Applying the standard set forth in *Rabidue v. Osceola Refining Co.*, 805 F. 2d 611, 620, 41 EPD 36,643 (6th Cir. 1986), cert. denied, 481 U.S. 1041 (1987), the court asserted that "the test for whether or not sexual harassment rises to the level of a hostile work environment is whether the harassment is 'conduct which would interfere with that hypothetical reasonable individual's work performance and affect seriously the psychological well-being of that reasonable person under like circumstances.'" *Harris*, 60 EPD 42,070 (quoting *Rabidue*, 805 F. 2d at 620). The district court concluded that Hardy's comments were not "so severe as to be expected to seriously affect [Harris'] psychological well-being," *id.*, and dismissed the complaint. In the court's view, "[a] reasonable woman manager under like circumstances would have been offended by Hardy, but his conduct would not have risen to the level of interfering with that person's work performance." *Id.* In a brief per curiam opinion, the Sixth Circuit affirmed the judgment for Forklift upon the Magistrate's reasoning. See *Harris v. Forklift Sys., Inc.*, 60 EPD 42,071 (6th Cir. 1992) (per curiam).

The Supreme Court granted certiorari, 507 U.S. (1993), to resolve a conflict among the circuits regarding whether a plaintiff must show psychological injury in order to prevail on a hostile environment sexual harassment claim.

The Opinion

At the outset, Justice O'Connor, writing for a unanimous Court, reaffirmed the standard set forth in *Meritor Savings Bank v. Vinson*, 477 U.S. 57, 40 EPD 36,159 (1986), that sexual harassment is actionable if it is sufficiently severe or pervasive to alter the conditions of the plaintiff's employment. The Court noted that an "objectively hostile or abusive work environment" is created when "a reasonable person would find [it] hostile or abusive," and the victim subjectively perceives it as such. *Harris*, slip op. at 4.

Rejecting the Sixth Circuit's psychological injury requirement, the Court noted that even though discriminatory incidents may not seriously affect an employee's psychological well-being,[1] a discriminatorily abusive work environment may, among other things, affect an employee's job performance or advancement. The Court concluded that even if harassing conduct produces no "tangible effects," a plaintiff may assert a Title VII cause of action if the "discriminatory conduct was so severe or pervasive that it created a work environment abusive to employees because of their race, gender, religion, or national origin." *Id.* According to the Court, "[w]hen the workplace is permeated with 'discriminatory intimidation, ridicule, and insult,' that is 'sufficiently severe or pervasive to alter the conditions of the victim's employment and create an abusive working environment,' Title VII is violated." *Id.* (quoting *Meritor*, 477 U.S. at 65, 67) (citations omitted).

In an attempt to clarify *Meritor*, the Court noted that *Meritor*'s reference to environments that completely destroy the emotional and psychological stability of members of minority groups was intended to illustrate egregious cases and was not intended to "mark the boundary of what is actionable." *Id.* at 5. The Court stated: "So long as the environment would reasonably be perceived, and is perceived, as hostile or abusive, there is no need for it also to be psychologically injurious." *Id.* (citation omitted).

Noting that the test for hostile environment is not "mathematically precise," the Court concluded that in assessing a hostile environment claim, the totality of the circumstances must be examined, including "the frequency of the discriminatory conduct; its severity; whether it is physically threatening or humiliating, or a mere offensive utterance; and whether it unreasonably interferes with an employee's work performance." *Id.* While psychological injury may be relevant, it is not required. See *id.* at 5–6.

Accordingly, the Court remanded the case for consideration of whether a hostile environment had been created. The Court concluded that the district court's concern with whether Harris suffered psychological injury "may well have influenced its ultimate conclusion, especially given that the court found this to be a 'close case.'" *Id.* at 6.

Justice Scalia and Justice Ginsburg issued separate concurring opinions. In his concurrence, Justice Scalia suggested that although the Court refined the *Meritor* standard, little certitude has been added. His concurrence noted that even though the Court adopted an objective standard for determining whether a hostile environment has been created and listed factors to be evaluated, it did not suggest how much of each factor is required, nor did it isolate a single factor as determinative. However, Justice Scalia asserted that he knew of "no alternative to the course the Court today has taken . . . I know of no test more faithful to the inherently vague statutory language than the one the Court today adopts." *Harris* (Scalia, J., concurring), slip op. at 2.

In her concurring opinion, Justice Ginsburg framed the critical issue in hostile environment cases as "whether members of one sex are exposed to disadvantageous terms or conditions of employment to which members of the other sex are not exposed." *Harris* (Ginsburg, J., concurring), slip op. at 1. Citing the Commission's brief, Justice Ginsburg suggested that the major inquiry in hostile environment cases should be "whether the discriminatory conduct has unreasonably interfered with the plaintiff's work performance." *Id.* According to Justice Ginsburg, all the plaintiff need establish is that the harassing conduct "[made] it more difficult to do the job." *Id.* at 1–2.

Analysis

The Court's decision in *Harris* reaffirmed *Meritor* and clarified, rather than altered, the elements necessary for proving hostile environment sexual harassment. The decision is fully consistent with the Commission's "Guidelines on Discrimination Because of Sex," 29 C.F.R. § 1604.11 and its Policy Guidance, "Current Issues of Sexual Harassment," EEOC Policy Guidance No. N-915–050, CCH 3114 (March 19, 1990). Accordingly, *Harris* requires no change in Commission policy or in the way the Commission investigates charges.

The Court in *Harris* adopted the "totality of the circumstances" approach which the Commission had previously set forth in its "Guidelines on Discrimination Because of Sex" and in its Policy Guidance "Current Issues of Sexual Harassment." Thus, in evaluating welcomeness and whether conduct was sufficiently severe or pervasive to constitute a violation, investigators should continue to "look at the record as a whole and at the totality of the circumstances, such as the nature of the sexual advances and the context in which the alleged incidents occurred." 29 C.F.R. § 1604.11(b).

The Court also noted that the factors that indicate a hostile or abusive environment may include the frequency of the discriminatory conduct, its severity, whether it is physically threatening or humiliating, and whether it unreasonably interferes with an employee's work performance.[2] The factors cited by the Court parallel those enumerated in the Commission's Policy Guidance "Current Issues of Sexual Harassment." See "Current Issues of Sexual Harassment," at 14. Moreover, both the Court and the Commission have stressed that an employee is not required to show any single factor in order to succeed on a hostile environment cause of action. See *Harris*, slip op. at 5–6; "Current Issues of Sexual Harassment," at 17. Based on the foregoing, investigators should continue to evaluate charges by considering the factors listed in *Harris* as well as any additional factors that may be relevant in the particular case.

The Court's rejection of the psychological injury requirement is also consistent with the Commission's policy. The Commission explicitly rejects the notion that in order to prove a violation, the plaintiff must prove not only that a reasonable person would find the conduct sufficiently offensive to create a hostile work environment, but also that his/her psychological well-being was affected. While investigators may consider psychological injury as a factor in assessing whether a hostile environment has been created, they should keep in mind that neither this nor any other single factor is required to state a cause of action for hostile environment harassment.[3] See generally "Current Issues of Sexual Harassment," at 15, n.20.

The Court in *Harris* used the "reasonable person" standard for assessing hostile environment claims. Previously, in its Policy Guidance on "Current Issues of Sexual Harassment," the Commission had adopted a "reasonable person" standard: "[i]n determining whether harassment is sufficiently severe or pervasive to create a hostile environment, the harasser's conduct should be evaluated from the objective standpoint of a 'reasonable person.'" "Current Issues of Sexual Harassment," at 14.

In defining the hypothetical "reasonable person," the Commission has emphasized that "[t]he reasonable person standard should consider the victim's perspective and not stereotyped notions of acceptable behavior." *Id.* at 15. In *Harris*, the Court did not elaborate on the definition of "reasonable person." The Court's decision is consistent with the Commission's view that a reasonable person is one with the perspective of the victim.[4] Thus, investigators should continue to consider whether a reasonable person in the victim's circumstances would have found the alleged behavior to be hostile or abusive.

> *Example—CP works in a thirty person advertising firm as a copywriter. CP is one of three female employees at the firm. After she had worked at the firm for about eight months, she was promoted to senior copywriter.*
>
> *Following her promotion, two of her supervisors stopped by her office to inform her of her new responsibilities. During this visit, the supervisors insinuated that CP was promoted because the firm needed to show potential clients "some good bodies" and "some nice legs" in higher positions. They also asked CP if she had slept with the head of personnel in order to obtain her promotion.*

Thereafter, these supervisors as well as some of CP's co-workers continued to taunt CP in front of other co-workers and sometimes before clients, suggesting that CP had been promoted because of her looks and because she was willing to succumb to the advances of clients and supervisors. CP complained to management and subsequently filed a charge with the Commission.

An investigator reviewing this charge should consider the behavior from the standpoint of the reasonable person in CP's position. A reasonable person in CP's position might take umbrage at the comments about "good bodies," "nice legs," or "sleeping one's way to a promotion" and thus might consider her co-workers' and supervisors' behavior to be hostile and offensive.

In *Harris* the Court stated that to violate Title VII, the challenged conduct must not only be sufficiently severe or pervasive objectively to offend a reasonable person, but also must be subjectively perceived as abusive by the charging party. See *Harris,* slip op. at 4. The Court noted that "[s]o long as the environment would reasonably be perceived, and is perceived, as hostile or abusive," Title VII would be violated. *Id.* at 5). There is nothing novel in the notion that a charging party must subjectively perceive a hostile environment in order to assert a violation of Title VII. It is well-settled that a charging party's claim will fail if the allegedly offensive conduct is found to be "welcome."[5]

Under the Commission's current policy, an investigator must consider whether the alleged harassment was "unwelcome . . . verbal or physical conduct of a sexual nature . . ." 29 C.F.R. § 1604.11(a); see *Meritor,* 477 U.S. at 2406 (requiring unwelcomeness analysis). Adopting the Eleventh Circuit's definition of unwelcome conduct, the Commission has stated that "conduct must be unwelcome 'in the sense that the employee did not solicit or incite it, and in the sense that the employee regarded the conduct as undesirable or offensive.'" "Current Issues of Sexual Harassment," at 7 (quoting *Henson v. City of Dundee,* 682 F. 2d 897, 903, 29 EPD 32,993 (11th Cir. 1982)). This policy requires investigators to examine whether the victim's conduct is consistent with an assertion that the alleged harassing behavior was both uninvited and offensive to the charging party. The second prong of the unwelcomeness inquiry, whether the employee considered the conduct offensive, is, in effect, synonymous with "subjectively perceiv[ing] the environment to be abusive." *Harris,* slip op. at 4.

In order to establish a subjective perception of abuse, the charging party must testify that s/he found the alleged conduct to be hostile or abusive at the time it occurred.[6] Unless the respondent produces evidence to the contrary, the subjective prong of the analysis will be satisfied.

Example—CP, a woman, has worked for A Corporation for three years. When she first began working for A Corporation, she joined in when her co-workers and supervisors would have sexual discussions. She herself would make sexual comments and lewd references.

After she had worked for A Corporation for about a year, her supervisors allowed her co-workers to post sexually explicit pictures on their office walls and in the hallways. Even though CP had not been offended by her co-workers' bawdy remarks, she believed that the posting of pornographic pictures demeaned women. She complained to her supervisor, who refused to ask the employees to remove the pictures. Shortly thereafter, more pictures were posted. After again receiving no response to her complaint, CP filed a charge.

Based on these facts, an investigator should find that the conduct was unwelcome, i.e., that CP subjectively considered the pornographic pictures to be abusive. Her willingness to engage in sexual banter is not material to assessing her perception of the pictures.

Note that an investigator may consider the prevalence of sexual banter in analyzing whether a hostile environment was created for other employees.

Finally, the *Harris* decision reinforces the Commission's position that conduct that constitutes harassment on any of the bases covered by Title VII is equally unlawful as a discriminatory term, condition, or privilege of employment. See *Harris,* slip op. at 4; see also *id.* at 2 (Ginsburg, J., concurring) (noting that harassment based on race, national origin, religion, and gender is equally unlawful). The Commission believes that Harris also applies to cases involving hostile environment harassment on the basis of age or disability. Accordingly, investigators should consider *Harris* applicable regardless of the anti-discrimination statute on which the charge is premised.[7]

Notes

[1]Prior to oral argument, the respondent conceded that psychological injury was not required in order to support a hostile environment cause of action under Title VII.

[2]In order to show that "[the alleged conduct] unreasonably interferes with . . . work performance," the employee need not show diminished performance but only that the alleged offensive conduct made it more difficult for him/her to do his/her job. See *Harris* (Ginsburg, J., concurring), slip op. at 1–2; see also *Harris,* slip op. at 4 ("even without regard to these tangible effects [such as detracting from employees' job performance], the very fact that the discriminatory conduct was so severe or pervasive that it created an environment abusive to employees because of their race, gender, religion, or national origin offends Title VII's broad rule of work place equality").

[3]Psychological injury may also be relevant for purposes of computing damages.

[4]For a more detailed discussion of this issue, see "Current Issues of Sexual Harassment," at 14. As explained there, although the reasonable person standard must take account of the victim's perspective, "Title VII does not serve 'as the vehicle for vindicating the petty slights suffered by the hypersensitive.'" *Id.* (quoting *Zabkowicz v. West Bend Co.,* 589 F. Supp. 780, 784, 35 EPD 34,766 (E.D. Wisc. 1984)).

[5]Note that even if a particular charging party has not been subjectively offended by the conduct in question, if a reasonable person would find the conduct offensive, the Commission itself may pursue relief for any other persons identified in the course of the investigation who subjectively found the environment to be hostile. See *General Telephone Co. of Northwest, Inc. v. EEOC,* 446 U.S. 318, 22 EPD 30,861 (1980).

[6]It is the Commission's position that "[w]hen there is some indication of welcomeness or when the credibility of the parties is at issue, the charging party's claim will be considerably strengthened if she [or he] made a contemporaneous complaint or protest." "Current Issues of Sexual Harassment," at 7. However, while making a complaint or issuing a protest may be helpful to charging party's case, "it is not a necessary element of the claim." *Id.* at 8.

[7]If one is subjected to taunts on the basis of race, national origin, etc., there is ordinarily no question that the comments are perceived as abusive and are therefore unwelcome. Nevertheless, before and after *Harris,* if the record shows that the comments are not unwelcome or perceived as hostile or offensive, the charging party will not prevail.

Bibliography

Age Discrimination in Employment Act (ADEA) (1967), 29 U.S.C. §§621 et. seq., available at: http://eeoc.gov/law/adea.html, and accompanying regulations at 29 C.F.R. §1625. Available at: www.access.gpo.gov/nara/cfr/waisidx_00/29cfr1625_00.html

Americans with Disabilities Act (ADA) (1990), 42 U.S.C. §§12101 et. Seq. Available at: http://eeoc.gov/laws/ada.html

Beard v. Flying J, Inc., 266 F. 3d 792 (8th Cir. 2001)

Bennett v. Progressive Corporation, 225 F. Supp. 2d 190 (N.D. N.Y. 2002)

Berdahl, J.L., Magley, V.J., & Waldo, C.R. (1996). The Sexual Harassment of Men. *Psychology of Women Quarterly, 20,* 527–547.

Bergman, M.E., Langhout, R.D., Palmieri, P.A., Cortina, L.M., & Fitzgerald, L.F. (2002). The (un)reasonableness of reporting: Antecedents and consequences of reporting sexual harassment. *Journal of Applied Psychology, 87,* 230–242.

Branscombe, N.R., Harvey, R.D., & Schmitt, M.T. (1999). Perceiving pervasive discrimination among African Americans: Implications for group identification and well-being. *Journal of Personality and Social Psychology, 77*(1), 135–149.

Brown v. Henderson, 155 F.S upp. 2d 502 (M.D. N.C. 2000)

Buchanan, N.T. (2001, December). *PTSD among sexually harassed African American women.* Presented at the meeting of the International Society for Traumatic Stress Studies, New Orleans.

Buchanan, N.T., & Ormerod, A.J. (2001, March). Using focus group methodology to examine the sexual and racial harassment experiences of African American women. Symposium at the annual meeting of the Association for Women in Psychology, Los Angeles, CA.

Burlington Industries, Inc. v. Ellerth, 524 U.S. 742, 118 S. Ct. 2257 (1998)

Cadena v. Pacesetter Corp., 224 F. 3d 1203 (10th Cir. 2000)

Cancelli, A.A., Ponterotto, J.G., Reynolds, A.L., & Utsey, S.O. (2000). Racial discrimination, coping, life satisfaction, and self-esteem among African-Americans. *Cultural Diversity and Ethnic Minority Psychology, 5*(4), 329–339.

Cardenas v. Massey, 269 F. 3d 251 (3rd Cir. 2001)

Casiano v. AT&T Corporation, 213 F. 3d 278 (5th Cir. 2000)

Castleberry v. Edward M. Chadbourne, Inc., 810 So. 2d 1028 (Fla. App. 2002)

Chavera v. Independent School District, 221 F. Supp. 2d 741 (S.D. Tex. 2002)

Cherry v. Menard, Inc., 101 F. Supp. 2d 1160 (N.D. Iowa 2000)

Church v. Maryland, 2002 WL 65992 (D. Md. 2002)

Cooke v. County of Suffolk (Unpublished) 2001 WL 637374 (2d Cir. 2001)

Cortina, L.M., Magley, V.J., Williams, J.H., & Langhout, R.D. (2001). Incivility in the workplace: Incidence and impact. *Journal of Occupational Health Psychology, 6*(1), 64–80.

Cortina, L.M., & Magley, V.J. (2002, June). Retaliation in the context of interpersonal mistreatment: The dangers of speaking out. Symposium conducted at the annual convention of the American Psychological Society.

Crawford v. Thomason, 2001 WL 329527 (Tenn. App. 2001)

Crowley v. L.L.Bean, Inc., 303 F.3d 387 (1st. Cir. 2002)

Culbertson, A.L., Rosenfield, P., Booth-Kewley, S., & Magnuson, P. (1992). *Assessment of sexual harassment in the Navy: Results of the 1989 Navy-wide survey,* TR-92–11. San Diego, CA: Naval Personnel Research and Development Center.

Dillard Department Stores, Inc. v. Gonzales, 72 S.W. 3d 398 (Tex. App. 2002)

Dockery v. Dayton-Hudson Corp. (Unpublished) 2001 WL 693094 (7th Cir. 2001)

Donovan, M.A., Drasgow, F., & Munson, L.I. (1998). The perceptions of fair interpersonal treatment scale: Development and validation of a measure of interpersonal treatment in the workplace. *Journal of Applied Psychology, 83*(5), 683–692.

Dowdy v. North Carolina (Unpublished) 2001 WL 1408456 (4th Cir. 2001)

Dowling v. The Home Depot, 2003 WL 40741 (E.D. Pa. 2003)

Duviella v. Counseling Service of the Eastern District of New York, 2001 WL 1776158 (E.D. N.Y. 2001) affirmed (Unpublished Opinion) 2002 WL 31628509 (2d Cir. 2002).

Equal Employment Opportunity Commission (1994). *Enforcement guidance, "Harris v. Forklift Systems."* Available at: http://eeoc.gov/docs/harris.html

Equal Employment Opportunity Commission v. Dial Corporation, 156 F. Supp. 2d 926 (N.D. Ill. 2001)

Equal Employment Opportunity Commission v. R&R Ventures, 244 F. 3d 334 (4th Cir 2001)

Equal Employment Opportunity Commission. (1990). *Policy guidance on employer liability under title VII for sexual favoritism.* Available at: http://eeoc.gov/docs/sexualfavor.html

Equal Employment Opportunity Commission. (1990). *Policy guidance on current issues of sexual harassment.* Available at: http://eeoc.gov/docs/current issues.html

Equal Employment Opportunity Commission. (1997). *Enforcement guidance: Application of EEO laws to contingent workers placed by temporary employment agencies and other staffing firms.* Available at: http://eeoc.gov/docs/conting.html

Equal Employment Opportunity Commission. (1998). *Compliance manual: Retaliation.* Available at: http://eeoc.gov/docs/retal.html

Equal Employment Opportunity Commission. (1999). *Enforcement guidance: Vicarious liability for unlawful harassment by supervisors.* Available at: http://eeoc.gov/docs/harassment.html

Equal Employment Opportunity Commission. (2000). *Guidelines on discrimination because of religion,* 29 C.F.R. §1605. Available at: www.access.gpo.gov/nara/cfr/waisidx_00/29cfr1605_00.html

Equal Employment Opportunity Commission. (2000). *Guidelines on discrimination because of sex,* 29 C.F.R. §1604. Available at: www.access.gpo.gov/nara/cfr/waisidx_00/29cfr1604_00.html

Equal Employment Opportunity Commission. (2000). *Guidelines on discrimination because of national origin,* 29 C.F.R. §1606. Available at: www.access.gpo.gov/nara/cfr/waisidx_00/29cfr1605_00.html

Equal Employment Opportunity Commission. (2002). *Rescission of enforcement guidance on remedies available to undocumented workers under federal employment discrimination laws.* Available at: http://eeoc.gov/docs/undoc-rescind.html

Equal Employment Opportunity Commission. (2002). *Compliance manual: National origin discrimination.* Available at: http://eeoc.gov/docs/national-origin.html

Faragher v. City of Boca Raton, 524 U.S. 775, 118 S. Ct. 2275 (1998)

Fielder v. United Airlines Corp., 218 F. 3d 973 (9th Cir. 2000)

Fitzgerald, L.F., Hulin, C., & Drasgow, F. (1995). The antecedents and consequences of sexual harassment in organizations: An integrated process model. In S. Sauter & G. Keita (Eds.), *Job Stress 2000: Emergent Issues.* Washington, DC: American Psychological Association.

Fitzgerald, L.F., Swan, S., & Fischer, K. (1994). Why didn't she just report him? The psychological and legal context of women's responses to sexual harassment. *Journal of Social Issues, 51,* 117–138.

Fitzgerald, L.F., Swan, S., & Magley, V.J. (1997). But was it really sexual harassment: Psychological, behavioral, and legal definitions of sexual harassment. In W.

O'Donohue (Ed.), *Sexual harassment: Research, theory, and treatment*. New York: Allyn & Bacon.

Franze, I.J., & Magley, V.J. (2001, March). Temporal sequencing of coping with sexual harassment. Symposium conducted at the meeting of the Association of Women in Psychology, Los Angeles.

Frederick v. Sprint/United Management Co., 246 F. 3d 1305 (11th Cir. 2001)

Gardenswartz, L., & Rowe, A. (1994). *Diverse teams at work*. New York: Irwin.

Gawley v. Indiana University, 276 F. 3d 301 (7th Cir. 2001)

Glomb, T.M. (2002). Workplace anger and aggression: Informing conceptual models with data from specific encounters. *Journal of Occupational Heath Psychology, 7*(1), 37–56.

Glomb, T.M., Richman, W.L., Hulin, C.L., Drasgow, F., Schneider, K.T., & Fitzgerald, L.F. (1997). Ambient sexual harassment: An integrated model of antecedents and consequences. *Organizational Behavior and Human Decision Processes, 71*, 309–328.

Greene v. Trustees of Columbia University, 2002 WL 31235796 (S.D.N.Y. 2002).

Gruber, J.E. (1998). The impact of male work environments and organization policies on women's experiences of sexual harassment. *Gender and Society, 3*(12), 301–329.

Gruber, J.E., Kauppinen-Toropainen, K., & Smith, M. (1996). Sexual harassment types and severity: Linking research and policy. In M. Stockdale (Ed.), *Women and work: Sexual harassment in the workplace* (Sec. III, Vol. 5). Thousand Oaks, CA: Sage.

Gutek, B. (1985). *Sex in the workplace*. San Francisco, CA: Jossey-Bass.

Gutek, B., & Koss, M.P. (1993). Changed women and changed organizations: Consequences of and coping with sexual harassment. *Journal of Vocational Behavior, 42*, 28–48.

Harris v. Forklift Systems, Inc., 510 U.S. 17, 114 S.Ct. 367 (1993)

Harrison v. Eddy Potash, Inc., 248 F. 3d 1014 (10th Cir. 2001)

Hatley v. Hilton Hotels Corp., 308 F. 3d 473 (5th Cir. 2002)

Haugerud v. Amery School District, 259 F. 3d 678 (7th Cir. 2001)

Henderson v. Simmons Food, 217 F.3d 612 (8th Cir. 2000)

Hertzberg v. SRAM Corporation, 261 F. 3d 651 (7th Cir. 2001)

Hesson-McInnis, M., & Fitzgerald, L.F. (1997). Sexual harassment: A preliminary test of an integrative model. *Journal of Applied Social Psychology, 27*(10), 877–901.

Hill v. American General Finance Incorporated, 218 F. 3d 639 (7th Cir. 2000)

Horkan v. United States Postal Service, EEOC Appeal No. 01976837 (April 6, 2000)

Howley v. Town of Stratford (2d Cir., 2000)

Hulin, C.L., Fitzgerald, L.F., & Drasgow, F. (1996). Organizational influences on sexual harassment. In M. Stockdale (Ed.), *Women and work: Sexual harassment in the workplace*. (Vol. 5), pp. 127–150. Thousand Oaks, CA: Sage.

Hussain v. Long Island Railroad Company, 2002 WL 31108195 (S.D. N.Y. 2002).

Jackson v. Arkansas Department of Education, 272 F. 3d 1020 (8th Cir. 2001)

Johnson v. West, 218 F. 3d 725 (7th Cir. 2000)

Jones v. Illinois Department of Transportation, 2001 WL 1545882 (N.D. Ill. 2001)

Jones v. Rent-a-Center, Inc., 2002 WL 31940707 (D. Kan. 2002)

Keashly, L. (2001). Interpersonal and systemic aspects of emotional abuse at work: The target's perspective. *Violence and Victims, 16*(3), 233–268.

Klonoff, E.A., Landrine, H., & Ullman, J.B. (1999). Racial discrimination and psychiatric symptoms among blacks. *Cultural Diversity and Ethnic Minority Psychology, 5*(4) 329–339.

Knutson v. Brownstein, 2001 WL 1661929 (S.D. N.Y. 2001)

Lagunovich v. Findlay City School System, 2001 WL 1734471 (N.D. Ohio 2001)

Little v. Windemere Relocation, Inc., 301 F.3d 958 (9th Cir. 2002)

Livingston, J.A. (1982). Responses to sexual harassment on the job: Legal, organizational, and individual actions. *Journal of Social Issues, 38*(4), 5–22.

Lockard v. Pizza Hut, Inc., 162 F.3d 1062 (10th Cir. 1998).

Lumhoo v. The Home Depot USA, 2002 WL 31409430 (E.D. N.Y. 2002)

Madison v. IBP, Inc., 257 F. 3d 780 (8th Cir. 2001)

Magley, V.J., Salisbury, J., Zickar, M., & Fitzgerald, L.F. (1997, April). *Evaluating the effectiveness of sexual harassment training.* Symposium conducted at the annual meeting of the Society for Industrial and Organizational Psychology, St. Louis.

Magley, V.J., Waldo, C.R., Drasgow, F., & Fitzgerald, L.F. (1999). The impact of sexual harassment on military personnel: Is it the same for men and women? *Military Psychology 11*(3), 283–302.

Marrero v. Goya of Puerto Rico, 304 F. 3d 7 (1st Cir. 2002)

Martindale, M. (1990). *Sexual harassment in the military: 1988.* Arlington, VA: Defense Manpower Data Center.

Matira v. Bald Head Island Management Incorporated, 259 F.3d 261 (4th Cir. 2001)

May v. AutoZone Stores, Inc., 2001 WL 1704158 (N.D. Miss. 2001)

McCowan v. Software Spectrum, Inc., 2002 WL 505138 (Tex. App. 2002)

McGrath v. Nassau County Health Care Corporation, 204 F.R.D. 240 (E.D. N.Y. 2001)

McIntosh, P. (1986, April). *White privilege and male privilege: A personal account of coming to see correspondences through work in women's studies.* Presented at the Virginia Women's Studies Association Conference, Richmond, Virginia.

Meadows v. County of Tulare (Unpublished) 1999 WL 685960 (9th Cir. 1999)

Meritor Savings Bank v. Vinson, 477 U.S. 57, 106 S. Ct. 2399 (1986)

Miller v. Woodharbor Molding & Millworks, 80 F. Supp. 1026 (N.D. Iowa 2000)

Mills, C.W. (1997). *The racial contract.* Ithaca, NY: Cornell University Press.

Molnar v. Booth, 229 F. 3d 593 (7th Cir. 2000)

Montero v. AGCO Corporation, 192 F. 3d 856 (9th Cir. 1999)

Munroe v. Compaq Computer Corporation, 229 F. Supp. 2d 52 (D. N.H. 2002)

Murrell, A.J. (1996). Sexual harassment and women of color: Issues, challenges, and future directions. *Women and Work: Sexual Harassment in the Workplace, Perspectives on Sexual Harassment in the Workplace* (Sec. II, Vol. 5). Thousand Oaks, CA: Sage.

New Hampshire Department of Corrections v. Butland, 797 A. 2d 860 (NH 2002)

Nichols v. Azteca Restaurant Enterprises, 256 F. 3d 864 (9th Cir. 2001)

O'Dell v. Trans World Entertainment Corporation, 153 F. Supp. 2d 378 (S.D. N.Y. 2001)

Oncale v. Sundowner Offshore Services, Inc., 523 U.S. 75, 118 S. Ct. 998 (1998)

Pacheco v. New Life Bakery, 187 F. 3d 1055 (9th Cir. 1999)

Passantino v. Johnson & Johnson Consumer Products, 212 F. 3d 493 (9th Cir. 2000)

Petet v. Equity Residential Properties Trust (Unpublished) 2000 WL 1171127 (9th Cir. 2000)

Pollard v. E.I. DuPont de Nemours Co., 523 U.S. 843, 121 S. Ct. 1946 (2001)

Pryor, J., Gledd, J., & Williams, K. (1995). A social psychological model for predicting sexual harassment. *Journal of Social Issues, 51*(1), 69–84.

Pryor, J.B., LaVite, C., & Stoller, L. (1993). A social psychological analysis of sexual harassment: The person/situation interaction. *Journal of Vocational Behavior, 42,* 68–83.

Pryor, J.B., & Whalen, N.J. (1997). A typology of sexual harassment: Characteristics of harassers and the social circumstances under which sexual harassment occurs. In W. Donohue (Ed.), *Sexual harassment: Theory, research and treatment.* Boston, MA: Allyn & Bacon.

Queener v. Windy Hill, Ltd. (Unpublished) 2001 WL 1685581 (Ohio App 2001)

Reed v. MBNA Marketing Systems, Inc., 2002 WL 31554405 (D. Maine 2002)

Reese v. Meritor Automotive Inc. (Unpublished) 2001 WL 227329 (4th Cir. 2001)

Robinson v. Shell Oil, 519 U.S. 337 (1997)

Rosales v. City of San Antonio, 2001 WL 1168797 (W.D. Tex. 2001)

Salisbury, J. (1996). *Healing the aftermath of harassment complaints: The final challenge.* Presented at the American Bar Association Institute on Sexual Harassment, Chicago.

Salisbury, J., & Jaffe, F. (1996). Individual training for sexual harassers. M.A. Paludi (Ed.) *Sexual harassment on college campuses.* Albany, NY: SUNY Press.

Schneider, K.T. (1996). *Bystander stress: Effects of sexual harassment on victims' co-workers.* Paper presented at a symposium on responses to sexual harassment at the annual conference of the American Psychological Association, Toronto, Ontario.

Schneider, K.T., Swan, S., & Fitzgerald, L.F. (1997). Job-related and psychological effects of sexual harassment in the workplace: Empirical evidence from two organizations. *Journal of Applied Psychology, 82,* 401–415.

Shupe, E.I., Cortina, L.M., Ramos, A., Salisbury, J., & Fitzgerald, L.F. (2002). The incidence and outcomes of sexual harassment among Hispanic and non-Hispanic white women: A comparison across levels of cultural affiliation. *Psychology of Women Quarterly, 26,* 298–308.

Smith v. First Union National Bank, 202 F. 3d 234 (4th Cir. 2000)

Stricker v. Cesford Construction Co., 179 F. Supp. 2d 987 (N.D. Iowa 2001)

Stringer, D., Remick, H., Salisbury, J., & Ginorio, A. (1990, Spring). The power and the reasons behind sexual harassment: An employer's guide to solutions. *Public Personnel Management, 19*(1), 187–196.

Talbot, M. (2002, October). Men behaving badly. *The New York Times Magazine.*

Taylor v. Nickels and Dimes, Inc., 2002 WL 1827659 (N.D. Tex. 2002)

Title VII (1964, as amended 1991) 29 U.S.C. §§2000e et. seq. Available at: http://eeoc.gov/laws/vii.html

Tutman v. WBBM-TV, Inc., 209 F. 3d 1044 (7th Cir. 2000)

Van Alstyne v. Ackerly Group, Inc. (Unpublished) 2001 WL 540379 (2d Cir. 2001)

Walker v. Thompson, 214 F. 3d 615 (5th Cir. 2000)

Wasti, S.A., & Cortina, L.M. (2002). Coping in context: Sociocultural determinants of responses to sexual harassment. *Journal of Personality and Social Psychology, 83*(2), 394–405.

Wilburn v. Fleet Financial Group, Inc., 170 F. Supp. 2d 219 (D. Conn. 2001)

Williams, J.H., Fitzgerald, L.F., & Drasgow, F. (1999). The effects of organizational practices on sexual harassment and individual outcomes in the military. *Military Psychology, 11*(3), 303–328.

Wright v. Anixter, Inc. (Unpublished) 1999 WL 638714 (9th Cir. 1999)

Wyatt v. Hunt Plywood Company, 297 F. 3d 405 (5th Cir. 2002)

Young v. R.R. Morrison and Son, Inc., 159 F. Supp. 2d 921 (N.D. Miss. 2000)

Zelaya v. Eastern & Western Hotel Corp. (Unpublished) 2001 WL 219897 (9th Cir. 2001)

Zemke, R., Raines, C., & Filipczak, B. (2000). *Generations at work: Managing the clash of veterans, boomers, xers, and nexters in your workplace.* New York: American Management Association.

Index

A

Accused harasser: debriefing of, 137–138, 168–169; failure to obtain input from, 100. *See also* Harassers

Ackerly Group, Van Alstyne v., 14

ADA (Americans with Disabilities Act), 10, 22

Addictive disorders, 35

ADEA (Age Discrimination in Employment Act), 10, 22

Administrative agency, 7

Adverse actions retaliation, 22–25

Affidavit, 7

Affirmative defense: defining, 7; EEOC guidance on effective investigative process for, 18–19; *Faragher/Ellerth*, 14

Age discrimination, 10, 22

Age harassment, 31–32

Allegations: clarifying the, 75; of criminal act, 105; procedures for investigating complaint, 63–65*fig. See also* Complaints

Appellate court, 6

Assumptions prior to investigation, 91

Attorney-client privilege: attorney work product doctrine and, 84; legal issues regarding, 83–84; waiver of work product and, 84

Attorneys: employee requesting an, 105; witnesses insisting on presence of their, 105

B

Bennett v. Progressive Corporation, 151

Berdahl, J. L., 30, 46

Bergman, M. E., 38

Body language, 96–97

Booth-Kewley, S., 37

Branscombe, N. R., 38

Buchanan, N. T., 45

Burden of proof, 91

Burlington Industries v. Ellerth. See Ellerth decision

C

Calendars, 114

CareerJournal.com, 26

"Chain of custody," 91–92

City of Boca Raton, Florida, Faragher v., 12–15, 16, 17

Civil vs. criminal investigations: assumptions, 91; burden of proof, 91; evidence gathering, 91–92; warnings and time limits, 92

Claims: common terms used in litigating, 7; stress of investigating harassment/discrimination, 3

Closing the investigation criteria: to avoid dragging out investigation, 100; to avoid premature closing, 100; behavior determined to be policy vs. legal violations, 116–117; credibility has been determined, 117*fig*–119; deciding on relevant/corroborating evidence, 120–121; determining, 78–79; identifying boorish behavior/bad management vs. harassment, 121; making a determination and, 122; risk factors for litigation after, 121–122

Complainant interviews: closure of, 111–112; learning the facts during, 110–111; preliminary issues of, 109–110

Complainants: debriefing the, 134–136, 168–169; failure to obtain input from, 100; fears of retaliation by, 103; interviewing the, 110–112; offering administrative leave/counseling/medical costs to, 136; problem with "I will handle it myself," 102; procedures for investigating allegations of, 63–65*fig*; requiring face-to-face confrontation between harasser and, 101–102; uncooperative, 103–104; who quits in the middle of investigation, 104; wish to remain anonymous by, 103. *See also* Employees; Plaintiffs; Retaliation; Victims

Complaints: defining, 5–6; filed with EEOC before investigation is finished, 106; HR and investigator roles in effective handling of, 67–68; by illegal aliens, 29; nontarget harassment, 28; off-duty conduct, 29;

procedures for investigating allegations of, 63–65*fig*; prompt, corrective action following, 125–131, 167; retaliation, 22–25; same sex harassment, 28; sexual favoritism, 26; system for intake of, 72; by temporary workers, 27–28; third-party harassment, 25–26; workplace dating, 26–27. *See also* Allegations

Computer calendars, 114

Computer records, 115

Conducting investigation: common problems that may arise during, 102–106; interviews and, 77–78, 92–99, 107–114; ten most common mistakes when, 100–102

Confidentiality: failure to maintain privacy and, 101; internal management of documentation and, 85; tips on sharing information and protecting, 89–91; ways to ask witnesses to protect, 90–91, 109; what you can't share, 90

"Constructive discharge," 18

Coping with harassment, 37–38

Corroborating evidence, 120–121

Cortina, L. M., 32, 33, 37, 38, 45

Counseling: offered to complainant, 136; offered to harasser, 137

Counseling Service of the Eastern *District of New York, Duviella v.*, 103–104

Criminal act allegations, 105

Criminal investigations. *See* Civil vs. criminal investigations

Crowley v. L.L. Bean, 29

Culbertson, A. L., 37

Cultural differences: body language and, 97; harassment in context of, 44–46; importance of investigator understanding, 45; sexual harassment and Mexican-American, 44–46

Culture of respect model, 60*fig*

D

Debriefing: of the accused, 137–138; benefits of, 133–134; checklist for, 142; of the complainant, 134–136; of employees and witnesses, 142; investigator training on, 168–169; leading the, 134; stages of, 139–141; of the workgroups, 138–139. *See also* Remedies

Defendants, 6

Demotions, 129

Depositions: defining, 7; taken from investigators, 144–145

Diaries, 115

Disability harassment: ADA definition of, 22; ADA prohibition on, 22; EEOC on employer liability for, 22; *Horkan v. United States Postal Service* decision on, 22; nature of, 31–32

Discipline: considerations in administering, 127–129; types of, 129–130

Discovery, 7

Discrimination: organization policies on preventing, 61–63; stress of investigating claims of, 3; training/education to prevent, 66–67, 130–131. *See also* Harassment

Discrimination law: investigator training in, 155–156;

relevant to EEO laws, 9–11; why investigators need to know, 9

Diversity: four layers of, 43*fig*; harassment in the context of, 42–47; investigation training regarding, 159–161; investigator's valuing/understanding of, 56; of race, ethnicity, other cultural differences, 44–46; tips for investigators regarding, 47

Documentation: adequate record keeping of, 81–82; attorney-client privilege relating to, 83–84; gathering evidence using, 91–92; gathering factual, 114–115; identifying pertinent, 76; internal management/confidentiality issues of, 85; investigator training on, 161–162; writing investigative report, 85–88. *See also* Investigative files

Donovan, M. A., 32

Drasgow, F., 30, 32, 39, 40, 65

Duty to investigate, 71–72

Duviella v. Counseling Service of the Eastern District of New York, 103–104

Dynamic organizational model: enforcement measures, 60; organizational values/vision/leadership practices, 59–60; preventative programs, 60; resolution strategies/resources, 61

E

EEOC Compliance Manual: adverse action retaliation addressed in, 23–25; on national origin discrimination, 21

EEOC Enforcement Guidance: on effect of employee's failure to complain, 19; on effective investigative process, 18–19; on policy/complaint procedure, 18; regarding illegal aliens, 29; regarding temporary workers, 27–28; on supervisory capacity, 17; on tangible employment action, 17–18

EEOC (Equal Employment Opportunity Commission): complaint filed before investigation is finished, 106; Compliance Manual of, 21; described, 6; disability harassment liability finding by, 22; governing harassment/discrimination, 9–11; guidance on supervisory harassment, 17–19; national origin harassment defined by, 21–22; race/color harassment defined by, 19–20; work-sharing agreements between state agencies and, 10

Electronic communications (e-mails), 115

Ellerth decision: affirmative defense as defined by, 14; EEOC Enforcement Guidance based on, 17–19; expanded to cover other forms of harassment, 19–22; hostile work environment defined in, 13; liability questions unanswered by, 16–17; liability standard when harasser is co-worker, 16*fig*; liability standard when harasser is victim's supervisor, 15*fig*; not applied to third-party harassment, 25; quid pro quo sexual harassment defined in, 13; tangible job injury definition/employer liability in, 12

Employees: dealing with distressed, 98–99; debriefing, 142, 168–169; effect of failure to complain by, 19; impact of harassment on individual, 39; insisting on attending with union representative, 105; remedies for aggrieved, 132–133; training/education on discrimination/harassment/retaliation, 66–67, 130–131; Weingarten rights of nonunion, 79–80. *See also* Complainants; Interviews

Employers: EEOC policy and complaint procedure guidelines for, 18; standards for liability of, 12–15, 22. *See also* Organizations; Tangible employment action

Enforcement of the heterosexual male gender role, 46

Enforcement measures, 60

Environmental factors, 40–41

Ethnic harassment, 31–32. *See also* Race/color harassment

Ethnicity differences: harassment in context of, 44–46; as sexual harassment factor, 44–45

Evidence: corroborating, 120–121; deciding what is relevant, 120; gathering of, 91–92

F

Face-to-face confrontation, 101–102

Failure to protect privacy, 101

Fair Practices Commission, 7

Faragher v. City of Boca Raton, Florida: affirmative defense defined by, 14; EEOC Enforcement Guidance based on, 17–19; expanded to cover other forms of harassment, 19–22; hostile work environment sexual harassment defined in, 13; liability questions unanswered by, 16–17; liability standard when harasser is co-worker, 16*fig*; liability standard when harasser is victim's supervisor, 15*fig*; liability standards when harasser is victim's supervisor, 15*fig*; not applied to third-party harassment, 25; quid pro quo sexual harassment defined in, 13; standard for employer liability in defined in, 12–15

FCRA (Fair Credit Reporting Act), 79

Ferina, S., 31

Filipczak, B., 45

Fisher, K., 37

Fitzgerald, L. F., 30, 33, 37, 38, 39, 40, 45, 65, 67

FTC (Federal Trade Commission), 79

G

Gardenswartz, L., 42, 43

Gender differences: responses to sexual harassment and, 47; types of sexual harassment and, 46–47

Gender harassment: enforcement of the heterosexual male gender role type of, 46–47; as sexual harassment, 44–45

Gender hostility, 31

Generational differences, 45–46

Ginorio, A., 34

Gledd, J., 33

Glomb, T. M., 32, 39

Gruber, J. E., 63

Gutek, B., 37, 38, 40

H

Harasser behavior: cultural/generational perspectives of, 44–46; factors motivating, 33; ignorance as reason for, 35–36, 46; judging severity of, 126–127*t*; personal crisis and, 35; personality or addictive disorders and, 35; power issues and, 34–35; sexism, racism, or stereotyping, 36

Harassers: debriefing the, 137–138, 168–169; discipline of, 127–130; factors motivating behavior of, 33; individual reasons for behavior of, 34–36; interviewing the alleged, 112–113; mistake to terminate prior to investigation, 101; quid pro quo, 33–34; requiring face-to-face confrontation between complainant and, 101–102; training for individual, 131, 138; who will not cooperate, 104. *See also* Accused harasser

Harassment: in the context of diversity, 42–47; hostile work environment sexual, 12; identifying boorish behavior/bad management vs., 121; long length of time since events of, 102–103; national origin, 21–22; organization policies on preventing, 61–63; quid pro quo sexual, 11; race/color, 19–20; religious, 20; role of HR and investigators in dealing with, 67–68; stress of investigating claims of, 3; supervisory, 12–19; Title VII definition of, 11. *See also* Discrimination; Psychology of harassment; Remedies

"Harassment Hot Line," 64

Harassment law: illegal aliens and, 29; impact of *Faragher* and *Ellerth* on, 12–22, 15*fig*, 16*fig*; investigator training in, 155–156; nontarget harassment under, 28; off-duty conduct under, 29; relevant to EEO laws, 9–11; same sex harassment under, 28; sexual favoritism under, 26; temporary workers and, 27–28; third-party harassment under, 25; why investigators need to know, 9; workplace dating under, 26–27

Harassment training: to implement organization policies, 66–67; for individual harassers, 131, 138; for workgroups, 130–131. *See also* Organization harassment policies; Training investigator program

Harvey, R. D., 38

Hesson-McInnis, M., 38

Hill-Thomas hearings, 37

Horkan v. United States Postal Service, 22

Hostile work environment sexual harassment: described, 12; nontarget harassment and, 28; standards of liability for, 13–15

HR (Human Resource) professionals: CareerJournal.com survey of, 26; intake coordinator of, 72; role in effective handling of complaints, 67–68

Hulin, C. L., 30, 33, 39

Human Rights Commission, 7

I

Ignorance/harasser behavior, 35–36, 46

Illegal aliens, 29

Intake coordinator, 72

"Internal" cop role, 4–5

Interviewing process: completing the, 114; introductory remarks with each witness, 109; tips on the, 107–108; universal issues of, 108–109; when interviewing the alleged harasser, 112–113; when interviewing the complainant, 110–112; when interviewing the witnesses, 113–114

Interviews: body language during, 96–97; civil vs. criminal investigation, 92–99; dealing with distressed employees, 98–99; order of, 99; questioning style during, 95–96; questioning techniques during, 93–94, 97; questions to avoid during, 97–98; setting atmosphere through manner/tone, 96; setting location/length/logistics of, 77–78; summarizing/reassuring during, 95–96. *See also* Employees; Investigators; Witnesses

Investigation notes, 83

Investigations: assuring that it is proceeding correctly, 73–75; civil vs. criminal, 91–99; criteria for closing the, 116–122; decision to terminate now and later do, 101; determining when complete, 78–79; documentation/record keeping during, 76, 81–88, 161–162; dragging out the, 100; duty to investigate and, 71–72; dynamic organization model conducive to, 59–61; lawsuit/administrative complaint filed before completed, 106; making a determination in, 122; procedures for investigating allegations, 63–65*fig*; "prompt and thorough," 106; role diversity may play during, 47; shortcutting the, 100

Investigations tips/techniques: for civil vs. criminal investigations, 91–99; common problems arising during, 102–106; for completing the process, 114–115; for conducting the investigation, 99–106; for confidentiality, 89–91; for interviewing process, 107–114; ten most common mistakes, 100–102

Investigative files: components of, 82; investigative notes, 83. *See also* Documentation

Investigative legal issues: FTC requirements for notice, 79; Weingarten rights of nonunion employees, 79–80

Investigative plan: assessing retaliation/safety/workgroup functioning issues, 76–77; to assure that investigation is proceeding correctly, 73–75; clarifying the allegations, 75; developing an, 72–77, 73*fig*; for gathering preliminary documents, 72; identifying applicable policies/procedures, 76; identifying potential witnesses/documents, 76; investigative training on developing, 163–164; legal issues to consider, 79–80; regarding size of investigation, 78–79; setting up interviews, 77–78

Investigative report: clear and concise language of, 85; disseminating the written, 88, 106; documenting follow-up activities in, 88; effective organization of, 87; issues to avoid, 86; recommendations to include in, 85–86; referencing policies at issue in, 86; when to write, 85

Investigator characteristics: ease with difficult behaviors/emotions, 52–53; emotional maturity/detachment, 55–56; excellent relationship with management, 54; having law enforcement background, 53–54; knowledge of hierarchy and culture, 55; legal knowledge, 53; presentation skills, 55; superior communication skills, 52; unbiased pursuit of the facts, 51–52; valuing and understanding diversity, 58

Investigator selection: attorney as, 57–58; factors involved in, 56–57; internal or external, 57; team approach to, 57

Investigator as witness: cross-examination of, 146–147; depositions taken from, 144–145; direct examination during trial, 146; possible questions asked, 143145

Investigators: characteristics of effective, 51–58; critical issues of retaliation complaints for, 24; differentiating between roles of decision maker and, 101; familiarity with harassment/discrimination law by, 9; greatest fears of, 3–5; greatest motivators of, 5; importance of understanding cultural offensiveness standards, 45; interpreting legal jargon, 5–6; judging severity of behavior, 126–127*t*; presenting issues to top management, 126; psychology of harassment and implications for, 38, 40, 41; "reasonable victim" standard applied by, 42; record keeping skills of, 81; role in effectively dealing with harassment/retaliation, 67–68; role in prompt, corrective action by, 125–131, 167; tips regarding diversity for, 47; uncovering widespread pattern of harassment, 32–33. *See also* interviews; Training investigator program

K

Keashley, L., 32
Klonoff, E. A., 44
Koss, M. P., 37, 38

L

Landrine, H., 44
Langhout, R. D., 32, 38
LaVite, C., 31, 34
Legal jargon, 5–6
Liability: co-worker/third-party harassment test of, 16–17; investigator's legal knowledge regarding, 53; standards for employer, 12–15, 22
Litigation: common terms used in, 7; cross-examination of investigator during, 146–147; direct examination of investigator during, 146; filed before completed investigation, 106; risk factors for, 121–122; under U.S. judicial system, 144
Livingston, J. A., 38
L.L. Bean, Crowley v., 29
Lockard v. Pizza Hut, 25

M

McIntosh, P., 40
Magley, V. J., 30, 32, 33, 38, 40, 46, 67
Magnuson, P., 37
Martindale, M., 37
MBNA Marketing Systems, Inc., Reed v., 29
Mexican-American women, 44–45
Mills, C. W., 31
Miranda warnings, 92
Munson, L. I., 32
Murrell, A. J., 44

N

National Labor Relations Board, 29
National origin harassment, 21–22, 31–32
Nature of harassment: coping with harassment, 37–38; harassers and, 33–36; impact of harassment on individuals, 39; impact of harassment on workgroups,

39–40; incivility and workplace aggression, 32–33; racial, ethnic, national origin, disability, or harassment, 31–32; sexual harassment and, 30–31
NLRB (National Labor Relations Board), 79–80
Nontarget harassment, 28

O

Off-duty conduct, 29
Oncale v. Sundowner Offshore Services, Inc., 28
Organization harassment policies: distribution of, 63; elements of effective, 61–62; investigation use of applicable, 76; prohibiting general harassment, 62–63; referencing in investigative report, 86; role of leadership in implementing, 65–66; role of training in implementing, 66–67, 130–131; zero tolerance, 125. *See also* Harassment training
Organization memos, 115
Organizational charts, 115
Organizations: culture of respect model of, 60*fig;* dynamic organizational model of, 59–61; policies to prevent discrimination/harassment/retaliation, 61–63; system for intake of complaints by, 72. *See also* Employers
Ormerod, A. J., 45

P

Palmieri, P. A., 38
Payroll records, 114
Personality disorders, 35
Personnel files, 114
Pictures (photo evidence), 115
Pizza Hut, Lockard v., 25
Plaintiffs: coping with harassment, 37–38; defining, 6. *See also* Complainants; Victims
Power relationships: extended to off-site situations, 36; as harassment issue, 34–35
Preventative programs, 60
Privacy issues. *See* Confidentiality
Progressive Corporation, Bennett v., 151
"Prompt and thorough" investigation, 106, 167
"Protected classes": described, 9; EEO laws on, 10–11
Pryor, J. B., 31, 33, 34
Psychology of harassment: coping with harassment, 37–38; environmental factors affecting harassment, 40–41; impact on individuals/workgroups, 39–40; implications for investigators, 41; nature of harassment, 30–36. *See also* Harassment

Q

Questioning style, 95–96
Questioning techniques, 93–94, 97
Quid pro quo harassers, 33–34
Quid pro quo sexual harassment: described, 11; standard for employer liability in, 12–14

R

Race/color harassment: coping with, 38; described, 19–20; nature of, 31–32; sexual harassment of African-American women and element of, 45. *See also* Ethnic harassment

Racial differences, 44–46
Racism behavior, 36
Raines, C., 45
Ramos, A., 45
"Reasonable victim" standard, 42
Reassignments, 130
Reed v. MBNA Marketing Systems, Inc., 29
Reflective questioning techniques, 97
Religious harassment, 20
Remedies: for aggrieved employees, 132–133; evaluation when cause is found, 136. *See also* Debriefing; Harassment
Remick, H., 34
Reprimands, 129
Resolution strategies/resources, 61
Respondents, 6
Retaliation: assessing issues of, 76–77; complainant fears of, 103; described, 22–23; nature of harassment, 33; organizational policies to prevent, 61–63; role of HR and investigators in dealing with, 67–68; training/education to prevent, 66–67, 130–131; victim fear of, 38. *See also* Complainants
Retaliation complaints: critical issues for investigators, 24; described, 22–23; EEOC Compliance Manual on, 23–25; important things to remember about, 24
Richman, W. L., 39
Rosenfield, P., 37
Rowe, A., 42, 43
Ryan, J., 46–47

S

Safety assessment, 76–77
Salisbury, J., 34, 40, 45, 67, 138
Same sex harassment, 28
Schmitt, M. T., 38
Schneider, K. T., 40
Scientific Colors, Inc., 20
September 11, 2001, 20, 21
Sexism behavior, 36
Sexual favoritism, 26
Sexual harassment: coping with, 37–38; gender differences and, 46–47; hostile work environment, 12; impact of gender/ethnicity on, 44–45; nature of, 30–31; quid pro quo sexual, 11; racial element of Black women and, 45
SHRM (Society for Human Resource Management), 26
Shupe, E. L., 45
Standards for employer liability: EEOC finding on disability harassment, 22; hostile work environment sexual harassment, 13–15; quid pro quo sexual harassment, 12–14; for supervisory harassment, 12–15
Statute of limitations, 92
Stereotypes: behavior related to, 36; sexual harassment of Black women and, 45; training investigator handout on, 178
Stoller, L., 31, 34
Stringer, D., 34
Sundowner Offshore Services, Inc., Oncale v., 28
Supervisor files, 115

Supervisory harassment: affirmative
defense/employer liability for, 12–15; EEOC's guidance on, 17–19; *Faragher/Ellerth* affirmative defense in, 12–15; unanswered questions about liability, 16–17; when harasser is co-worker, 16*fig*; when the harasser is supervisor, 15*fig*

Supervisory harassment (EEOC guidelines): defining supervisory capacity, 17; defining tangible employment action, 17–18; on effect of employee's failure to complain, 19; on effective investigative process, 18–19; on policy and complaint procedure, 18

Suspension, 129

Swan, S., 30, 37, 38, 40

T

Talbot, M., 46

Tangible employment action: defining, 12; EEOC guidelines on supervisory harassment, 17–18. *See also* Employers

Tangible job injury, 12

"Telephone" game, 90–91

Termination: as disciplinary action, 130; mistake prior to investigation close, 101

Terminology: additional terms used in manual, 8; legal jargon, 5–6; used in litigating claims, 7

Third-party harassment: liability for, 25; *Lockard v. Pizza Hut* decision on, 25

Time sheets, 114–115

Title IV (Civil Rights Act of 1964), 10

Title VI (Civil Rights Act of 1964), 10

Title VII (Civil Rights Act of 1964), 10, 11

Title XI (Civil Rights Act of 1964), 10

"Tomb of skeletons," 4

Training investigator handouts: Case Studies, 174–176; Debriefing the Workgroup Exercises, 194; Forming an Investigative Plan, 182–183; Four Layers of Diversity, 177; Microcosm Respectful Workplace Anti-Harassment Policy, 171–173; Remedies, Healing, and Aftermath, 193; Role Play Feedback Guidelines, 192; Role Play Preparation and Feedback Forms, 190–191; Self-Evaluation Form, 170; Stereotypes and Generalizations, 178; Triad Role Play, 180–181; Witness Statement: Tom Torrance, 186; Witness Summary: B.J. Raymond, 188; Witness Summary: David Lee, 187; Witness Summary: Michelle Cline, 189; Witness Summary: Willima Michaels, 184–185; You as a Diverse Entity, 179; Your Organization's Follow-Up Issues, 195

Training investigator program: goals of, 151; handouts for, 170–195; instructions for, 153–169; outline of, 152–153; overview of, 151. *See also* Harassment training; Investigators

Training investigator program instructions: I. opening activity, 154; II. characteristics of effective investigator, 154; III. introduction to law of harassment and discrimination, 155–156; IV. elements of effective policy, 156–157; V. psychology of investigating, 157–159; VI. diversity issues in investigating, 159–161; VII. documenting investigation, 161–162;

VIII. triad role play, 162–163; IX. forming investigative plan, 163–164; X. questioning skills, 164; XI. role play (skill practice), 164–166; XII. reaching a conclusion, 166–167; XIII. prompt, corrective action, 167; XIV. healing the aftermath, 168–169; XV. conclusion, 169

Transfers, 130

Trial court, 6

U

Ullman, J. B., 44

United States Postal Service, Horkan v., 22

U.S. judicial system, 144

V

Van Alstyne v. Ackerly Group, 14

Victims: coping with harassment, 37–38; fear of retaliation by, 38; liability standard when harasser is co-worker, 16*fig*; liability standard when harasser is supervisor, 15*fig*; procedures for investigating allegations of, 63–65*fig*; "reasonable victim" standard and, 42. *See also* Complainants; Plaintiffs

W

Waiver of attorney-client/work product privileges, 84

Waldo, C. R., 30, 46

Wasti, S. A., 37

Weingarten rights, 79–80

Whalen, N. J., 33

Williams, J. H., 32, 40, 65

Williams, K., 33

Witnesses: bias impairing impartiality of, 118; character of, 118; civil vs. criminal warning requirements for, 92; contradiction/consistency of, 119; dealing with distressed, 98–99; debriefing, 142, 168–169; demeanor of, 119; identifying potential, 76; inherent improbability of, 119; insisting the presence of their attorney, 105; interviewing the, 113–114; introductory remarks when interviewing, 109; investigator as, 143–147; no longer working for organization, 104–105; order of interviews, 99; prior inconsistent statements by, 118; refusing to be interviewed, 104; setting up interviews with, 77–78; ways to ask them not to share information, 90–91, 109; who do not speak English, 104. *See also* Interviews

Workgroups: debriefing, 138–139, 168–169; harassment training for, 130–131; impact of harassment on, 39–40; investigation assessment of functioning, 76–77

Workplace: hostile work environment in the, 12, 13–15, 28; incivility and aggression in, 32–33; sexual material pervading the, 31

Workplace dating, 26–27

Z

Zembe, R., 45

Zero tolerance policy, 125

Zickar, M., 40, 67

About the Authors

Jan C. Salisbury, M.S., is the president of Salisbury Consulting, which specializes in organization development, implementing diversity in U.S. and global organizations, leadership development, team building, and change. For the past twenty-three years, she has, through interventions, investigations, and training, facilitated the resolution of hundreds of harassment and discrimination complaints throughout the country. She was worked extensively in a broad range of organizations, including local and federal governments, high tech, law enforcement, agricultural production, education, manufacturing, and service. She has conducted research and published extensively in the area of harassment and abuse in the workplace and has been an invited speaker at national psychological and legal conferences. She has also been an expert witness in over eighty lawsuits, evaluating the effectiveness of organizational responses to harassment and discrimination.

Bobbi Killian Dominick, J.D., SPHR, was a shareholder in a Boise law firm for over seventeen years, practicing employment law and successfully defending companies accused of discrimination and harassment. In the course of her work, she conducted many investigations into allegedly discriminatory behavior, both as counsel for the organization and as lead investigator. As a defense counsel in harassment cases, she reviewed many investigations conducted by others to observe their effectiveness. Her many clients represented such diverse interests as mining, agriculture, high tech, education, manufacturing, retail, banking, and public entities. She now leads her own consulting company, providing training and investigation services for organizations seeking to prevent and correct problems with harassment and discrimination in the workplace. She provides expert witness services in employment litigation. She also serves as counsel to the law firm of Gjording & Fouser, providing advice on employment defense and other litigation.

How to Use the CD-ROM

System Requirements

Windows PC

- 486 or Pentium processor-based personal computer
- Microsoft Windows 95 or Windows NT 3.51 or later
- Minimum RAM: 8MB for Windows 95 and NT
- Available space on hard disk: 8 MB Windows 95 and NT
- 2X speed CD-ROM drive or faster

Macintosh

- Macintosh with a 68020 or higher processor or Power Macintosh
- Apple OS version 7.0 or later
- Minimum RAM: 12MB for Macintosh
- Available space on hard disk: 6MB Macintosh
- 2X speed CD-ROM drive or faster

NOTE: This CD-ROM requires Netscape 3.0 or MS Internet Explorer 3.0 or higher. You can download these products using the links on the CD-ROM Help Page.

Getting Started

Insert the CD-ROM into your drive. The CD-ROM will usually launch automatically. If it does not, click on the CD-ROM drive on your computer to launch. After you click to agree to the terms of the Copyright Page, the Home Page will appear.

Moving Around

Use the buttons at the left of each screen to move among the menu pages. To view a document listed on one of the menu pages, simply click on the name of the document. To quit a document at any time, click the box at the upper right-hand corner of the screen.

To quit the CD-ROM, you can click the Exit button or hit Alt-F4.

To Download Documents

Open the document you wish to download. Under the File pulldown menu, choose Save As. Save the document onto your hard drive with a different name. It is important to use a different name, otherwise the document may remain a read-only file.

You can also click on your CD drive in Windows Explorer and select a document to copy it to your hard drive and rename it.

In Case of Trouble

If you experience difficulty using this CD-ROM, please follow these steps:

1. Make sure your hardware and systems configurations conform to the systems requirements noted under "Systems Requirements" above.

2. Review the installation procedure for your type of hardware and operating system. It is possible to reinstall the software if necessary.

3. Have a question, comment, or suggestion? Contact us! We value your feedback, and we want to hear from you.

For questions about this or other Pfeiffer products, you may contact us by:

E-mail: customer@wiley.com
Mail: Customer Care Wiley/Pfeiffer
               10475 Crosspoint Blvd.
               Indianapolis, IN 46256
Phone: (U.S.) 800-274-4434 (Outside the U.S. 317-572-3985)
Fax: (U.S.) 800-569-0443 (Outside the U.S. 317-572-4002)

To order additional copies of this product or to browse other Pfeiffer products visit us online at www.pfeiffer.com.

To speak with someone in Product Technical Support, call 800-762-2974 or 317-572-3994 Monday through Friday 8:30 a.m. to 5 p.m. (EST). You can also contact Product Technical Support and get support information through our website at http://www.wiley.com/techsupport

Before calling or writing, please have the following information available:

- Type of operating system
- Any error messages displayed
- Complete description of the problem

It is best if you are sitting at your computer when making the call.

Pfeiffer Publications Guide

This guide is designed to familiarize you with the various types of Pfeiffer publications. The formats section describes the various types of products that we publish; the methodologies section describes the many different ways that content might be provided within a product. We also provide a list of the topic areas in which we publish.

FORMATS

In addition to its extensive book-publishing program, Pfeiffer offers content in an array of formats, from fieldbooks for the practitioner to complete, ready-to-use training packages that support group learning.

FIELDBOOK Designed to provide information and guidance to practitioners in the midst of action. Most fieldbooks are companions to another, sometimes earlier, work, from which its ideas are derived; the fieldbook makes practical what was theoretical in the original text. Fieldbooks can certainly be read from cover to cover. More likely, though, you'll find yourself bouncing around following a particular theme, or dipping in as the mood, and the situation, dictates.

HANDBOOK A contributed volume of work on a single topic, comprising an eclectic mix of ideas, case studies, and best practices sourced by practitioners and experts in the field.

An editor or team of editors usually is appointed to seek out contributors and to evaluate content for relevance to the topic. Think of a handbook not as a ready-to-eat meal, but as a cookbook of ingredients that enables you to create the most fitting experience for the occasion.

RESOURCE Materials designed to support group learning. They come in many forms: a complete, ready-to-use exercise (such as a game); a comprehensive resource on one topic (such as conflict management) containing a variety of methods and approaches; or a collection of like-minded activities (such as icebreakers) on multiple subjects and situations.

TRAINING PACKAGE An entire, ready-to-use learning program that focuses on a particular topic or skill. All packages comprise a guide for the facilitator/trainer and a workbook for the participants. Some packages are supported with additional media—such as video—or learning aids, instruments, or other devices to help participants understand concepts or practice and develop skills.

- *Facilitator/trainer's guide* Contains an introduction to the program, advice on how to organize and facilitate the learning event, and step-by-step instructor notes. The guide also contains copies of presentation materials—handouts, presentations, and overhead designs, for example—used in the program.

- *Participant's workbook* Contains exercises and reading materials that support the learning goal and serves as a valuable reference and support guide for participants in the weeks and months that follow the learning event. Typically, each participant will require his or her own workbook.

ELECTRONIC CD-ROMs and web-based products transform static Pfeiffer content into dynamic, interactive experiences. Designed to take advantage of the searchability, automation, and ease-of-use that technology provides, our e-products bring convenience and immediate accessibility to your workspace.

METHODOLOGIES

CASE STUDY A presentation, in narrative form, of an actual event that has occurred inside an organization. Case studies are not prescriptive, nor are they used to prove a point; they are designed to develop critical analysis and decision-making skills. A case study has a specific time frame, specifies a sequence of events, is narrative in structure, and contains a plot structure—an issue (what should be/have been done?). Use case studies when the goal is to enable participants to apply previously learned theories to the circumstances in the case, decide what is pertinent, identify the real issues, decide what should have been done, and develop a plan of action.

ENERGIZER A short activity that develops readiness for the next session or learning event. Energizers are most commonly used after a break or lunch to stimulate or refocus the group. Many involve some form of physical activity, so they are a useful way to counter post-lunch lethargy. Other uses include transitioning from one topic to another, where "mental" distancing is important.

EXPERIENTIAL LEARNING ACTIVITY (ELA) A facilitator-led intervention that moves participants through the learning cycle from experience to application (also known as a Structured Experience). ELAs are carefully thought-out designs in which there is a definite learning purpose and intended outcome. Each step—everything that participants do during the activity—facilitates the accomplishment of the stated goal. Each ELA includes complete instructions for facilitating the intervention and a clear statement of goals, suggested group size and timing, materials required, an explanation of the process, and, where appropriate, possible variations to the activity. (For more detail on Experiential Learning Activities, see the Introduction to the *Reference Guide to Handbooks and Annuals*, 1999 edition, Pfeiffer, San Francisco.)

GAME A group activity that has the purpose of fostering team sprit and togetherness in addition to the achievement of a pre-stated goal. Usually contrived—undertaking a desert expedition, for example—this type of learning method offers an engaging means for participants to demonstrate and practice business and interpersonal skills. Games are effective for team-building and personal development mainly because the goal is subordinate to the process—the means through which participants reach decisions, collaborate, communicate, and generate trust and understanding. Games often engage teams in "friendly" competition.

ICEBREAKER A (usually) short activity designed to help participants overcome initial anxiety in a training session and/or to acquaint the participants with one another. An icebreaker can be a fun activity or can be tied to specific topics or training goals. While a useful tool in itself, the icebreaker comes into its own in situations where tension or resistance exists within a group.

INSTRUMENT A device used to assess, appraise, evaluate, describe, classify, and summarize various aspects of human behavior. The term used to describe an instrument depends primarily on its format and purpose. These terms include survey, questionnaire, inventory, diagnostic, survey, and poll. Some uses of instruments include providing instrumental feedback to group members, studying here-and-now processes or functioning within a group, manipulating group composition, and evaluating outcomes of training and other interventions.

Instruments are popular in the training and HR field because, in general, more growth can occur if an individual is provided with a method for focusing specifically on his or her own behavior. Instruments also are used to obtain information that will serve as a basis for change and to assist in workforce planning efforts.

Paper-and-pencil tests still dominate the instrument landscape with a typical package comprising a facilitator's guide, which offers advice on administering the instrument and interpreting the collected data, and an initial set of instruments. Additional instruments are available separately. Pfeiffer, though, is investing heavily in e-instruments. Electronic instrumentation provides effortless distribution and, for larger groups particularly, offers advantages over paper-and-pencil tests in the time it takes to analyze data and provide feedback.

LECTURETTE A short talk that provides an explanation of a principle, model, or process that is pertinent to the participants' current learning needs. A lecturette is intended to establish a common language bond between the trainer and the participants by providing a mutual frame of reference. Use a lecturette as an introduction to a group activity or event, as an interjection during an event, or as a handout.

MODEL A graphic depiction of a system or process and the relationship among its elements. Models provide a frame of reference and something more tangible, and more easily remembered, than a verbal explanation. They also give participants something to "go on," enabling them to track their own progress as they experience the dynamics, processes, and relationships being depicted in the model.

ROLE PLAY A technique in which people assume a role in a situation/scenario: a customer service rep in an angry-customer exchange, for example. The way in which the role is approached is then discussed and feedback is offered. The role play is often repeated using a different approach and/or incorporating changes made based on feedback received. In other words, role playing is a spontaneous interaction involving realistic behavior under artificial (and safe) conditions.

SIMULATION A methodology for understanding the interrelationships among components of a system or process. Simulations differ from games in that they test or use a model that depicts or mirrors some aspect of reality in form, if not necessarily in content. Learning occurs by studying the effects of change on one or more factors of the model. Simulations are commonly used to test hypotheses about what happens in a system—often referred to as "what if?" analysis—or to examine best-case/worst-case scenarios.

THEORY A presentation of an idea from a conjectural perspective. Theories are useful because they encourage us to examine behavior and phenomena through a different lens.

TOPICS

The twin goals of providing effective and practical solutions for workforce training and organization development and meeting the educational needs of training and human resource professionals shape Pfeiffer's publishing program. Core topics include the following:

Leadership & Management

Communication & Presentation

Coaching & Mentoring

Training & Development

E-Learning

Teams & Collaboration

OD & Strategic Planning

Human Resources

Consulting

Printed and bound by CPI Group (UK) Ltd, Croydon, CR0 4YY

23/04/2025

14661015-0005